Projects for
Woodworkers
Volume 3

Projects for Woodworkers
Volume 3

The Editors of *The Woodworker's Journal*

Madrigal Publishing Company

We at Madrigal Publishing have tried to make this book as accurate and correct as possible. Plans, illustrations, photographs, and text have been carefully researched by our in-house staff. However, due to the variability of all local conditions, construction materials, personal skills, etc., Madrigal Publishing assumes no responsibility for any injuries suffered or damages or other losses incurred that result from material presented herein. All instructions and plans should be carefully studied and clearly understood before beginning any construction.

For the sake of clarity, it is sometimes necessary for a photo or illustration to show a power tool without the blade guard in place. However, in actual operation, always use blade guards (or other safety devices) on power tools that are equipped with them.

Printed in the United States of America.

Second Printing: October 1992

Library of Congress Cataloging-in-Publication Data:
(Revised for volume 3)

Projects for woodworkers.

     Includes indexes.
     1. Woodwork.   I. Woodworker's journal.
TT185.P76   1987   684'.08   87-15414
ISBN 0-9617098-1-2 (pbk. : v. 1)
ISBN 0-9617098-5-5 (v. 3)

Madrigal Publishing Company
517 Litchfield Road
P.O. Box 1629
New Milford, CT 06776

Table of Contents

(continued on next page)

Introduction

There are many ways to enjoy the craft of woodworking. Happily, most of them are unrelated to skill level, or shop size, or the number of hand and power tools we have. Much of our enjoyment from woodworking comes from simple pleasures. The sweet fragrance of freshly cut pine. The comfortable feel of a well-tuned hand plane slicing through a cherry plank. The satisfaction that comes from working with a clear sense of purpose — and seeing that work through to completion. The opportunity to explore our creative energies — to turn a jumbled pile of rough-sawn boards into something of lasting beauty and function. The quiet moments when a workshop becomes a place of relaxation and reflection — where we work at our own pace, marking time not to the breakneck speed of a computer chip, but to the steady rhythm of the mallet and chisel. It's little wonder our hobby is enjoyed by so many.

We think you'll find many hours of simple pleasures within the pages of *Projects for Woodworkers, Volume 3*. It's the latest in our popular series, and offers 60 more great projects, all of them selected from the 1983 issues of *The Woodworker's Journal* magazine. The projects address a wide range of woodworking interests — toys, lamps, cupboards, chests, cabinets, tables, planters, mirrors, and much more. Happy woodworking!

Also, we want to extend our thanks to the following individuals whose valuable project contributions helped make this book possible:

Sam Allen, Old World Weather Forecaster; **Warren W. Bender, Jr.**, Canning Jar Storage Shelves: **J.J. Ciciarelli**, Collector's Plate Stand; **C.W. Comfort**, Key Holder; **Donald E. Cornue**, Porch Swing; **Brian Diehm**, Chinese Tea Table; **Glen Firmender**, Oak Pedestal Table; **Thomas A. Gardner**, Chippendale Mirror; **Ronald E. Harr**, Butler's Tray Table; **Brian Johnson**, Display Pedestal; **Paul Levine**, End Grain Table Lamp and Nesting Tables; **C.J. Maginley**, Toy Dump Truck, Steam Roller, Car with Boat and Trailer, Tractor with Cart, Pumper Firetruck, Airplane, Train; **Steve Perkins**, Record and Tape Cabinet; **Charlie Plumb**, Contemporary Clock; **Roger E. Schroeder**, Carved Eagle; **Gary F. Walden**, Oriental Table.

In addition, our thanks to **Cherry Tree Toys** for the Elephant Push Toy, **Joe Gluse** who did the technical art for the Butler's Tray Table, Chinese Tea Table, Oriental Table, Lighted Wall Planter, Waterbed, and Coal Scuttle; **Gene Marino III** who did the technical art for the Toy Car with Boat and Trailer, Record and Tape Cabinet, Toy Tractor with Cart, Toy Pumper Firetruck, Toy Airplane, Early American Wall Secretary, and Toy Train; and **John Kane** of **Silver Sun Studios** for the cover photo and many of the project photos.

The Editors

Tinsel-Art Mirror

In the 1840's, clipper ship captains discovered tinsel pictures in China and began bringing examples of this lovely art form home to New England where the technique was soon imitated.

Our black and white photo hardly does justice to the vibrant colors in the tinsel picture of this lovely small mirror. The frame is made of ordinary nose and cove molding with a strip glued to the back. The reverse glass tinsel picture can be reproduced with very little, if any, artistic ability.

Make the molding (part A) first. About six feet of nose and cove molding is required; it can be purchased at most lumberyards. You'll also need six feet of backing strip (part B) cut to $3/8$ in. thick and $3/8$ in. wide. Set up the table saw to rip $1/8$ in. of molding stock along one edge as shown in Detail A. Next, glue the backing strip to the molding using brads to hold it in place as it dries. Don't drive the brads all the way; leave the heads exposed so they can be pulled out with pliers after drying.

With the miter gauge set to 45 degrees, cut the four miter joints as shown. Apply glue to the joints, then assemble using two small finishing nails at each corner.

Lay out the location of the notch for the divider backing (D), then cut it out using a sharp chisel. Cut part D to size ($1/4$ in. by $3/8$ in. by $7^{1}/4$ in.) and secure in the notch with glue. The divider (part C) can now be cut ($3/16$ in. by $3/4$ in. by $6^{1}/4$ in.) and glued in position. Use care when cutting it to length so that it fits snugly between the molding.

Fill the finishing nail holes, then give the frame a complete sanding. Ours was finished with two coats of Minwax's Puritan Pine Wood Finish followed by an application of their Antique Oil Finish. Two small hook-eyes and a short length of picture wire will allow the mirror to be easily hung.

Cut the mirror (H) and $1/8$ in. hardboard (I) to size, then install in the back rabbet. Use several small brads to secure both parts.

To reproduce the tinsel picture you'll need the glass, waterproof India ink, a drawing pen (we used a crow quill pen), a couple of small camel's hair brushes, flat black enamel and three tubes of oil colors.

Start by centering the clean pane of glass over the full size drawing and using the drawing pen and India ink, trace the drawing on the glass. When the ink has dried, use a small brush to carefully outline flowers, stems and leaves with flat black enamel. When the outlining has been done, continue to paint the entire background black. Two coats will probably be needed and this should be allowed to dry completely before proceeding.

Squeeze small amounts of Prussian blue, alizarin crimson and thalo green on a non-absorbent surface (an old saucer makes a good palette). Using a small camel's hair brush, mix a small amount of green with turpentine and paint this transparent mixture over all the leaves and stems. Try to cover all areas smoothly without brushing the paint out too much.

Use alizarin crimson for the rose on the left and Prussian blue for the flower on the right. Remember to keep the paint thinned enough to be transparent. The upper flower is painted purple by mixing crimson and blue.

Set the pane aside to dry, which may take a couple of days, then go over the painting in the areas indicated by diagonal lines, applying darker colors to the centers of the leaves and flowers. Don't lay the paint on too thickly; just make it darker than the previous work. Try to work with smooth strokes but don't worry

about some streaking as it will not be very noticeable in the finished picture.

When the painting is completely dry, cut a piece of ordinary aluminum foil to the size of the glass. Carefully crumple the foil, then flatten it out and lay it shiny side down on the painted glass. Cover this with the $1/8$ in. hardboard backing and fasten this "sandwich" to the frame (see Detail B). That's all there is to it.

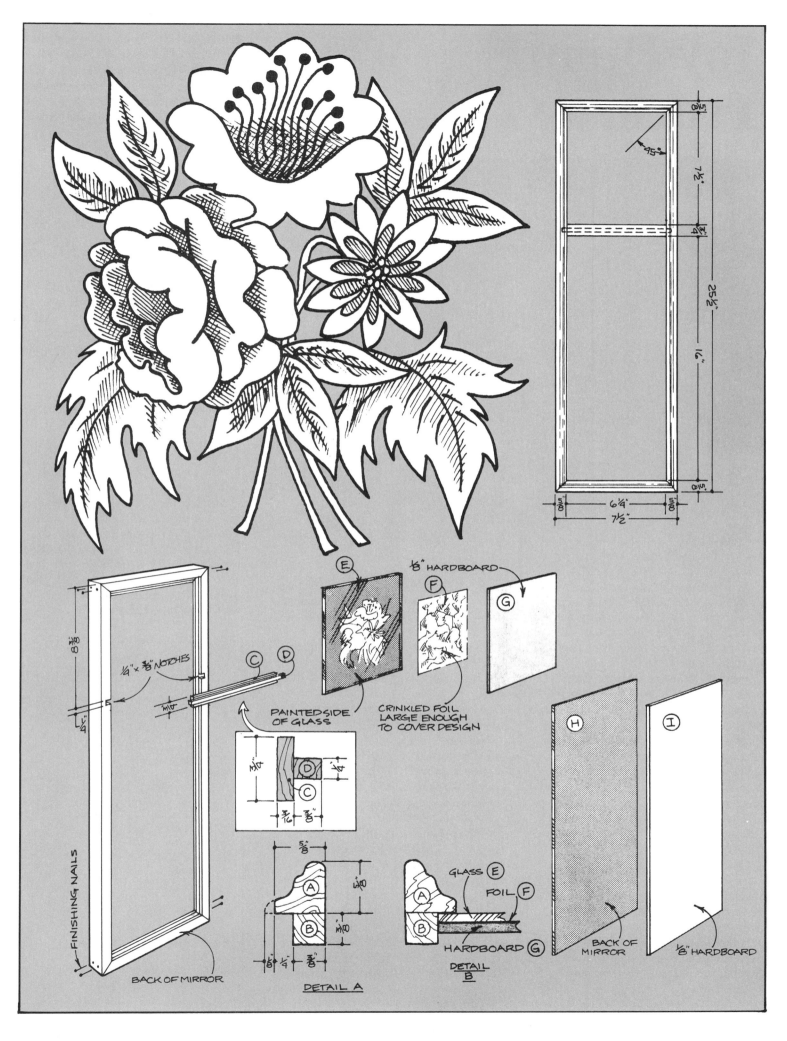

5/8"

7½"

3/4"

25½"

16"

5/8"

5/8" 6¼" 5/8"
7½"

95°

E

⅛" HARDBOARD

F

G

CRINKLED FOIL
LARGE ENOUGH
TO COVER DESIGN

PAINTED SIDE
OF GLASS

3/8"

⅛" x ⅜" NOTCHES

1/16"

¼"

C D

3/4"   ¼"
D
C
1/16" ⅜"

5/8"

3/8"

⅜" ¼" ⅜"

A

B

3/8"

GLASS E

FOIL F

A

B

HARDBOARD G

DETAIL
B

H

I

BACK OF
MIRROR

⅛" HARDBOARD

FINISHING NAILS

BACK OF MIRROR

DETAIL A

3

Toy Dump Truck

A sturdy, well built toy will provide countless hours of fun for a child. Since a toy like this will take a pretty good beating, it's best to use a hardwood. This one is made of poplar, but maple or oak are also good choices.

Make the lower cab (part A) first. Cut to the dimensions shown, then make four "headlights" by drilling 5/16 in. diameter by 1/4 in. deep holes. Use a file or rasp to round over the "nose," then smooth with sandpaper.

The upper cab (B) is cut from 1 1/8 in. thick stock to a width of 1 7/8 in. The front bevel can be cut with a block plane.

Apply glue to the mating surfaces of both parts and clamp in place. Allow to dry overnight.

The two frame parts (C) are made next. Cut to dimensions shown in the Bill of Materials, then round over the back end as shown. Lay out the location of the pivot dowel (P) holes, then use a 1/4 in. drill bit to drill each hole. As shown in the detail, one hole is drilled completely through, the other is only 1/2 in. deep.

After the undercarriage (part D) is cut to size it can be glued to the two frame parts (C). Apply glue to the mating surfaces, then clamp securely. Be sure the pivot dowel holes are exactly opposite each other. Allow to dry overnight.

The bumper (part E), the axle supports (parts F), and the cab assembly (parts A and B) can now be glued to parts C and D. Again, apply clamps and allow to dry. Be sure to drill the 5/16 in. diameter axle holes in parts F before assembly.

Next, cut the bottom (K) to size from 3/4 in. hardwood plywood (solid stock can also be used here). To hide the plywood edge at the back, an edge strip (part L) is glued as shown.

The pivot block (part J) can now be cut to size as shown in the Bill of Materials. Referring to the drawing detail, note that a 5/16 in. diameter hole is drilled through the block at a point 1/2 in. from the top edge and 7/8 in. from the back.

Parts M, the two sides, can now be cut to size. In each piece drill a 3/16 in. diameter hole for the tailgate pivot (Q). The hole location is shown in the Detail. Also, at this time, drill a 1/2 in. diameter by 1/2 in. deep hole in the left side to take the dumping peg (R).

After the front (part N) is cut to size, the sides (M), the bottom (K), and part N can be joined with glue and finishing nails as shown. The pivot block (J) can now be glued to the underside of the bottom (K). It should be located so that it is flush with the back of the edge strip (L) and centered along the width of part K. Three dowels (parts S) serve to reinforce the joint. Be sure to locate the dowels so they do not interfere with the pivot dowel (P).

Set the sub-assembly consisting of parts J, K, L, M, and N in position on the sub-assembly of parts C and D. Apply glue to the 1/4 in. diameter by 1/2 in. deep hole in part C, then drive the pivot dowel (P) into place.

Cut the tailgate (O) to length and width before drilling a 3/16 in. diameter by 3/4 in. deep hole in each end. Apply a generous radius to the top corners. To install the tailgate, put a small amount of glue into the 3/16 in. diameter holes in the tailgate, then drive in the tailgate pivot (Q).

The wheels (G) can be made to the dimensions shown, or purchased ready-made from Woodcraft Supply Corp., 21 Wood County Industrial Park, P.O. Box 1686, Parkersburg, WV 26102-1686. Ask for part no. 50N41 (2 3/8 in. diameter by 9/16 in. thick).

Note that the front axle (H) has a single wheel glued to each end, while the rear axles (I) have two wheels on each end.

Give the entire piece a complete sanding. Remove any sharp edges and round all corners. Clean up any spots where excess glue squeezed out. The best non-toxic finish is no finish at all.

Bill of Materials
(all dimensions actual)

Part	Description	Size	No. Req'd.
A	Lower Cab	1 3/4 x 4 1/2 x 3 1/2	1
B	Upper Cab	1 1/8 x 4 1/2 x 1 7/8	1
C	Frame	3/4 x 1 x 10	2
D	Undercarriage	1 x 2 x 8	1
E	Bumper	1/2 x 1 x 5	1
F	Axle Support	1 x 1 1/4 x 3 1/2	3
G	Wheel	2 1/2 dia. x 1/2 thick	10
H	Front Axle	1/4 dia. x 4 3/4	1
I	Rear Axle	1/4 dia. x 5 3/4	2
J	Pivot Block	1 x 2 x 1 3/4	1
K	Bottom	3/4 x 4 1/2 x 6 1/4	1
L	Edge Strip	1/8 x 3/4 x 4 1/2	1
M	Side	3/4 x 2 1/2 x 8	2
N	Front	3/4 x 2 1/2 x 4 1/2	1
O	Tailgate	3/4 x 3 1/8 x 4 1/2	1
P	Pivot Dowel	1/4 dia. x 3 1/4	1
Q	Tailgate Pivot	3/16 dia. x 1 1/2	2
R	Dumping Peg	1/2 dia. x 1 1/4	1
S	Dowels	1/4 dia. x 1 3/8	3

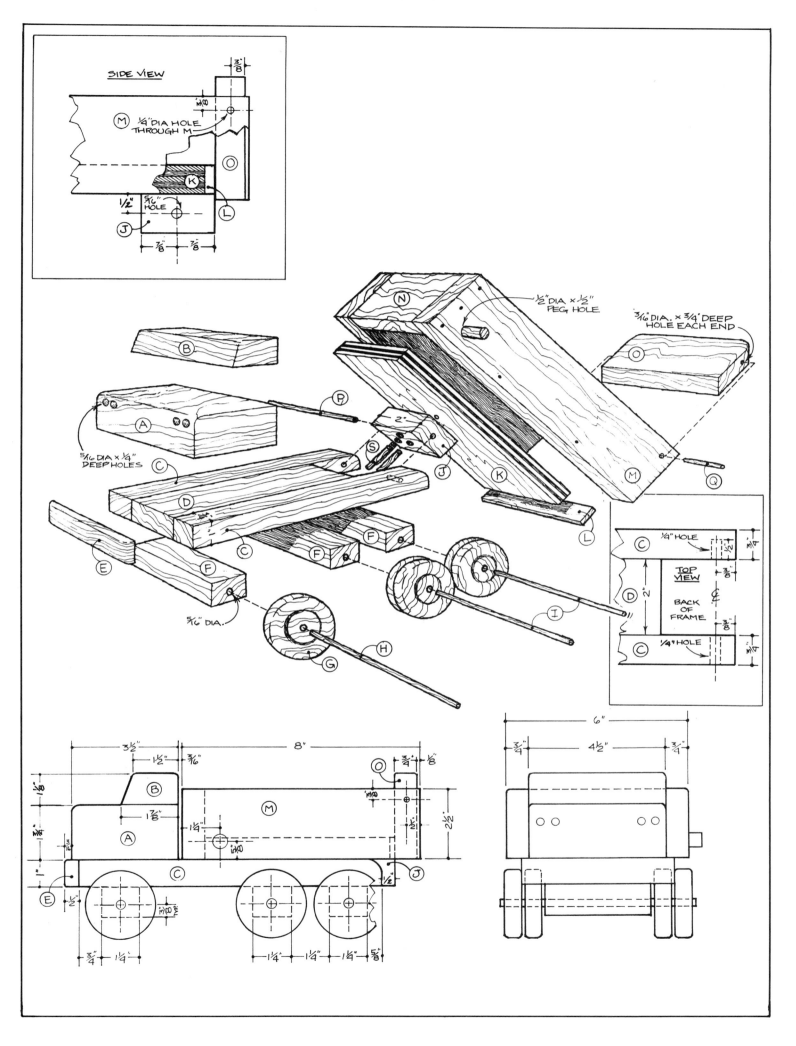

SIDE VIEW

¾"

⅛"

Ⓜ ¼" DIA HOLE THROUGH M

Ⓞ

Ⓚ

Ⓛ

Ⓙ

½"

5/16" HOLE

⅞"   ⅞"

Ⓝ

½" DIA × ½" PEG HOLE

3/16" DIA. × ¾" DEEP HOLE EACH END

Ⓞ

Ⓑ

Ⓟ

Ⓐ

5/16" DIA × ¼" DEEP HOLES

Ⓢ

2"

Ⓒ

Ⓓ

Ⓙ

Ⓚ

Ⓒ

Ⓕ   Ⓕ   Ⓕ

Ⓛ

Ⓔ

Ⓕ

Ⓜ

Ⓠ

5/16" DIA.

Ⓘ

Ⓗ

Ⓖ

Ⓒ   ¼" HOLE

TOP VIEW

BACK OF FRAME

Ⓓ   2"

Ⓒ   ¼" HOLE

¼"

⅜"

3½"

1½"

8"

3/16"

¾"

⅛"

Ⓑ

Ⓞ

1⅞"

1¼"

Ⓐ

⅜"

2½"

Ⓜ

1"

Ⓒ

Ⓙ

½"

Ⓔ   ½"

¾" ¼"

1¼" 1¼" 1¼" ⅝"

6"

¾"   4½"   ¾"

Bang-a-Peg Toy

There's nothing new about this toy — it's been entertaining small-sized aspiring woodworkers for generations. The kids bang the pegs in on one side of the board, then turn it over and bang from the other side. Ours is big and sturdy, and since very little stock is required, the scrap box may yield all the material that is needed.

Obviously a hardwood must be used here, preferably maple or oak. We used maple for the pegs and oak for the board. The hammer has an oak head with a maple handle.

Cut the peg board to size, then lay out and mark the locations of the six peg holes. Keep in mind that the diameters of the peg holes and the pegs are critical. Too much slop and the pegs will fall through the holes, too tight and they won't go through at all. Ideally, the hole diameters should be about $1/16$ in. less than the peg diameters. However before starting, it's a good idea to make some trial holes and pegs.

We used 1 in. diameter dowel stock for the pegs, then drilled a $15/16$ in. hole. To make a $15/16$ in. drill bit we simply filed down a 1 in. spade bit.

Two $1/16$ in. wide slots are cut in each peg. This allows it to compress when driven into the hole. Note that the cuts start at opposite ends and are at 90 degrees to each other. The slots can best be cut with a band saw, although a panel saw, used with care, will also do the job.

After a thorough sanding, several coats of Watco Danish Oil were applied as a final finish.

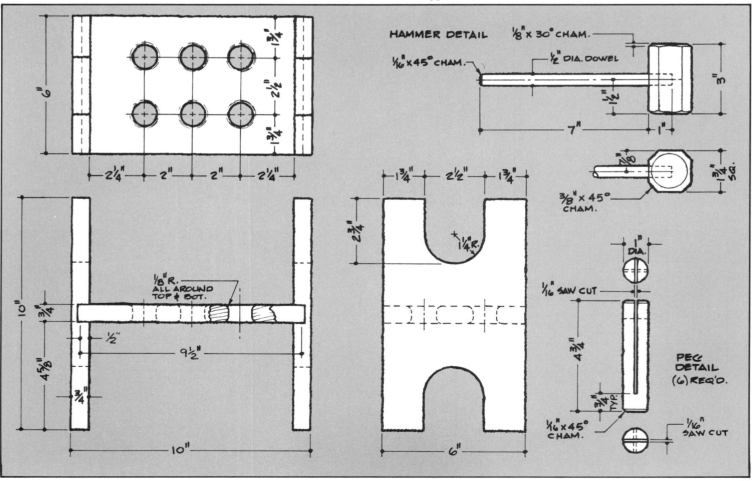

Key Holder

T his easy-to-make key rack will provide a handy place to hang the keys when you come into the house.

We used pine for ours, but just about any wood species will do. Since little stock is required, you may find your scrap box will provide plenty of material.

Cut to length and width, then transfer the pattern to the stock. Use a saber, band, or jigsaw to cut the profile. A 1 in. diameter spade bit is used to cut the 1/2 in. deep keyhole. The dovetail is cut to the same depth with a sharp chisel. We

painted the bottom of the hole with a coat of flat black paint.

Give the part a complete sanding, taking care to make sure the edges are well smoothed. Two coats of polyurethane varnish will yield a durable clear final finish. Five 3/4 in. brass cup hooks, available in hardware stores, will complete the project.

Secure to the wall with a wood screw through the keyhole. Paint the screw head with flat black paint.

I SQUARE = 1/2 "

3/4 " THICK STOCK

End Grain Table Lamp

Next, make the frame (parts B and C) to fit around the panel molding. Part C is joined to part B with a simple butt joint. Later, this joint will be further reinforced when it is assembled to the leg. Check to see that the panel molding fits in the flat frames, and adjust if necessary. Make the eight frame caps (parts D) as shown, then make the four legs (parts A).

Assemble the lamp without glue to see if any of the joints need adjustment. If all is well, begin by gluing up two sides. When these are dry, final assembly is accomplished by adding the other two sides. Use glue sparingly. If any squeezes out, leave it to be chipped off after it is dry.

Fit the light bracket (part H) and assemble the light socket. A spot of glue will hold part H in place. The bulb size is not critical, but lower wattages are desirable because this lamp is for accent light and not for reading.

The finish is applied after final checking for glue squeeze-out and a fine sanding. Watco Danish Oil or any good quality penetrating oil finish will result in an attractive final finish.

Bill of Materials (all dimensions actual)			
Part	Description	Size	No. Req'd.
A	Leg	1 x 1 x 20	4
B	Frame Rail	1/4 x 1 1/2 x 8 1/2	8
C	Frame Stile	1/4 x 1 1/2 x 6 3/8	8
D	Frame Cap	1/2 x 3/4 x 8	8
E	Panel Molding	1/2 x 1 x 6	8
F	Panel Molding	1/2 x 1 x 6 7/8	8
G	Panel	1/8 x 6 3/8 x 5 1/2	4
H	Light Bracket	3/8 x 2 x 8 5/8	1

A band saw can be used to cut pine strips for panel (part G).

Pipe clamp is used to edge-glue pine strips for panel G. Blocks on each end serve as clamp pads. Plastic wrap keeps excess glue from sticking to workbench.

T his lovely lamp will provide any room with warm accent lighting. It's made entirely from mahogany and pine scrap lumber so the price is right too.

Start by making the four panels (parts G) from 1 by 6 no. 2 common pine. Slice thin strips 1/8 in. to 3/16 in. thick from the board (see photo). Sand the fuzzy edges, then apply glue to the edges and glue up on a sheet of plastic wrap (see photo). Clamp using end blocks and let dry overnight.

Sand the panels and keep them standing on edge until they are assembled to the finished lamp. Next, choose the kind of lumber you wish to use (the lamp in the photo is mahogany), and begin to cut up all the necessary pieces as shown in the Bill of Materials. The panel molding (parts E and F) is made by cutting 1/2 in. by 1 in. stock. Round over two edges with a 3/16 in. router bit with a guide bearing. Cut the rabbet and kerf as shown, then sand. Once the molding is made, miter and fit it to the panels, leaving a small allowance for the panel. The allowance will permit the panel to expand and contract. After mitering, test dry-fitting the pieces and then glue up.

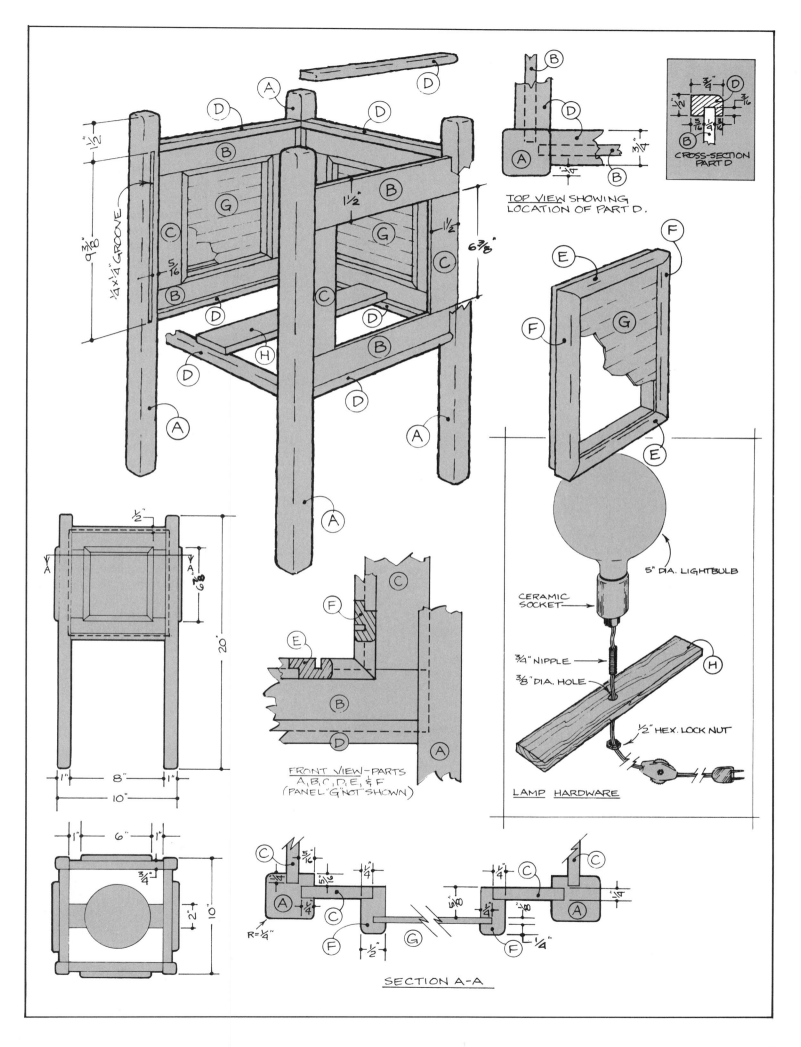

TOP VIEW SHOWING
LOCATION OF PART D.

CROSS-SECTION
PART D

¼"×¼" GROOVE

5" DIA. LIGHTBULB

CERAMIC
SOCKET

¾" NIPPLE

⅜" DIA. HOLE

½" HEX. LOCK NUT

LAMP HARDWARE

FRONT VIEW—PARTS
A, B, C, D, E, & F
(PANEL "G" NOT SHOWN)

R = ¼"

SECTION A-A

Butler's Tray Table

A butler's tray table is truly a classic piece of furniture. Because it can be used with many styles of furniture, it has become very popular in recent years. But like many other styles that are copied for hundreds of years, some of the butler's tray tables made today are very different from the original article.

This tray table is a reproduction of one in a home in Abingdon, Virginia. According to the owner, the model is more than 100 years old. The top was completely original. However, the original folding base had been lost years ago, so the owner had commissioned a local craftsman to make a replacement. The original base held the top about waist high, a convenient service height for the butler. The replacement base holds the top at coffee table height.

The panels (parts J) were made from solid stock, which could result in problems since they tend to shrink and swell with changes in humidity. To avoid this, make the panels from 1/2 in. mahogany stripe plywood. A 24 in. by 24 in. piece is available from Constantine, 2050 Eastchester Road, Bronx, NY 10461. Honduras mahogany solid stock is used for all other project parts.

Begin by cutting the panel to 5³/4 in.

Bill of Materials
(all dimensions actual)

Part	Description	Size	No. Req'd.
A	Front & Back Apron	3/4 x 2¹/2 x 23¹/2	2
B	End Apron	3/4 x 2¹/2 x 13³/4	2
C	Legs	1¹/2 x 1¹/2 x 18¹/2	4
D	Base Rail	3/4 x 1 x 13¹/2	2
E	Stretcher	3/4 x 1 x 24¹/8	1
F	Frame End	1/2 x 2¹/2 x 15	2
G	Frame Front & Back	1/2 x 2¹/2 x 27¹/2	2
H	Top Rail	1/2 x 2¹/2 x 10¹/2	2
I	Stile	1/2 x 2¹/2 x 13¹/2	1
J	Panel	1/2 x 5³/4 x 10¹/2	4
K	Front & Back Leaf	1/2 x 4 x 27¹/2	2
L	End Leaf	1/2 x 4 x 18	2
M	Cleat	1/2 x 1 x 12¹¹/16	2
N	Hinge	Woodcraft 16R22	8

wide by 10¹/2 in. long. Following this, a 1/4 in. by 1/4 in. tongue is cut around all four edges as shown in the detail.

The frame end (part F) is cut to length and width, then a 1/4 in. by 5/16 in. groove (see Detail) is cut along the inside edge. Also, a 1/4 in. by 1⁵/8 in. by 1 in. tenon is cut on each end.

Part G has a stopped groove along the inside edge, along with a mortise to take the part F tenon. Make the mortise slightly more than 1 in. deep in order to allow for excess glue.

Parts H and I have grooves along both

edges and 1/4 in. by 1/4 in. tongues on each end.

Assemble the top as shown using glue and pipe clamps. Check to make sure the top is flat before setting aside to dry overnight.

Parts K and L were cut out of the same 1/2 in. stock. Handle-hole cuts were traced from a cardboard template and then cut with a jigsaw. A saber saw or coping saw would also work. Then the curved edges of these pieces, as well as the handle cutouts, were rounded over with a 1/4 in. radius bit in a hand router. A shaper table would be easier to use for this.

Although many modern copies of these tables use round-end hinges, the original tables used rectangular hinges. Be sure to get ''Butler's Tray'' hinges so that the flaps will lock in the up and down positions. I found some beautiful 1¹/2 by 2¹/2 English brass hinges sold by Woodcraft Supply Corp., 210 Wood County Industrial Park, P.O. Box 1686, Parkersburg, WV 26102-1686 (order part no. 16R22). Recess these into the top using a router guided by a template. Finish the corners of the hinge mortises with a sharp chisel. Two strips of wood (part M) screwed across the bottom of the top assembly serve to strengthen the top and position it properly on its base.

The base construction is fairly simple. The mortise and tenon is used for all joints. The outside edge of each leg was chamfered before assembly. Hand sanding of machined edges gave the base a finished appearance.

Any finishing method will work, although the original was French polished. Stain the tray table with Watco alcohol stain and then apply a Danish oil finish followed by several coats of paste wax. The end result is a beautiful piece of furniture, one that looks a lot harder to build than it really is.

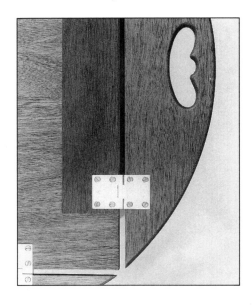

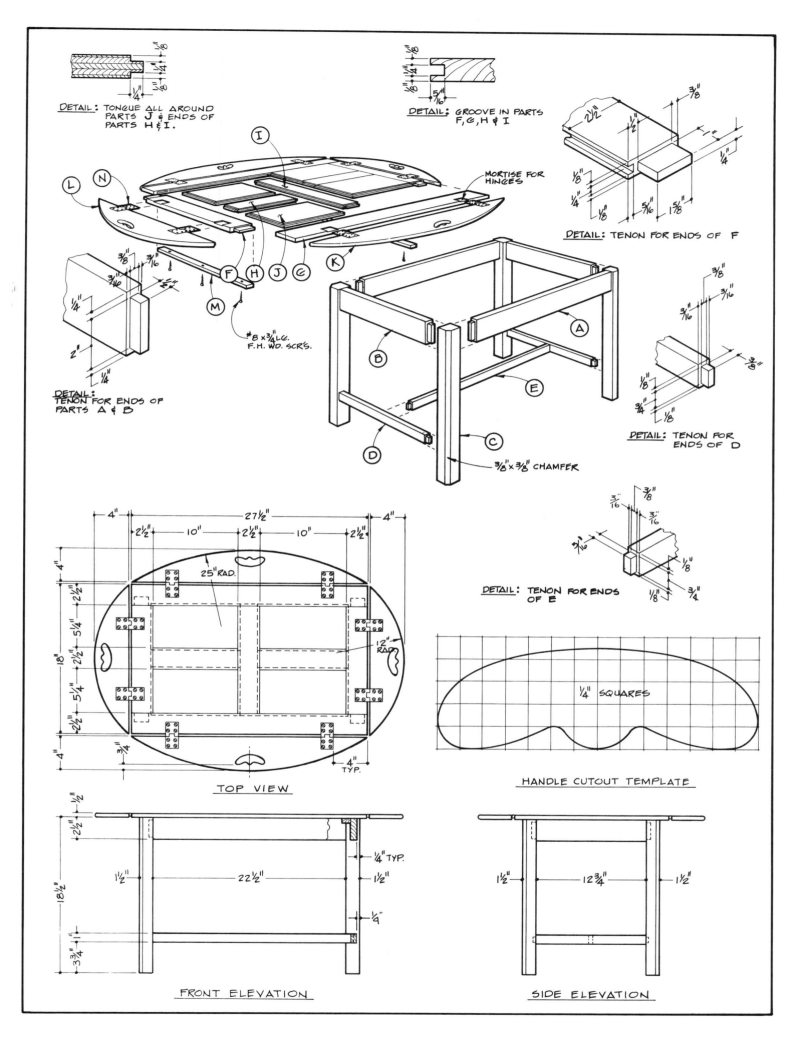

DETAIL: TONGUE ALL AROUND
PARTS J & ENDS OF
PARTS H & I.

DETAIL: GROOVE IN PARTS
F, G, H & I

DETAIL: TENON FOR ENDS OF F

MORTISE FOR
HINGES

DETAIL:
TENON FOR ENDS OF
PARTS A & B

DETAIL: TENON FOR
ENDS OF D

#8 x 3/4" LG.
F.H. WD. SCR'S.

3/8" x 3/8" CHAMFER

DETAIL: TENON FOR ENDS
OF E

25" RAD.

12" RAD.

TOP VIEW

1/4" SQUARES

HANDLE CUTOUT TEMPLATE

FRONT ELEVATION

SIDE ELEVATION

11

Contemporary Clock

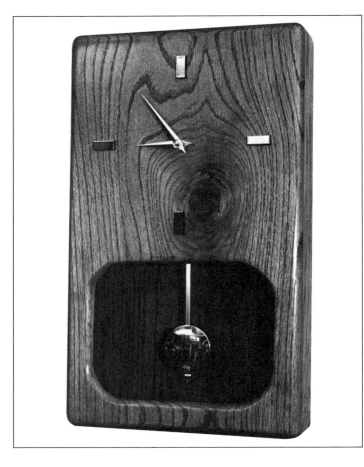

*Editor's Note: Our thanks to Charlie Plumb for making these plans available to us. Charlie is the author of the book **How You Can Make Battery Operated Clocks...Easily.** The clock shown is one of many that are described in his book. Readers who would like a copy of the book (softcover) can order it from Charlie Plumb, 2525 West Main St., Littleton, CO 80120.*

There seems to be a surprisingly large number of woodworkers who feel that to do any kind of clockmaking requires exceptional skills and years of practice. No doubt that's true for some clock designs, but certainly not for all of them. Many kinds of clocks are remarkably easy to make, especially since the advent of battery-powered quartz movements.

This attractive contemporary clock falls well within the skill level of even a beginning woodworker. Oak solid stock is used throughout and the joinery is basic. If you've never built a clock before and would like to try, this is a good one to cut your teeth on.

The front and back are made from $^5/8$ in. thick stock. Since the wood has so much to do with the appearance of the clock, try to select stock with a pleasing figure. Cut both parts to a width of $10^3/4$ in. and a length of $18^1/4$ in. Check to be sure the cuts are square. Lay out the location of the openings in each part, then drill a $^3/8$ in. hole in the waste stock. With this hole as a starting point, use a saber saw to cut out the openings. Also at this time, lay out and drill a $^3/8$ in. hole in the front part for the movement shaft.

The frame is made from $^3/4$ in. thick stock. The top and bottom measure $2^3/4$ in. wide by $10^3/4$ in. long. The sides measure the same width but are $18^1/4$ in. long. To make the miters, set the table or radial-arm saw blade to 45 degrees. Since the angle must be exact, don't rely on the crude gauges that most saws have. Instead use a draftsman's 45-degree triangle to check the angle.

After the miters have been cut, the frame can be assembled. The oak miters will really soak up the glue, so it's best to apply one coat, let it soak in, then add a second coat. Use corner clamps to secure each joint (see photo), then set aside to dry overnight. A web clamp can also be used to clamp the frame. After the frame is dry, make a crosscut through the center of the top and bottom. When the front and back are assembled to the frame, the space this crosscut creates allows for wood movement.

Next the front and back can be joined to the frame. Apply glue to the mating surfaces, then clamp using C-clamps (see photo). Be sure to use clamp pads to protect the clock case. Brads with the heads clipped off will keep the two frame halves from slipping out of register. Keep the sides flush to maintain the $^1/8$ in. space.

When dry, use a router with a $^1/2$ in. rounding-over bit to round over all edges. Following this give all surfaces a thorough sanding. A poorly sanded clock case won't look good, so spend plenty of time with the sandpaper. An application of Deftco penetrating oil will result in an attractive final finish.

The battery-operated quartz pendulum movement is available from Klockit, P.O. Box 636, Lake Geneva, WI 53147. Order part no. 11907H (includes pendulum). Hands are also included at no extra charge. Ask for part no. 67907H, brass. If you choose to use another movement, be sure that the shaft is long enough for a $^5/8$ in. thick dial face. Klockit also sells the four dashes, specify part no. 60060H.

Mount the movement. The opening in the back makes for easy access. A size "C" alkaline battery supplies the power.

Mitered frame is assembled with corner clamps.

Clock case back is glued to mitered frame. Note clamp pads used to protect stock.

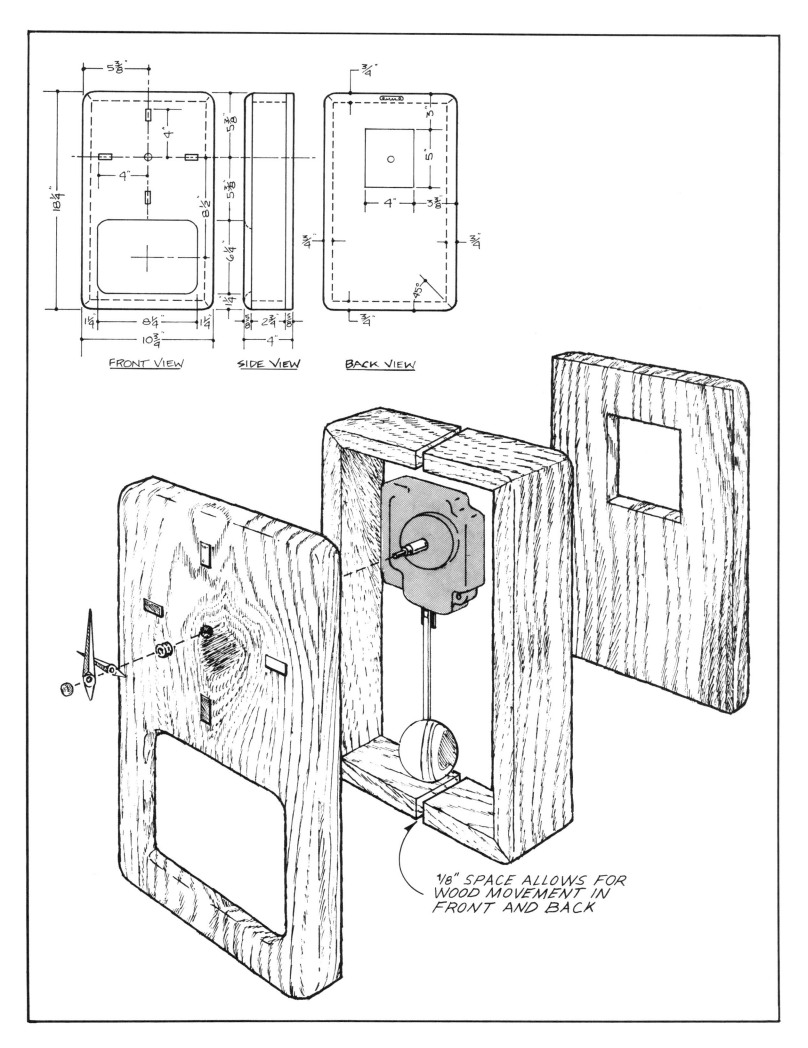

FRONT VIEW

SIDE VIEW

BACK VIEW

⅛" SPACE ALLOWS FOR
WOOD MOVEMENT IN
FRONT AND BACK

13

| Bill of Materials | | | |
| (all dimensions actual) | | | |
Part	Description	Size	No. Req'd.
A	Front	3/4 x 5 x 22 1/4	2
B	Side	3/4 x 11 5/8 x 22 1/4	2
C	Stile	3/4 x 2 1/2 x 20 3/4	2
D	Rail	3/4 x 2 1/2 x 17	2
E	Panel	3/4 x 15 1/2 x 16 1/4	1
F	Bottom	3/4 x 11 x 29 1/4	1
G	Shelf	3/4 x 11 x 29 1/4	1
H	Top	3/4 x 12 3/4 x 31 1/2	1
I	Back	1/4 x 29 1/4 x 20 7/8	1
J	Turnbutton	see detail	1
K	Knob	see detail	1

Pine Cabinet

This small early American style cabinet can be put to use in just about any room in the house, especially if some extra storage space is needed. It's made from number two common pine, to keep costs to a minimum, although almost any kind of wood can also be used.

The two front pieces (parts A) can be made first. Cut to the length and width as shown in the Bill of Materials, checking to be sure all cuts are square. The 3/8 in. by 3/4 in. rabbet can best be cut with a dado head cutter, but if you don't have one, repeated passes with a table or radial arm saw blade will produce satisfactory results. The 1 1/2 in. bottom radius can be cut with a band or saber saw.

Next, the sides (parts B) can be cut to length and width. Referring to the drawing, lay out and mark the location of the 3/8 in. by 3/8 in. dadoes for the shelf (G) and the bottom (F). Cut out using the dado head cutter or use the repeated pass technique. Note that part B also has a 1/4 in. by 3/8 in. rabbet along the inside back edge to take the back (part I).

The bottom (part F) and the shelf (part G) are identical parts. Cut to size, then apply the 3/8 by 3/8 in. rabbet on each end as shown. Try to cut the rabbet for a tight fit in the side (B) dado. Later, when parts F and G are sanded, a good snug fit should result.

The top (Part H) is made from 3/4 in. thick stock cut to a width of 12 3/4 in. and a length of 31 1/2 in. If you can't get stock that's at least 12 3/4 in. wide, it will be necessary to edge-glue two or more narrower boards. Three or four 1/4 in. diameter by 1 1/2 in. long dowel pins in each edge-joint will make it easier to align the boards. Apply a thin coat of glue to each edge, then clamp firmly with bar or pipe clamps. Allow to dry thoroughly.

Note that the back edge of part H has a 1/4 in. by 3/8 in. rabbet that's stopped at a point 1 1/8 in. from the corner. Later, the back (part I) will fit into this rabbet. This cut can best be made using a router equipped with a 1/4 in. piloted rabbet bit. The cut will be round where it is stopped, but this can quickly be squared-up with

a sharp chisel.

Knotty pine plywood is a good choice for the back (part I), although fir plywood can be used, especially if the cabinet is to be located where the back can't be seen.

The door components, parts C, D, and E, can be made next. Both the stiles (C) and rails (D) are made from 3/4 in. stock ripped to a 2 1/2 in. width. Note also that both parts require a 1/4 in. wide by 3/8 in. deep groove along their inside edge. A dado head cutter can cut this groove, although a few passes with the table or radial arm saw will also do the job.

The tenon on each end of parts D can be cut by using any of several methods, but perhaps the easiest one is to use a table saw tenon jig. With the saw blade set to a height of 1 in., adjust the jig to cut the 1/4 in. wide tenon.

A 1/4 in. mortising chisel will make quick work of the mortise in part C. Make it slightly deeper than 1 in. to allow for any excess glue or wood chips.

The large center panel (E) is made of 3/4 in. stock although 1/2 in. material can also be used if it's available. Like the top, the panel will probably require edge-gluing in order to get enough width. The gluing techniques are the same.

Cut the panel to length and width, then use the dado head to make the 1/4 in. by 3/8 in. rabbet as shown. This step is not necessary if 1/2 in. stock is used. The bevel can be cut on the table saw with the blade tilted to about 8 degrees. Adjust the rip fence to properly locate the bevel, then pass the stock, on edge, over the blade. When you approach the end of each cut, make sure the panel is firmly supported at the back of the table to avoid any tendency for the stock to dip into the blade.

Give all parts a thorough sanding, then assemble as shown using glue and clamps. Join parts A to B first. Allow glue to dry, then drill holes and add the dowel pins. Next, assemble parts G and F, again adding dowels after the glue has dried. The top (part H) can now be secured to the case with glue and dowel pins as shown. The back (I) is now added with glue and finishing nails.

The door components are assembled at one time. The mortise and tenon joints are glued, but the panel (E) is not. It must be free to expand and contract with changes in humidity.

The 1 1/2 in. brass butt hinges are mortised into both the front (A) and the door stile (C). The knob can be turned to the shape shown, although a similar profile can be found in most hardware stores. The small turnbutton (J) will serve to keep the door closed.

Give all parts a final sanding, then stain and finish to suit. We applied two coats of Minwax's Golden Oak Wood Finish followed by an application of their Antique Oil Finish.

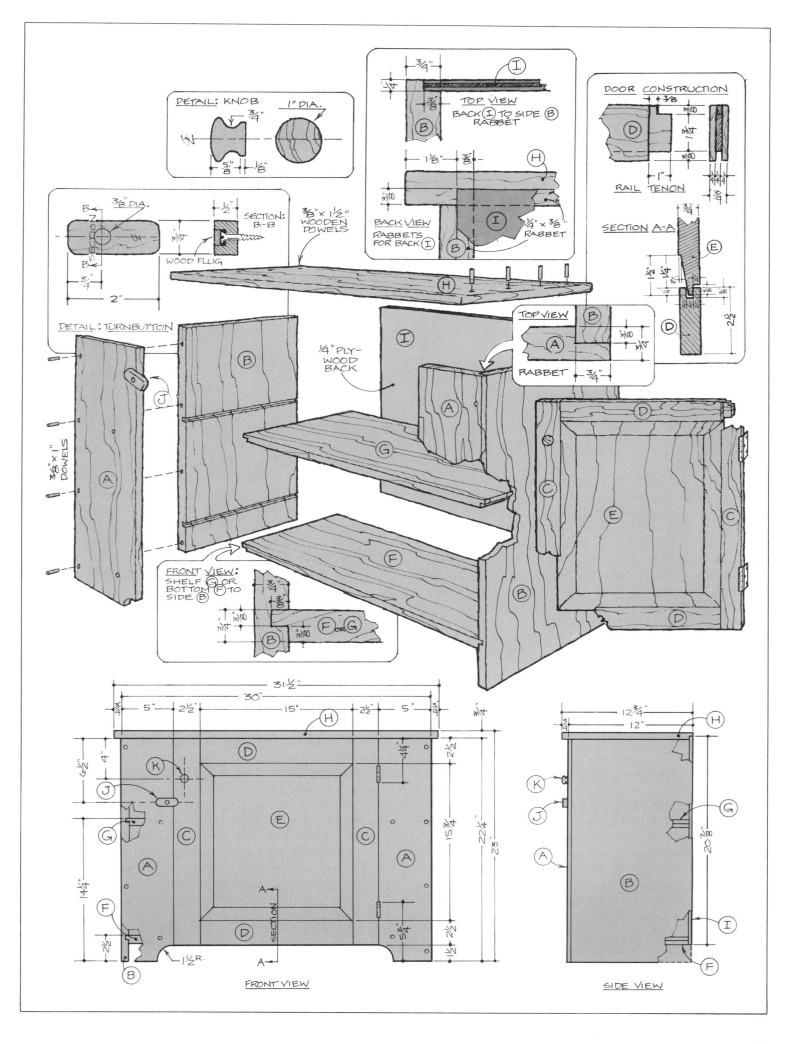

DETAIL: KNOB

1" DIA.

3/4"

5/8"   1/8"

DETAIL: TURNBUTTON

3/8" DIA.

SECTION: B-B

WOOD PLUG

1/2"

2"

3/4"

3/8" x 1/2" WOODEN DOWELS

3/8" x 1" DOWELS

FRONT VIEW: SHELF G OR BOTTOM F TO SIDE B

TOP VIEW BACK I TO SIDE B RABBET

3/4"

3/8"

BACK VIEW RABBETS FOR BACK I

1/8"   3/8"

1/4" x 3/8" RABBET

TOP VIEW RABBET

3/4"

DOOR CONSTRUCTION

3/8"

RAIL TENON

1"

SECTION A-A

3/4"

1/2"   1/4"

2 1/2"

1/4" PLY-WOOD BACK

31 1/2"

30"

5"   2 1/2"   15"   2 1/2"   5"

4 1/4"

2 1/2"

15 3/4"

22 1/4"

25"

4"

6 1/2"

14 1/4"

2 1/2"

1 1/2" R.

5 3/4"

1/2"   2 1/2"

FRONT VIEW

12 3/4"

12"

20 7/8"

SIDE VIEW

15

This very attractive pine cabinet owes much of its charm to the door panel which consists of a stenciled design on the back of a pane of glass. When covered with black enamel, the metallic powders used in the design catch the light and seem to glow from within.

The techniques for creating such panels are fairly simple and the materials needed are inexpensive. Once you've mastered the basics, you'll probably want to incorporate stenciled designs into many other woodworking projects.

Basically, the process of reverse-glass stenciling consists of cutting stencils and positioning them on a slightly tacky varnish surface. Using the fingertip wrapped in chamois, very fine metallic powders are rubbed on the varnish within the stencil units. The entire stenciled design is then covered with black enamel.

All of the design units used in the fruit and bowl design are shown full-size on page 18. To make stencils you only have to trace the designs on smooth paper or preferably architect's linen. The linen is semi-transparent so you can trace directly on it, dull side up, using a fine tip black felt-tip pen. Architect's linen is available at drafting supply stores. It's easy to cut and the stencils can be reused many times. When tracing, be sure to leave about 1 in. of space around each unit.

Cutting out the stencil units is best done with a pair of straight cuticle scissors sharpened right up to the tip. A small razor knife can also be used, working on a cardboard pad. After cutting the stencils, mark each unit with the color of metallic powder to be used, as shown in the key on page 18.

The metallic bronzing powders in this design are extra brilliant pale gold, extra brilliant copper and brilliant aluminum. The powders are sold in 1 oz. bottles and will last a long time since only small amounts are needed for one design.

Many stores that carry paints, wallpaper and decorating supplies also carry bronzing powders. If you cannot find them locally, or have the paint store order them for you, they can be obtained from Wood Finishing Enterprises, 1729 North 68th St., Wauwatosa, WI 53213. They carry a full line of colors.

After the stencils have been cut, you're ready to varnish the pane of glass. Apply one coat of unthinned varnish to one side of the glass and make sure that all of the glass is covered. Finish off with the tip of the brush to pick up tiny bubbles on the surface, then set the glass aside in a dust-free place and wait for the varnish to become almost, but not quite dry. The proper stage has been reached when the surface is very slightly tacky but the fingertip leaves no mark.

On a piece of paper, pour small amounts of each of the three colored powders. The first unit to be stenciled is the bowl so place your stencil (shiny side down if architect's linen is used) on the varnished surface so that the bowl is centered as shown in the photo. It's a help to work over a black background.

Fold a piece of chamois (or velvet) around your index finger so

that the tip is smoothly covered. Pick up a very small amount of gold powder with the fingertips and, with a light circular touch, apply the powder around the edges of the stencil. Take up more powder as needed and try to keep the brightest areas near the edges. After the brightest parts are done, go over them with more pressure to burnish the powder. Lift the stencil carefully, taking care to keep stray specks of powder off other areas of the glass.

The other units of the drawing are added in much the same way using the indicated colors. Note that the fruit and leaf units are not covered completely with powder but rather, the powder is applied around the edges of the stencil and allowed to fade. Separate stencils are used for the centers of flowers and the grapes and leaves are done by simply moving one or two single stencils around.

Wall Cabinet
with Reverse-Glass Stenciling

When the design has been completed, set it aside to dry for a few days; then cover the entire stenciled surface with flat black enamel from a spray can. If your first attempt is not quite right, you can clean the glass off with turpentine and try it again.

The cabinet sides (^{3}/4 in. by 6^1/2 in. by 15^1/4 in.) can be cut to size from standard 1 by 8 stock. Try to select good flat stock that has a pleasing figure. Referring to the drawing, lay out the locations of the holes for the shelf support pins, then bore holes to a depth of ^{3}/8 in. Next, cut the top (^{3}/4 in. by 6^1/2 in. by 12^1/4 in.) to length and width, then set up the dado head to cut the ^{1}/4 in. by ^{3}/8 in. rabbet for the back panel as shown. Also, at this time cut the two rabbets in the side pieces.

The base is cut to size (^{3}/4 in. by 7 in. by 14 in.), then a router equipped with a ^{3}/8 in. rounding-over bit (piloted) is used to apply a bead to the front and sides.

After cutting the rail (^{3}/4 in. by 2 in. by 11^1/2 in.) to size, give all parts a complete sanding. The case can be assembled as shown. Use glue on all joints and clamp securely. Six counterbored wood screws secure the base. The ^{1}/4 in. plywood back can now be cut to fit.

The molding (see detail) can be purchased at most lumberyards. Miter the two corners and join to the case with glue and countersunk finishing nails.

All door rails and stiles are ^{3}/4 in. thick and 1^1/4 in. wide. A tenon jig used in conjunction with the table saw will simplify cutting the four slip joints. Take care when cutting the joints so they result in a good snug fit. Assemble with glue and clamps. When dry, use a ^{3}/8 in. rabbet bit (piloted) to cut the door rabbet. The router bit will leave rounded corners which can be cleaned up with a sharp chisel.

Cut the adjustable shelf to size (^{3}/4 in. by 5^1/2 in. by 11^3/8 in.) before giving the entire project a thorough sanding. Ours was stained with two coats of Minwax Golden Oak finish followed by an application of Watco Danish Oil. Four strips of ^{1}/4 in. quarter round molding, mitered at the corners are tacked in place to secure the glass.

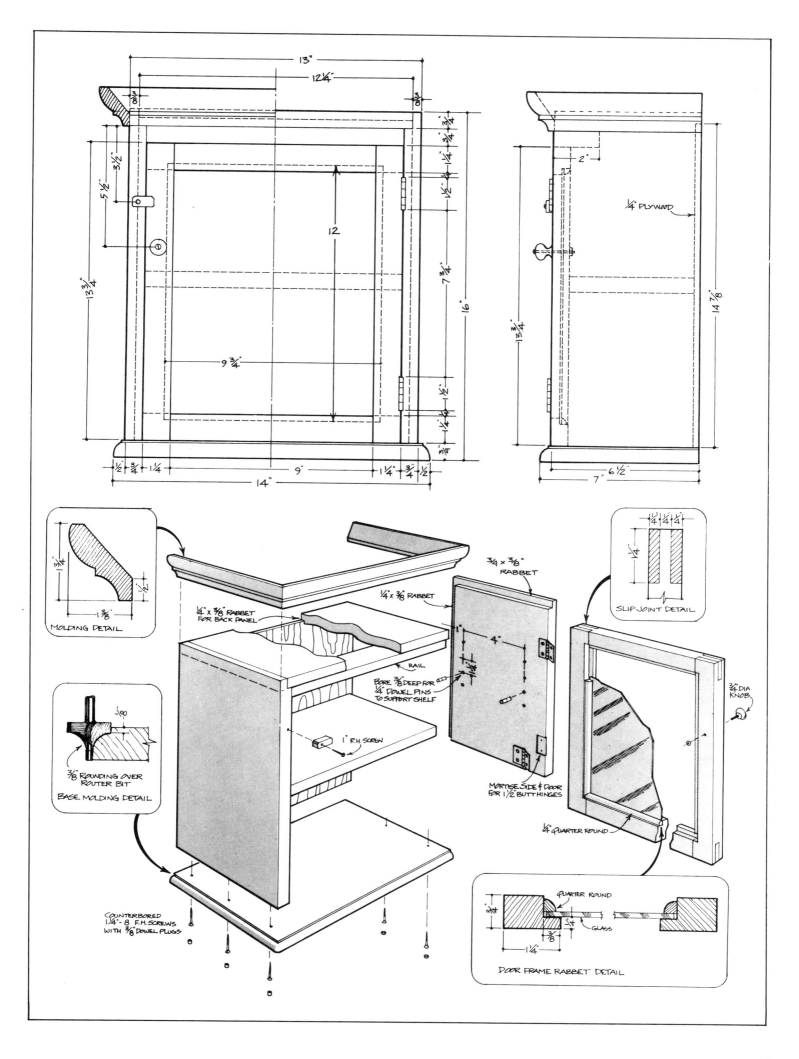

MOLDING DETAIL

BASE MOLDING DETAIL

3/8" ROUNDING OVER ROUTER BIT

COUNTERBORED
1/4"-8 F.H. SCREWS
WITH 3/8" DOWEL PLUGS

1/4" x 3/8" RABBET
FOR BACK PANEL

1/4" x 3/8" RABBET

3/4 x 3/8"
RABBET

RAIL

1" R.H. SCREW

BORE 3/8" DEEP FOR
1/4" DOWEL PINS
TO SUPPORT SHELF

MORTISE SIDE & DOOR
FOR 1/2" BUTT HINGES

SLIP JOINT DETAIL

1/4" QUARTER ROUND

3/4" DIA.
KNOB

1/4" PLYWOOD

QUARTER ROUND

GLASS

DOOR FRAME RABBET DETAIL

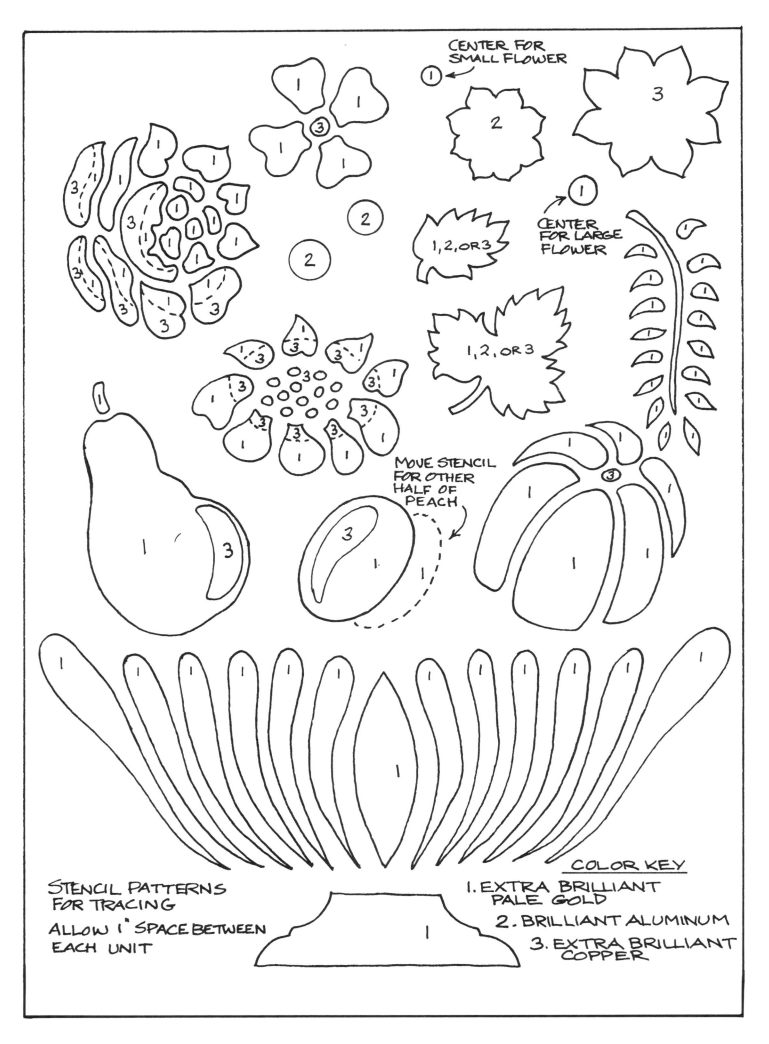

CENTER FOR SMALL FLOWER

CENTER FOR LARGE FLOWER

MOVE STENCIL FOR OTHER HALF OF PEACH

STENCIL PATTERNS FOR TRACING

ALLOW 1" SPACE BETWEEN EACH UNIT

COLOR KEY
1. EXTRA BRILLIANT PALE GOLD
2. BRILLIANT ALUMINUM
3. EXTRA BRILLIANT COPPER

Punched Tin Spice Cabinet

(D) as shown. Next, referring to the drawing, drill five pairs of $1/4$ in. diameter by $1/4$ in. deep holes in each side for the shelf adjusting pegs. The bottom (D) and shelf (E) can now be cut to size.

The base (B) and top (C) are cut from $3/4$ in. thick stock and a molding applied to the front and sides. To make the molding, use a $3/8$ in. roundover bit with pilot to apply the $3/8$ in. radius and $1/8$ in. step. The $1/4$ in. radius is applied with a file or Surform tool.

Now assemble the top, base, sides, and bottom, checking to be certain that the cabinet is square. Note that counterbored 1 in. by no. 6 flat head wood screws secure the top and base to each side. Make sure that the bottom is flush with the sides at the front. Plug your screw holes, and sand the plugs off flush after the glue has dried.

Next, use a $1/4$ in. bearing-guided rabbeting bit, set for a $1/4$ in. depth, to rout the $1/4$ in. by $1/4$ in. rabbet all around the back of the cabinet to accept the back (F). Note that where the bottom sets into the sides, you'll need to stop and then restart the rabbet, since the bottom will interfere with the bearing. However, as the dado for the bottom is also $1/4$ in. deep, you shouldn't have to do much cleaning up to keep the rabbet consistent. A little hand work with the chisel will square the corners to accept the square back, or as an alternate you could round the corners of the back to match the radius of your rabbeting bit.

Select good flat stock for the door rails (H), stiles (G) and divider (I). Cut to size and check their fit to the cabinet opening.

Made from pine, this small piece makes a handsome and versatile cabinet for home or apartment. The pierced tin panels provide a nice detail and can be made with little effort. The project requires only a small amount of lumber so you may find your scrap box will yield enough material. And if you don't have enough scraps around, it can be made from the judicious use of a 6 ft. length of 1 by 8 stock.

The two sides (A) are cut to length and width, and a $1/2$ in. wide by $1/4$ in. deep dado is cut into each to accept the bottom

Bill of Materials
(all dimensions actual)

Part	Description	Size	No. Req'd.
A	Side	$1/2$ x 6 x $16^{1}/_2$	2
B	Base	$3/4$ x $6^{5}/_8$ x $10^{3}/_4$	1
C	Top	$3/4$ x $6^{5}/_8$ x $10^{3}/_4$	1
D	Bottom	$1/2$ x $5^{3}/_4$ x 9	1
E	Shelf	$1/2$ x $5^{1}/_4$ x $8^{1}/_2$	1
F	Back	$1/4$ x 9 x 17	1
G	Door Stile	$1/2$ x 1 x 13	2
H	Door Rail	$1/2$ x 1 x $8^{1}/_2$	2
I	Door Divider	$1/2$ x 1 x $8^{1}/_2$	1
J	Tin Panel	.010 x $5^{1}/_2$ x 7	2
K	Door Knob	$5/8$ in. ceramic	1
L	Turnbutton	see detail	1
M	Drawer Front	$5/8$ x 3 x $8^{1}/_2$	1
N	Drawer Side	$1/2$ x 3 x $5^{1}/_4$	2
O	Drawer Back	$1/2$ x $2^{1}/_2$ x $7^{7}/_8$	1
P	Drawer Bottom	$1/4$ x $5^{1}/_{16}$ x $7^{3}/_4$	1
Q	Drawer Knob	$3/4$ in. ceramic	1
R	Molding	$1/4$ in. quarter-round as req'd.	
S	Drawer Stop	$1/4$ x $3/4$ x $1^{1}/_2$	1

Next, cut a 1/4 in. deep by 1 in. wide lap joint on the ends of all pieces and a 1/4 in. deep by 1 in. wide dado centered halfway up the back of the stiles to accept the divider as shown. Glue and clamp the frame and check for squareness. When dry, use a router with a 1/4 in. piloted rabbet bit to cut 5/16 in. deep recesses for the tin panels (J) in the inside of the door frame and divider. Use a chisel to square the corners.

Cut the drawer (parts M, N, 0 and P) to dimensions shown then cut a 3/8 in. deep by 9/16 in. wide rabbet on each side of the front to accept the sides as shown. Cut a 1/4 in. deep by 1/2 in. wide dado 1/4 in. from the back end of each side to fit back (0). With a 1/4 in. straight router bit or with the dado head, cut a slot 1/4 in. deep by 1/4 in. wide on the inside of the front and sides to accept the bottom. Note that the back fits flush with the sides at the top and rests on the bottom (P).

Use glue to assemble the drawer parts as shown. Nail the sides to the front with small finishing nails. Clamp securely and check for squareness. Next, cut the turnbutton (L), drawer stop (S), molding for tin panels (R) and 1/4 in. diameter by 3/4 in. long shelf pegs. Glue the drawer stop in position on the base as shown.

Mount the door to the cabinet with two 1 in. by 1 in. loose pin brass hinges. Remove the hinges, sand, and stain the door and all other parts with one coat of Minwax Golden Oak Stain (No. 210B) and finish with Watco Danish Oil. Add the shelf, then secure the back with small finishing nails. Apply the turnbutton with a 1 in. by no. 6 brass flathead wood screw. The tin panels are held into place with 1/4 in. quarter-round molding tacked into place. Finally, mount the door and affix the ceramic knobs to the door and drawer.

Tin for the panels (J) can be purchased via mail-order from Country Accents, P.O. Box 437, Montoursville, PA 17754. Write to them for price and ordering information.

If desired, the tin can be made to have an antique finish, much like the look of pewter. Working in one direction only use very fine (220-grit) garnet or aluminum oxide paper and give the sheet a thorough sanding. Use even pressure and continue sanding until the bright shine is dulled. You'll find it easier to hold the tin if you place it on a rubber sink mat.

Next, wash the tin and dry it thoroughly, then place it in a shallow non-metallic container — a glass baking disk or plastic dish pan will do fine. Add vinegar to the dish until the tin is covered with about 1/4 in. of vinegar. The longer the tin soaks in the vinegar, the darker it will get, but we found that 6-8 hours gives good results. If you have a small piece of scrap tin, it's not a bad idea to use it for a test. When you are satisfied with the results, remove the tin, then wash thoroughly and dry.

Now transfer the full-size pattern to the tin and place the panel on a scrap board for piercing. A variety of tools can be used for piercing — awls, nailsets, screwdrivers, even square flooring nails.

Each tool imparts its own distinctive mark when struck with a hammer. For this project we used a 1/32 in. nailset to punch the holes to about 1/16 in. diameter. The holes were spaced about 1/8 in. apart.

PATTERN
PIERCED TIN DESIGN:
FULL SIZE

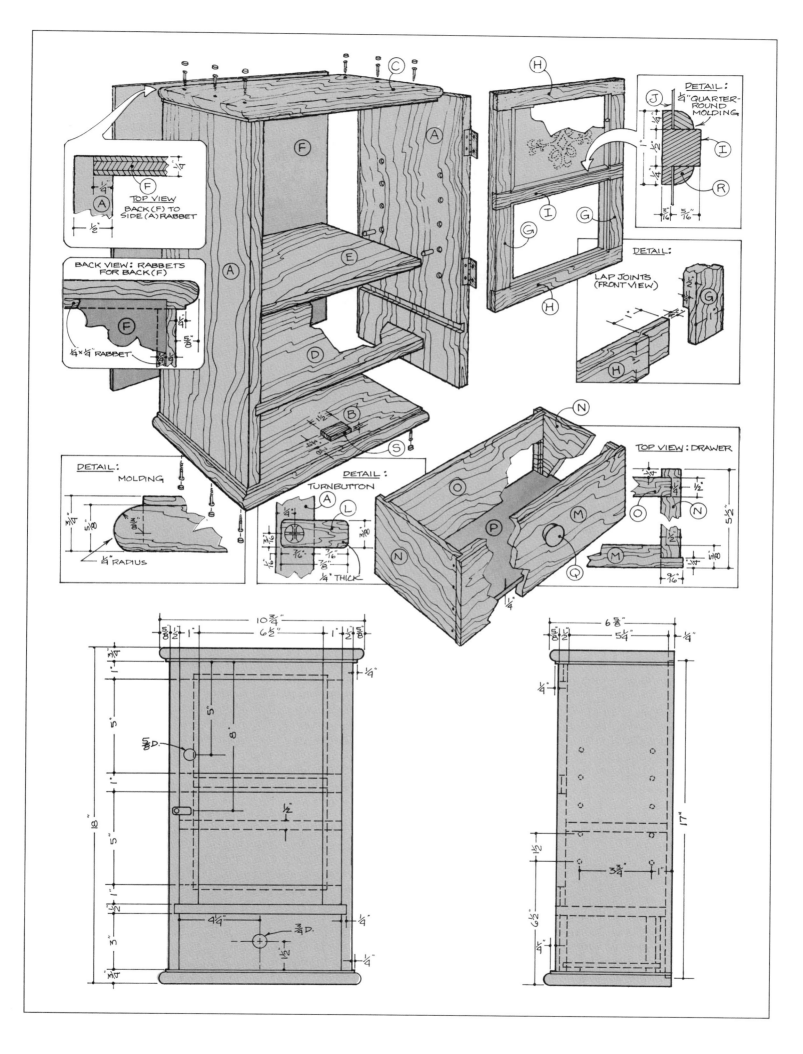

DETAIL:
"QUARTER-
ROUND
MOLDING

TOP VIEW:
BACK (F) TO
SIDE (A) RABBET

BACK VIEW: RABBETS
FOR BACK (F)

¼" × ¼" RABBET

LAP JOINTS
(FRONT VIEW)

DETAIL:
MOLDING

¼" RADIUS

DETAIL:
TURNBUTTON

¼" THICK

TOP VIEW: DRAWER

10¾"

6½"

5"

5"

⅝" D.

18"

5"

1"

4¼"

¾" D.

6⅝"

5¼"

17"

6½"

3¾"

Porch Swing

This rugged swing can be built in just a few hours, either out of redwood, or if you plan to paint it, out of regular construction lumber. The one shown was finished with an exterior semi-transparent gray stain. It measures five ft. overall, but the length can certainly vary depending upon available space.

Start by cutting all the 2 by 4 stock to the proper length, then nip off all the corners to soften the exposed ends and take away any rough edges. Next, make notches in seat supports (B) and (C) 3 in. back from the front end to accept the 2 by 4 swing support (A). Now, using a 30 - 60 degree draftsman's triangle, mark the locations of the notches as shown on the ends of support struts (F). Cut out with a saber saw and check for fit over part A. Now, make a 30-degree angle cut on one end of both arm rest supports (E). Take the back support (D) and lay it down over the seat support (C) in the position of the seat, then drill a $^3/8$ in. hole through both pieces and fasten them together with a $^3/8$ in. by 4 in. bolt (K), washers (N) and hex nut (O). Tighten down so that the two pieces form an "L" shape at about 10 degrees from a right angle.

Take parts E and F and lay them down in the proper position over the pieces just assembled so that the notches line up with each other and the upper end of part E is parallel with the seat support (C). Drill a $^3/8$ in. hole through all three 2 by 4's in the lower end where shown, insert a $^3/8$ in. by $5^1/2$ in. bolt (L) and washer and secure them with another washer and hex nut. Also drill through Parts F and D in the position shown and fasten together with a $^3/8$ in. by 4 in. bolt (K) with washers and hex nut. Now follow the same procedure for the other end except do it in the opposite direction so that when set up for assembly, all bolt heads will face outward. After both ends are assembled, drill a $^3/8$ in. hole $1^1/2$ in. from the top of back supports (D) to accept the $^3/8$ in. by 2 in. eyebolts (M). While you're at it, do the same to either end of swing support (A)

and secure those two eyebolts with nut and washer.

To finish the two brace assemblies, cut the arm rests (G) to size out of 1 by 8 stock, then nip off three corners as shown. On the remaining corner, cut a $1^1/2$ in. by $3^1/2$ in. notch. Fit this notch into the back support (D) resting it on the rearward end of the support strut (F). Position arm rest support (E) so that the arm rest (G) sits squarely upon its 30-degree angle and drive three 6d coated box nails through the arm rest and into part E as shown. Toenail two more nails into the back support (D), then follow this same procedure with the other end.

Now drop the two end brace assemblies down over swing support (A) into the notches you cut earlier so that the outermost edges of support struts (F) are 3 in. in from the ends of the swing support. Drive a 10d common nail through brace assembly and into swing support to be sure they stay in place, then positioning the center seat support (B) exactly in the middle, do the same to that. You're now ready for the final step.

Taking your remaining 1 by 8 stock, rip all of it to $3^1/2$ in. width and cut the pieces to the lengths required. Notice that these lengths vary depending upon where they go. Round off or bevel all exposed square edges slightly for appearance and comfort. Lay the four seat slats down, making sure to space them apart evenly, (approximately $^3/4$ in.). Overhang the front slat about $^3/4$ in. Secure all four seat slats with $1^1/2$ in. long galvanized deck screws. Now flip the seat onto its back, place the last three slats into position (one below

the arm rest, two above), and secure these in the same manner.

When fastening hooks into your porch ceiling, be sure to position them at least 12 in. further apart than the length of your swing so that the chain doesn't rub against the arm rests. Be sure too, that your hooks hit something good and solid to prevent any painful surprises. Cut your chain into two equal lengths and secure a link to the ceiling hooks approximately 15 in. off center; the shorter length goes to the back, the longer to the seat. Now lift your swing into place and fasten with "S" hooks adjusting until it hangs level and swings properly. To make it more comfortable, hang the seat so it tilts back slightly. When you're sure it hangs the way you want it, snip off any excess links and test it for weight. Then chase the kids away and enjoy.

Bill of Materials
(all dimensions actual)

Part	Description	Size	No. Req'd.
A	Swing Support	$1^1/2$ x $3^1/2$ x 60	1
B	Center Seat Support	$1^1/2$ x $3^1/2$ x 16	1
C	End Seat Support	$1^1/2$ x $3^1/2$ x 21	2
D	End Back Support	$1^1/2$ x $3^1/2$ x $21^1/2$	2
E	Arm Rest Support	$1^1/2$ x $3^1/2$ x $13^1/2$	2
F	Support Strut	$1^1/2$ x $3^1/2$ x 20	2
G	Arm Rest	$3/4$ x $3^1/2$ x $21^1/2$	2
H	Slat	$3/4$ x $3^1/2$ x 52	2
I	Slat	$3/4$ x $3^1/2$ x 51	3
J	Slat	$3/4$ x $3^1/2$ x 48	2
K	Hex Head Bolt	$3/8$ x 4	4
L	Hex Head Bolt	$3/8$ x $5^1/2$	2
M	Eyebolt	$3/8$ x 2	4
N	Washer	$3/8$	16
O	Hex Nut	$3/8$	10

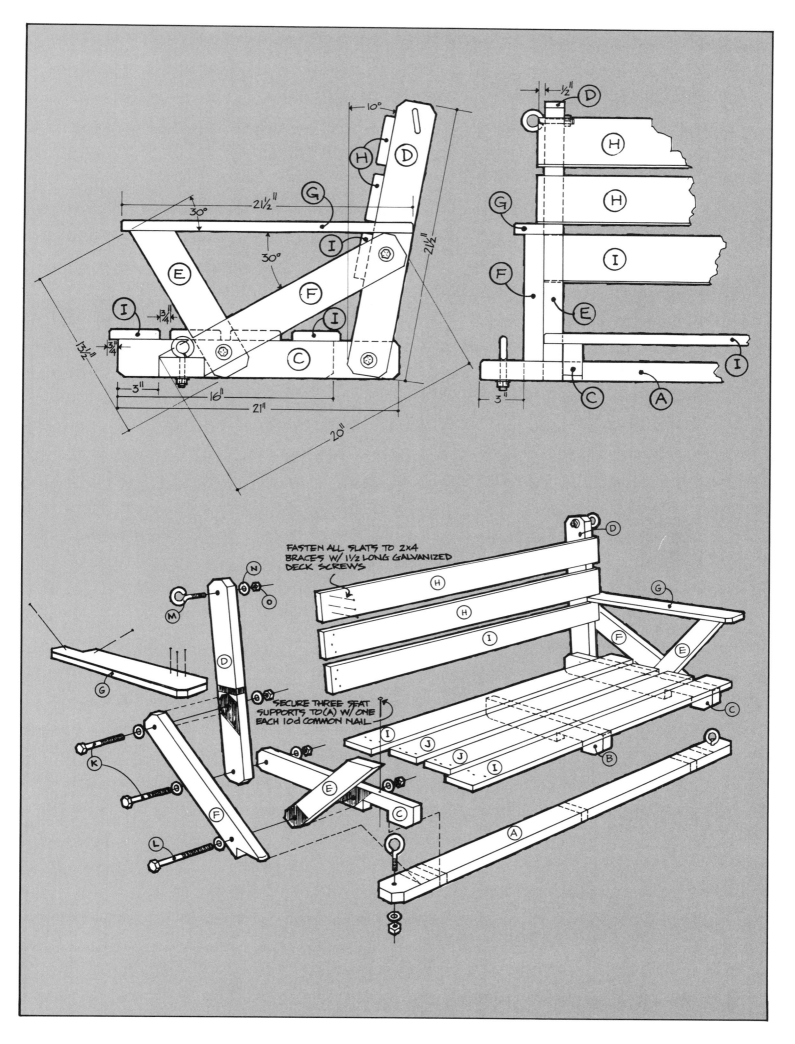

10°

21½"

30°

30°

E

G

I

D

H

F

I

C

I

3¾"

13½"

¾"

3"

16"

21"

20"

21½"

½"

D

H

H

G

I

F

E

C

A

I

3"

FASTEN ALL SLATS TO 2x4
BRACES W/ 1½ LONG GALVANIZED
DECK SCREWS

SECURE THREE SEAT
SUPPORTS TO (A) W/ ONE
EACH 10d COMMON NAIL

N
M
O
D
K
L
E
F
C
G

D
H
H
I
G
F
E
C
I
J
J
I
B
A

Cheval Mirror

The frame members square and shape after gluing up. The top (B) can be band sawn to shape and the curve sanded before assembly.

The mortises should be cut first based on the dimensions of the tenon shown in the detail. Lay out and mark their locations, then use a drill press to remove most of the waste. Clean out the waste with a sharp chisel. The tenon can be made on the table saw using the miter gauge. Using the mortised piece as a gauge to set the blade height, lower the blade to the height of the cheek of the mortise. Make a test cut in scrap material and adjust the blade if necessary. Use a stop to set the width of cut, then make repeated passes to cut out one side of the tenon. We usually take a piece of scrap of the same size and make the full cut as well. If necessary, reset the blade for the other side, then flip the scrap piece and make a trial cut. Try for a snug fit that can be forced together by hand. It's helpful to start by making the tenon too fat, then gradually raise the blade and thin it down until it fits just right.

Glue and assemble the mortises when you're satisfied with the fit. When dry, sand all joints flush and mold the edges as shown. Make the rabbet with a pilot bearing rabbeting bit in a router. The cut is $3/8$ in. wide and $1/2$ in. deep. The face is coved on the inside, again with a bearing on the bit. This is a $3/8$ in. cove. Take care not to take too deep a cut with the coving bit, otherwise you may cut into the tenons at the inside frame corners.

Back view shows batten (F) screwed to frame.

On the outside of the frame use a $3/8$ in. beading bit with a bearing. Give all parts a good sanding and set the frame aside.

Cut up stock for the feet (D) from four pieces of $3/4$ in. pine. Dado them as shown and glue together. When dry, trace the pattern and band saw the shape.

Shape the uprights and check the bottom for a good fit in the feet. Give the feet and uprights a good sanding, then glue up.

Cut the stretcher (I). When the feet assemblies are dry, join them with the stretcher. You may need an extra pair of hands to glue this up, or you can temporarily join the parts with finishing nails before clamping. The nails can be punched in afterward and the holes filled. Don't put the nails where the dowels will go. Mark and drill for the $3/8$ in. by 3 in. dowels and cut the dowel stock oversize. When clamping, apply glue sparingly with a sliver of wood. An overdose of glue will be trapped by the dowel and possibly split the stretcher open. Drive in the dowels and sand flush.

Cut the back (G) from $1/4$ in. plywood and the three battens from $3/4$ in. by $1 1/4$ in. stock. Screw the battens on with $1 1/4$ in. by no. 6 flathead wood screws. Use a $1/4$ in. threaded insert and $1/4$ in. threaded rod (or a carriage bolt with the head cut off) to hold the frame in the carriage. When drilling the $3/8$ in. diameter holes in the frame sides to take the threaded inserts, take care to keep the hole from spoiling the mirror rabbet cut. Epoxy wooden knobs over the $1/4$ in. threaded rod.

Give all parts a thorough final sanding with 220-grit aluminum oxide sandpaper. Any areas of glue squeeze-out should be cleaned

This lovely tilting mirror will make a practical addition to an entry hall or bedroom. We made ours from mostly clear $3/4$ in. and $1 1/8$ in. thick pine, but just about any good cabinet grade hardwood can also be used.

Begin by making the frame (parts A, B and C). Cut the members from $1 1/8$ in. thick no. 2 common pine. With a little selective cutting you should be able to get clear stock (no knots). Mortise and tenon joints are used to join the frame parts together. Leave all out with a sharp chisel. Take particular care to sand any rough areas within the cove cut. Any sharp edges should be rounded over slightly.

Of course, the type of final finish is a matter of personal preference. We chose to stain ours with Minwax's Golden Oak Stain, applying one coat. A small foam brush makes for easy application of the stain, although a rag can also be used with good results. Allow the stain to dry thoroughly. For a clear final finish we applied two coats of polyurethane varnish, sanding lightly between coats.

Bill of Materials
(all dimensions actual)

Part	Description	Size	No. Req'd.
A	Frame Side	1 1/8 x 1 1/2 x 55*	2
B	Frame Top	1 1/8 x 4 x 18	1
C	Frame Bottom	1 1/8 x 1 1/2 x 18	1
D	Foot	3/4 x 6 x 18	4
E	Upright	1 1/8 x 4 x 39	2
F	Batten	3/4 x 1 1/4 x 17 1/4	3
G	Back	1/4 x 15 5/8 x 53 1/8	1
H	Mirror	1/4 x 15 5/8 x 53 1/8	1
I	Stretcher	1 1/8 x 3 1/2 x 18 1/2	1

* includes tennons

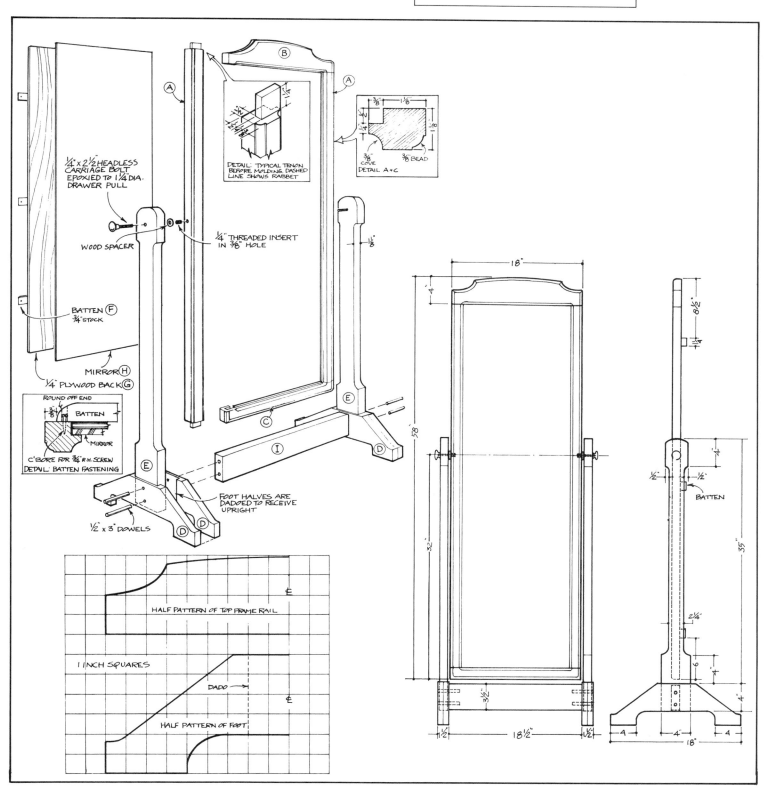

25

Television Stand/End Table

This handsome stand, made from white oak, is sturdy enough to take even the heaviest TV. There's a spacious shelf on the bottom to accommodate video equipment, books or magazines, and a convenient drawer to store things out of sight.

Joint edges and glue up the required width. For the sides (A) this will be 16⁵/₈ in. wide; for the top (B) and bottom (C) it will be 15⁵/₈ in. wide. Allow to dry thoroughly, at least one full day in a heated space. Scrape off the excess glue, then plane and sand the surface. Trim to size and lay out the cuts to be made on the inside faces of the sides.

The plywood back (D), which is glued into a ¹/₄ in. wide by ³/₈ in. deep groove all around, gives the piece considerable strength. It also means that there will be a left and a right side for parts A.

With a ³/₄ in. straight bit in the router, make a ³/₈ in. deep by ³/₄ in. wide dado in the sides. Note that the dado stops 1¹/₈ in. from each edge. Slowly lower the bit in to start the cut, then run it to the end of the cut. Back it up slightly and let the bit stop before lifting the router. Use an edge-guide to control the placement of the bit,

or clamp a straightedge at the appropriate distance from the cut. A sharp carbide bit will be able to remove this much material in one pass if driven by a 1 hp or larger motor. If you use a smaller machine, make the cuts in two or more passes.

To make the grooves for the back (D) use a ¹/₄ in. straight bit and run the groove into the dadoes already made for the top and bottom. Next, using the same setup, cut the groove for the back in the underside of the top, and the top surface of the bottom. The groove will be ¹/₂ in. closer to the edge on the top than it is on the sides. This is important to remember if you use the edge guide, because you must change the setting. Round over the edges with a ³/₈ in. radius rounding over bit.

Cut the back to size and glue up the sides (A), the top (B), the bottom (C) and the back (D) with yellow glue. Clamp and let dry overnight.

Cut the base pieces (E) and glue in place. It will help to pre-sand all pieces before assembly.

While you are waiting for the glue to dry on the carcase you can begin to make the drawer. The drawer front and back

(G) are joined to the drawer sides (F) with a rabbet and dado joint. A ¹/₄ in. by ¹/₄ in. groove is cut around the inside for the bottom (K). Dry fit with the bottom. If everything is alright, the parts can be glued up. Make sure the assembly is square and sits on a flat surface while the glue is drying. You can glue the bottom in place if you use plywood. If you use solid stock, let it "float" in the groove.

Cut out the stock for the drawer face (H) from particleboard or plywood, then cover it with white plastic laminate. Edge the face with ¹/₈ in. thick oak strips (I). Mount the drawer face by screwing to the front of the drawer with two 1¹/₄ in. by no. 8 flathead wood screws.

Before mounting the drawer face, use a router to groove the sides of the drawer ³/₈ in. deep by ³/₄ in. wide for the guides (J). The guides are screwed to the side with two 1 in. by no. 6 flathead wood screws. Be sure to use oversize holes at the back end of the guide to allow for wood movement. Note that the drawer guide is sized to allow space between it and the back, again to permit wood movement.

Install the drawer and check for a good sliding fit. If there is any tendency to bind, the drawer guides can be slightly sanded or shaved as needed.

Now give the entire project a thorough sanding. Use a sharp chisel to remove any areas of glue squeeze-out. Final sand with 220-grit sandpaper.

Watco Danish Oil was used for a final finish. This easy-to-apply penetrating oil soaks into the wood and then hardens to form a durable finish that looks most attractive on a piece like this. A coat of wax to the drawer guides will help keep the drawer operating smoothly. If you'd like a cabinet that can be rolled around, install four casters to the bottom so that the base is about ¹/₂ in. off the floor.

Bill of Materials
(all dimensions actual)

Part	Description	Size	No. Req'd.
A	Side	³/₄ x 16⁵/₈ x 19¹/₂	2
B	Top	³/₄ x 15⁵/₈ x 28¹/₂	1
C	Bottom	³/₄ x 15⁵/₈ x 28¹/₂	1
D	Back	¹/₄ x 15⁵/₈ x 28¹/₂	1
E	Base	³/₄ x 2¹/₂ x 28¹/₂	2
F	Drawer Side	³/₄ x 5 x 12	2
G	Drawer Front & Back	³/₄ x 5 x 27¹/₄	2
H	Drawer Face	³/₄ x 6 x 27¹/₂	1
I	Drawer Face Trim	¹/₈ x ³/₄	As req'd.
J	Drawer Guide	⁵/₈ x ³/₄ x 12	2
K	Drawer Bottom	¹/₄ x 11³/₄ x 26¹/₄	1

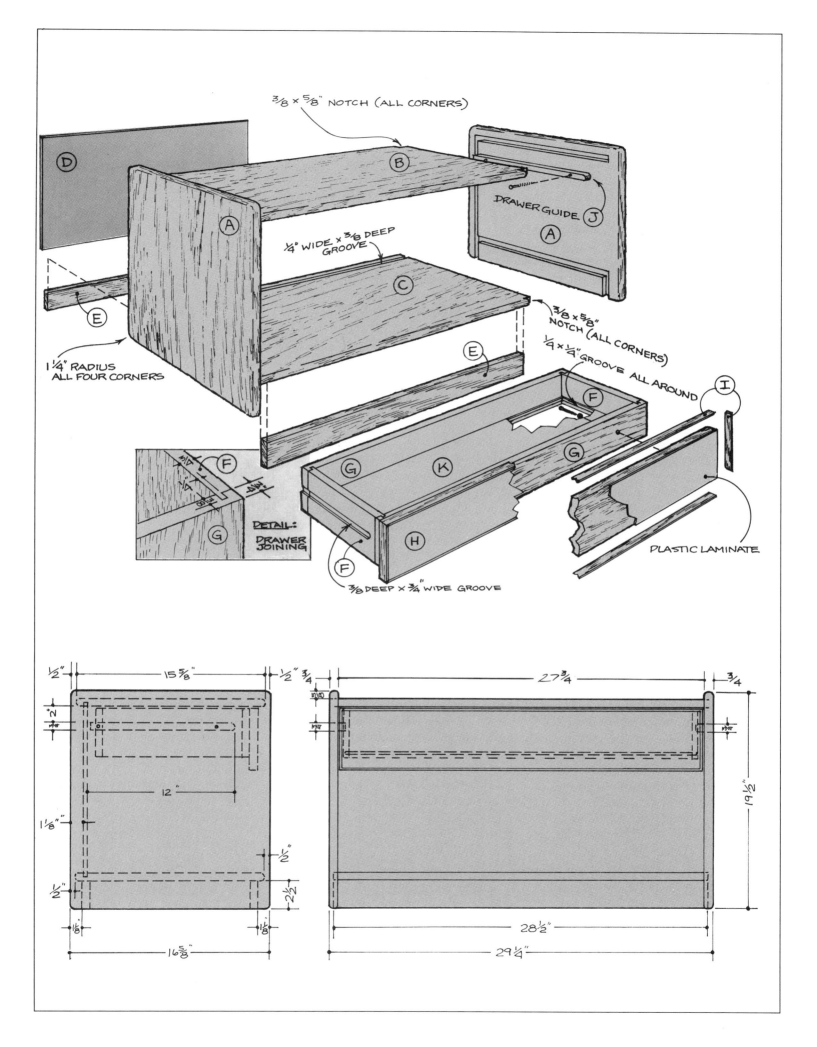

3/8 × 5/8" NOTCH (ALL CORNERS)

D

B

A

DRAWER GUIDE

J

A

1/4" WIDE × 3/8 DEEP GROOVE

C

3/8 × 5/8" NOTCH (ALL CORNERS)

1/4 × 1/4" GROOVE ALL AROUND

E

1 1/4" RADIUS ALL FOUR CORNERS

I

F

E

F

G

K

G

F

DETAIL: DRAWER JOINING

G

H

PLASTIC LAMINATE

3/8 DEEP × 3/4" WIDE GROOVE

1/2"   15 5/8"   1/2" 3/4   27 3/4   3/4

2"

3/4"

12"

1 1/8"

1/2"

19 1/2"

1/2"   2 1/2"

1/8   1/8

16 5/8"   28 1/2"

29 1/4"

27

Resembling the heavy block-and-tackle rigs that were common to all old-time sailing ships, this handsome pine lamp has a look that is unquestionably nautical. It requires only standard $^4/_4$ ($^3/_4$ in. thick) and $^5/_4$ ($1^1/_8$ in. thick) stock, and since construction is fairly basic, even the novice woodworker should be able to build it with little difficulty.

Begin by making the two outer shells (parts A) and the inner shell (part B). For each part cut $^5/_4$ stock (which actually measures $1^1/_8$ in. thick) to 7 in. wide by 9 in. long, then transfer the shape of the oval pattern from the grid pattern to the stock. On the two parts A, also mark the location of the 1 in. diameter center hole. On part B, mark the location of the $^1/_2$ in. wide by 5 in. long slot and the $^3/_8$ in. top and bottom hole. By the way, this slot simply serves as a means to shorten the length of the $^3/_8$ in. drill hole. Without the slot, the drill hole would have to run the entire length of part B.

To make the slot, drill a $^1/_2$ in. diameter hole at the top and bottom of the slot, then cut out the remaining material with the saber saw. The $^3/_8$ in. top and bottom holes are best cut with a drill press, but they can be done by hand if care is taken to insure that the hole is square. Parts A and B can now be cut to shape using a band or saber saw. Following this, the 1 in. diameter hole is bored in each part A as shown.

Parts C and D are made from $^3/_4$ in. thick stock. Transfer the shape from the grid pattern, then cut out and give all edges a good sanding. Although it is possible to glue and clamp the entire block assembly at once, we found it easier to first assemble parts C and D to part A. At this point we also checked the rope for an easy sliding fit. When dry, these two sub-assemblies were joined to part B. Glue and clamp securely at each stage. Before gluing, though, drive a couple of short brads, then clip the heads off so that about $^1/_8$ in. is exposed. The brads will keep the mating parts from sliding when clamped. Just be sure the brads are not in line with the location of the $^1/_2$ in. dowel pin holes that will be drilled later to join the base to the shell. When the shell has dried, cut 1 in. diameter dowel plugs to length and glue in place in the side holes. Cut the plugs slightly long, then sand the excess flush.

The base is made from $1^1/_8$ in. stock cut to 7 in. wide and 9 in. long. A compass is used to scribe a $1^1/_4$ in. radius at each corner. This radius is then cut out with a band or saber saw. A shallow cove is

Nautical Table Lamp

applied all around with a piloted $^3/_8$ in. cove bit. Locate and mark the center point on the underside of the base, then drill a 1 in. diameter by $^3/_4$ in. deep hole. At the center point of this hole, finish boring through the base with a $^1/_2$ in. diameter drill bit. Connecting the 1 in. hole to the back edge of the base is a $^1/_4$ in. diameter hole.

On the top of the base, lay out and mark the location of the two $^1/_2$ in. diameter by $1^1/_4$ in. long dowel pins that secure the base to the shell. Drive a short brad into the center point of each hole location, then clip off the heads so that about $^1/_8$ in. is exposed. Sand a slight flat area across the shell bottom, then center the shell on the base. Be sure the hole in the base is aligned with the slot in the shell, then carefully press the shell to the base so that the brad points mark the shell bottom. Now separate the shell from the base and remove the brads with a pair of pliers. Using the brad holes as centers, drill $^{11}/_{16}$ in. deep holes to accept the $^1/_2$ in.

diameter dowel pins. Also at this time, locate and drill the four holes for the rope ends.

Give all parts a thorough sanding, particularly the edges of the shell, then assemble the shell to the base. Use glue and clamp firmly. Stain to suit and final finish with two coats of polyurethane varnish.

Cut $^3/_4$ in. diameter rope (hemp) to length, taking care to tape the ends tightly before cutting. Insert in the holes and glue in place. If necessary, a finishing nail can be added to further secure each rope end.

A 5 in. length of $^1/_8$ in. I.P. threaded lamp pipe is inserted into the shell to a depth of $^3/_4$ in. The lamp cord is then fed through the base and up through the shell and out the lamp pipe. A $^5/_8$ in. spacer and 4 in. long brass tube slip over the lamp pipe. The harp is added and the cord is connected to the socket. The socket then threads to the top of the lamp pipe. The addition of a bulb and lamp shade completes the project.

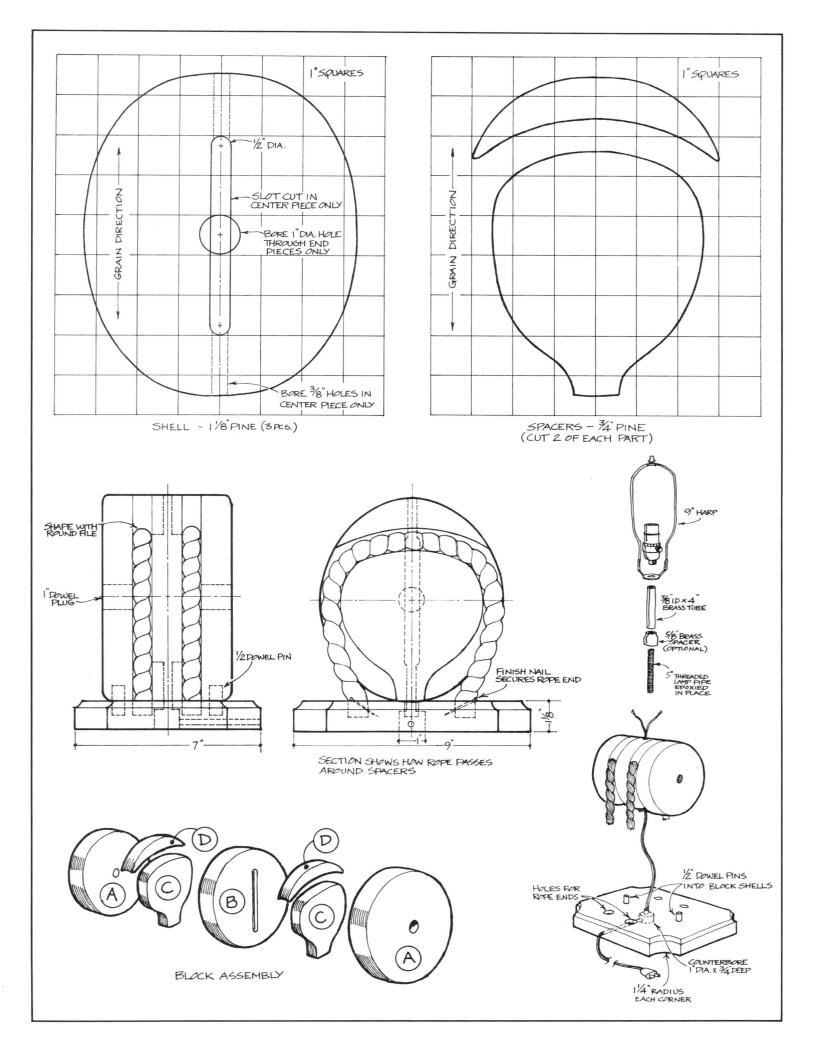

1" SQUARES

GRAIN DIRECTION

½" DIA.

SLOT CUT IN
CENTER PIECE ONLY

BORE 1" DIA. HOLE
THROUGH END
PIECES ONLY

BORE ⅜" HOLES IN
CENTER PIECE ONLY

SHELL - 1⅛" PINE (3 PCS.)

1" SQUARES

GRAIN DIRECTION

SPACERS - ¾" PINE
(CUT 2 OF EACH PART)

SHAPE WITH
ROUND FILE

1" DOWEL
PLUG

½" DOWEL PIN

7"

FINISH NAIL
SECURES ROPE END

⅛"

1"

9"

SECTION SHOWS HOW ROPE PASSES
AROUND SPACERS

9" HARP

⅜" ID x 4"
BRASS TUBE

⅝" BRASS
SPACER
(OPTIONAL)

5" THREADED
LAMP PIPE
EPOXIED
IN PLACE

BLOCK ASSEMBLY

A
C
D
B
D
C
A

HOLES FOR
ROPE ENDS

½" DOWEL PINS
INTO BLOCK SHELLS

COUNTERBORE
1" DIA. x ¾" DEEP

1¼" RADIUS
EACH CORNER

Beam Balance

Occasionally it's fun to make something that doesn't really have a function other than to be purely decorative. Undoubtedly, this project falls into that category. However, we've found one thing it can do, and that is generate quite a bit of conversation. More than likely you'll be asked if it actually works. If made carefully, the answer is yes, it's a reasonably accurate balance.

The base (B) and the scales (D) can best be made by faceplate turning the stock, although it's also possible to make both parts with a router. If a router is used, part B must be made from two pieces of stock, one piece 1 in. thick, the other 3/4 in. thick. The two pieces are glued up after the routing is completed on each piece.

Because we lathe-turned ours, we used maple stock in order to take advantage of its excellent turning qualities. Cherry would be another good choice.

Begin by making the base (part B). Cut 1³/4 in. thick stock to 7 in. square, then scribe corner-to-corner diagonal lines to locate the center point. From this center point, use a compass to scribe three circles, the first to match the diameter of your faceplate (ours was 6 in. dia.), the second to 6¹/2 in. diameter, and the third to 6³/4 in. diameter. Next, use a band or saber saw to cut the stock to the 6³/4 in. diameter circle.

With the scribed circle as a centering guide, the faceplate can now be screwed to the stock and then the entire unit attached to the lathe. Use the gouge to true up the stock, turning it down to the scribed 6¹/2 in. diameter circle. With the lathe still turning, use a pencil to mark a line 1 in. from the faceplate. Keeping this 1 in. thickness, use the parting tool to make a ¹/2 in. deep cut. Working left to right, continue making ¹/2 in. deep cuts until a ³/4 in. wide step is formed. Next, use a pencil to mark a line establishing the ¹/4 in. step for the ¹/2 in. radius cove, then use a gouge or roundnose scraper to form the cove. The ¹/2 in. outside radius can now be applied with the skew.

With the stock still in the lathe, give it a thorough sanding. Start with 100-grit aluminum oxide paper to remove any rough turning marks. Follow this with 150-, then 220-grit. Remove the base from the faceplate and fill the screw holes

with wood filler.

On the top surface of the base, lay out and mark the location of the ³/8 in. thick by 1¹/2 in. wide by 1⁵/16 in. deep mortise. Most of the mortise can be cut by drilling a series of holes with a ³/8 in. drill bit. The remaining waste stock can be removed with a sharp chisel. Note that the mortise is cut slightly deeper than the tenon length to allow room for any excess glue.

To make the scales (part D), cut ³/4 in. thick stock to 4¹/2 in. square, then scribe corner-to-corner diagonal lines to locate the center point. From this center point use a compass to scribe two circles, one measuring 3³/4 in. diameter, the other measuring 4 in. diameter. Use a band or saber saw to cut out to the 4 in. diameter.

Since the underside of the scales can be seen, the faceplate can't be screwed directly to the scale. If it is, the unsightly filled screw holes will show. Instead the faceplate is screwed to a backing block which is then glued (with paper in between to allow easy removal) to the scale. To make the backing block, cut ³/4 in. thick stock (pine is suitable) to 3¹/2 in. square. Scribe diagonal lines to locate the center, then use the compass to scribe two circles, the first to match the diameter of

your faceplate (ours was 3 in. diameter), the second to 3¹/4 in. diameter. Now use the band or saber saw to cut the backing block stock to the 3¹/4 in. diameter.

At this point, to aid when centering the backing block on the scale, it's a good idea to add a 3¹/4 in. diameter circle to the scale stock. With a piece of heavy (brown grocery bag) paper in between, glue (with wood glue) the backing block to the scale stock, taking care to center it on the scribed circle. The two parts will have a tendency to slide over each other, so before gluing, drive two small brads into the scale stock, then clip off the heads so about ¹/8 in. is exposed. Just make sure the brads are located a safe distance from where the turning tools will cut. When dry, the faceplate can be screwed to the backing block and then the entire unit attached to the lathe.

To insure that the stock rotates smoothly, it's a good idea to first true up the backing block using the parting tool. Use the gouge to true up the scale stock, turning it down to the scribed 3³/4 in. diameter. A ¹/2 in. gouge will do a good job of rounding the outside edge to the profile shown on the drawing. In order to shape the entire curve, though, it will be necessary to partially cut into the backing block.

Next, arrange the tool rest so that it faces the face surface of the stock. To dish out the scale, begin by using a pencil to mark a 3³/₈ in. diameter on the turned stock. This establishes the diameter of the dished-out area. With this line as a guide, use a parting tool to make a ¹/₄ in. deep cut. Working toward the center from this groove, use a ¹/₂ in. gouge to remove the remaining material. Sand completely using the same procedure as was used for the base. Remove the stock from the lathe. Now remove the faceplate, then use a chisel and mallet to knock off the backing block. Sand off the remaining paper before

drilling three ¹/₈ in. chain holes located 120 degrees apart.

The post (part C) is cut to 1⁷/₈ in. wide by 12¹/₂ in. long. The tenon can be cut in a variety of ways, but we chose to use the dado head in conjunction with the table saw. No matter what method you choose, though, make sure the tenon fits snugly in the base mortise. The ¹/₄ in. wide notch for the beam (A) can also be cut in a variety of ways. We used a tenon jig. With the table saw blade set for a height of 2¹/₈ in., the notch was cut with three or four passes over the blade. Next, use a ruler to scribe the top-to-bottom taper, then a smooth or jack plane to cut to shape. Add the ¹/₄ in. chamfer with a file or drawknife.

The beam (A) is made next. If you don't have ¹/₄ in. thick stock it can be resawn from thicker stock on the band or table saw. Transfer the grid pattern shown, then cut to shape. A ¹/₈ in. ring hole is added at each end.

Sand part A so that it pivots freely in the post notch. A ¹/₄ in. dowel pin is glued in place and sanded flush with the surface. Several coats of Deftco Danish Oil produces a nice finish.

We used brass cafe curtain rings and light brass chain available at most hardware stores. The links were opened to fit in the scale holes, then closed over. A piece of felt, glued to the bottom, completes the project.

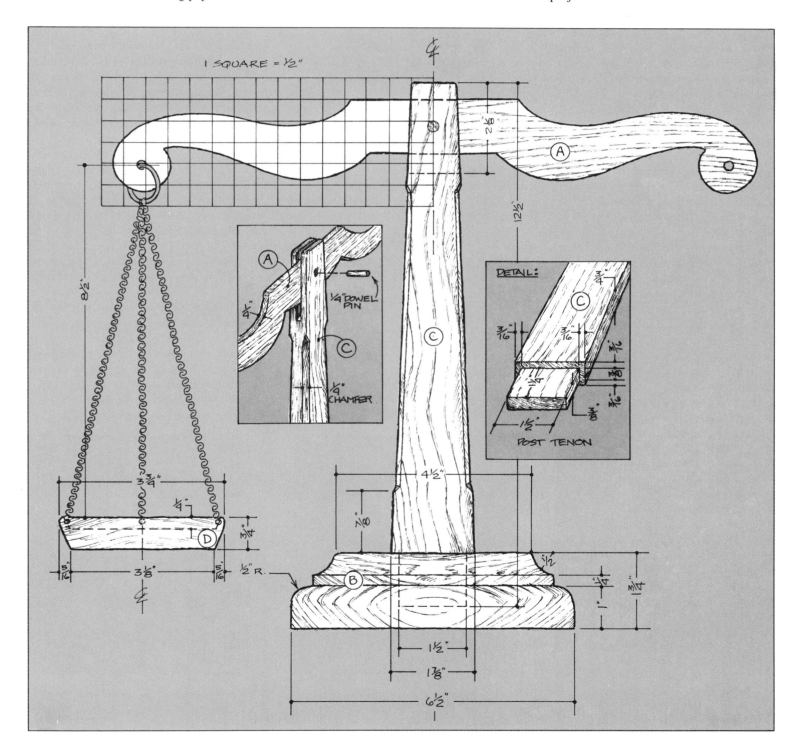

Nesting Tables

These three little tables will nest out of the way when not in use, or form a set of serving tables that are both attractive and functional.

All three tops are the same size, 16 in. square and 3/4 in. thick. They are made from strips 2 in. wide by 16 1/2 in. long. Allow the extra length so you can trim to final size. Saw up the strips (eight pieces) and keep them arranged the way they came off the saw. This way they will not amplify the error if your blade is not perpendicular to the table.

Glue the top strips by spreading yellow (aliphatic resin) glue on both edges of the joint. Apply a thin coat and rub the pieces together. Clamp with bar clamps, alternating top and bottom to apply even pressure and minimize bowing the top. Apply only enough pressure to close the joints. Do not touch the glue squeeze out. Let it harden and scrape it off. However, don't let the glue come into contact with the bar clamps. If it does, the glue will turn black. When dry, sand thoroughly and trim to size. If you find the top has a slight bow, assemble it convex side up.

The leg frames are made from 24 pieces of 1 1/4 in. wide by 16 1/8 in. long by 3/4 in. thick white oak. They are 1/8 in. oversize so you can sand them flush.

When all the stock is cut to size, mark out the slip joints with a fine pencil or scribe. Cut on the outside of the tenon line for the tenons with a backsaw or the band saw (see photo). Don't forget to allow 1/16 in. extra at each end. Now, saw off the cheeks at the tenons. On scrap stock, saw on the inside of the open mortise lines and chisel out the waste. Try the fit. If everything looks satisfactory, make all the pieces.

Clamp up the frames with yellow glue and bar clamps. You will also need C-clamps to close the cheeks of the mortise tight to the tenons. Be careful to apply only light pressure with the bar clamps or you will bow the legs. When dry, sand flush and drill a 3/8 in. hole in the frame corners. Don't drill all the way through or you will tear out material when you set your dowels. With a 3/8 in. dowel cutter make long grain dowels from scrap stock. Round the tips and apply a very small amount of glue to the holes with a sliver of wood. Drive the dowels home and sand flush when dry.

Drill and countersink each frame for three screws. To allow for wood movement, elongate the two outside screw holes. After final sanding, screw the leg frames to the tops with six 1 1/2 in. by no. 8 flathead wood screws for each table. The first table (see drawing) has its legs flush with the edge of the top. The legs of the second table are located to fit with slight clearance inside the first table. The legs of the third table are located to fit just inside the second table. Finish with a penetrating oil and wax if desired.

The band saw is used to make face cuts for tenons.

A radial-arm saw cuts off tenon cheeks.

C-clamps close cheeks of the mortise tight to tenons. Note clamp pads to protect stock.

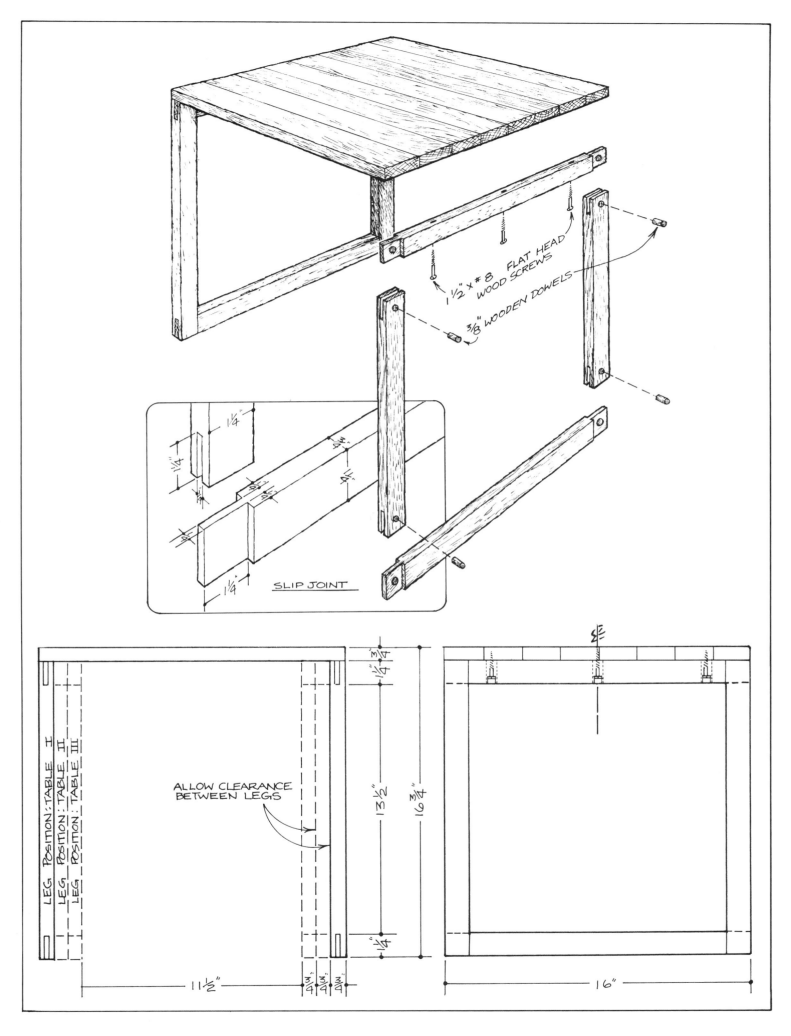

1 1/2" x #8 FLAT HEAD
WOOD SCREWS

3/8" WOODEN DOWELS

1/4"

1/4"

1/4"

3/4"

1/4"

1/4"

SLIP JOINT

LEG POSITION: TABLE I
LEG POSITION: TABLE II
LEG POSITION: TABLE III

ALLOW CLEARANCE
BETWEEN LEGS

3/4"
1/4"

13 1/2"

16 3/4"

1/4"

11 1/2"

3/4" 3/4" 3/4"

3/8"

16"

Toy Steam Roller

Kids will find that backyard construction can be even more fun with a sturdy steam roller toy like this. Poplar was used for all parts, although maple or oak would also be good choices. Of course, even pine can be used, but it's much more susceptible to dents and scratches.

The hood (part A) can be made first. Cut to length, width and thickness, then lay out and mark the location of the 1¼ in. radius as shown. Use a band or saber saw to cut out the curve.

The floor (part B) and the undercarriage (part C) can now be cut to size and joined together. Use wood glue and clamp securely. Before gluing, drive a couple of short brads in part C (don't locate them in line with axle holes), then clip the heads off so that about ⅛ in. is exposed. This will keep the two parts from sliding when clamped. Allow to dry thoroughly. Now, parts B and C can be glued to part A, again using clipped brads, glue and clamps. When dry, mark the location of the wheel axle hole on part C, then drill a ⁷⁄₁₆ in. diameter through hole as shown.

The steering bar (part D) and the roller support (part E) are made next. Cut to the dimensions shown in the Bill of Materials, then drill the ¼ in. diameter holes for the roller axle (L) as shown. Round the

bottom of parts E before gluing and clamping to part D. Note that parts E are set back ⅛ in. from each end of part D. When dry, drill for ¼ in. diameter by 1¼ in. long pins as shown. Cut the pins a little on the long side, then glue in place. When dry, sand flush with the surface.

Part F, the pivot pin, can be lathe-turned to the dimensions shown. Lacking a lathe, a similar pin can be ordered from Cherry Tree Toys, P.O. Box 369,

Bill of Materials
(all dimensions actual)

Part	Description	Size	No. Req'd.
A	Hood	1½ x 2 x 4	1
B	Floor	¾ x 1½ x 2½	1
C	Undercarriage	1 x 1½ x 4	1
D	Steering Bar	⅝ x ¾ x 4⅝	1
E	Roller Support	⅝ x ¾ x 2⅛	2
F	Pivot Pin	(see Detail)	1
G	Seat	½ x ⅝ x 1	1
H	Seat Back	¼ x 1 x 1⅛	1
I	Steering Post	³⁄₁₆ dia. x 1⅛ long	1
J	Steering Wheel	1 dia. x ¼ thick	1
K	Roller	2½ dia. x 3 thick	1
L	Roller Axle	¼ dia. x 4⅝ long	1
M	Wheel	3½ dia. x 1⅛ thick	2
N	Spacer	(see Detail)	2
O	Wheel Axle	⅜ dia. x 6½ long	1

Belmont, OH 43718. Their part no. 10 has a ⁵⁄₁₆ in. diameter shaft and is 1⁹⁄₁₆ in. long, so the shaft will need to be shortened and a ⅜ in. diameter hole drilled.

Cut part I to length before gluing the steering wheel (J) in place. The steering wheel can be cut from ¼ in. thick stock with a 1 in. diameter hole saw. Drill a ½ in. deep hole in the hood (A) for part I, then sand part I so that it turns freely in this hole. Glue parts G and H together before gluing them both to part B. When glued in place, part G will prevent the steering wheel (J) and post (I) from coming out, yet the wheel and post will be free to turn in the hole.

The roller (K) is made from four pieces of ¾ in. thick by 3 in. square stock glued together and lathe-turned to 2½ in. The center hole in the drum should be just large enough so that it will revolve easily on the axle (L).

Part M, the wheels, can be lathe-turned or cut out with the band saw or saber saw. Sand the edges smooth. The spacer (N) can be a 1 in. diameter dowel, or a wooden thread spool, or it can be lathe-turned to the shape shown.

Give all parts a complete sanding, taking care to remove sharp edges. Complete assembly as shown. No final finish is necessary.

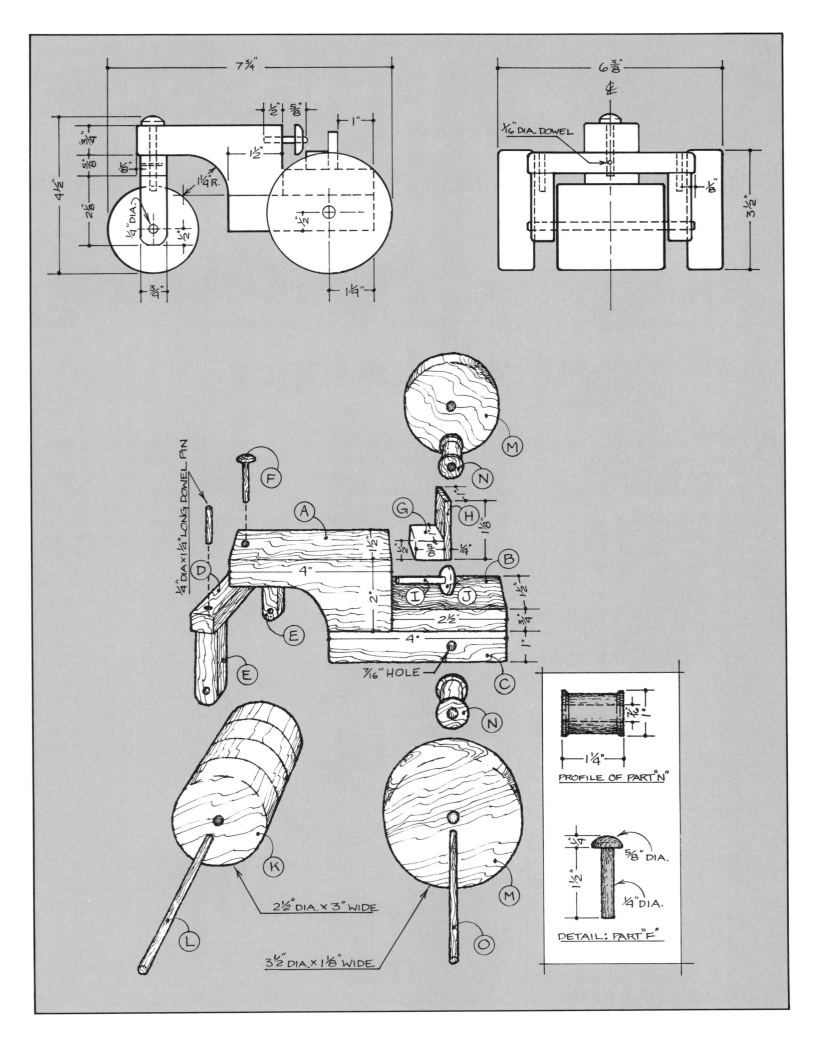

7¾"
4½"
½" 5/8"
¾"
3/16"
5/8"
1/8"
1"
¼" R.
1½"
¼" DIA.
½"
½"
2 1/8"
¾"
1¼"

6 3/8"
3½"
1/16" DIA DOWEL
1/8"

¼" DIA X 1½ LONG DOWEL PIN
F
M
N
A
G
H
1"
1/8"
½"
5/8"
¼"
2½"
D
B
4"
2"
I
J
½"
1"
¾"
E
2½"
4"
E
C
7/16" HOLE
N

K
L
2½" DIA. X 3" WIDE

M
O
3½" DIA. X 1/8" WIDE

7/16"
1"
1¼"
PROFILE OF PART "N"

¼"
5/8" DIA.
1½"
¼" DIA.
DETAIL: PART "F"

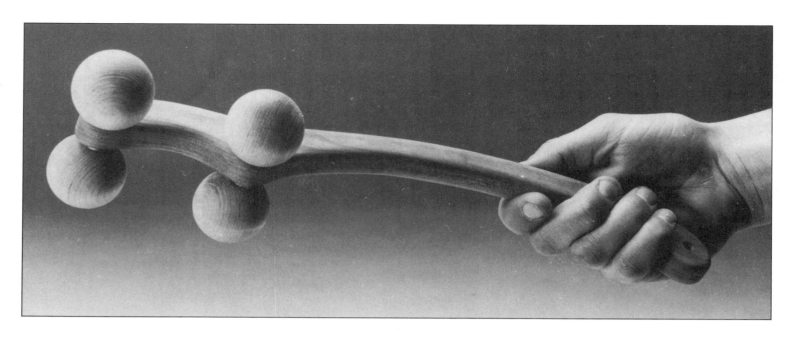

Back Massager

Aching backs will welcome this gadget. When rolled across suffering muscles it generates a gentle massaging action that feels just great. In fact, even pampered backs will enjoy it.

Most any type of wood can be used for the handle — ours was made with cherry. The $1^{1}/_{2}$ in. diameter hardwood balls were ordered from Meisel Hardware Specialties, P.O. Box 70, Mound, MN 55364-0070. Order part no. 1346.

From $^{3}/_{4}$ in. thick stock, use a band saw or saber saw to cut the handle to the profile shown. Drill $^{7}/_{16}$ in. diameter holes for the two axles and a $^{1}/_{4}$ in. diameter hole for the hanger as shown. Use a file or Surform tool to apply a generous radius to all edges. Sand the file marks, starting with coarse (80 grit) sandpaper, then working to 100, 150, and finally, 220 grit.

In order to accurately locate the axle hole in the center of the wooden ball, it's a good idea to make a jig like the one shown. Using the dado head cutter, make two cuts at right angles to each other, each one $^{3}/_{8}$ in. deep by $^{3}/_{4}$ in. wide.

Carefully measure and mark the exact center point where the dadoes crisscross. Clamp the jig in the drill press so that this center point is in line with the center point of the drill bit. Place a ball in the jig so that it is supported by the four corners. Use a handscrew to hold the ball, then drill a $^{3}/_{8}$ in. diameter hole to a depth of $^{1}/_{2}$ in. Repeat this procedure for the other three balls.

Cut the axles to length, then assemble the balls with glue. Allow to dry before applying a clear final finish.

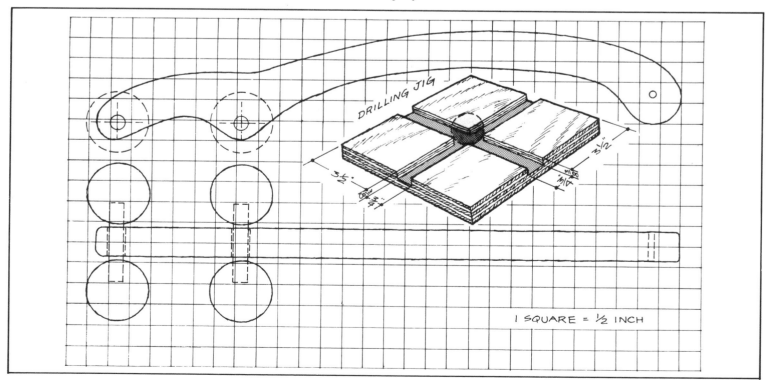

DRILLING JIG

1 SQUARE = $^{1}/_{2}$ INCH

Mailbox

A minimum of stock and a few evenings in the workshop are all that's needed to construct this sturdy mailbox. Ours is made from pine, but cedar is also a good choice, especially if it will be exposed to the weather. To help keep rain from getting inside, we've added a cove along the cleat (F) and inset the back (C) and cleat so that rain traveling down the outside of a building will run behind the mailbox. For further weatherproofing, it's important to use brass hinges, galvanized nails, and a water-resistant glue such as the plastic resin type.

Begin by cutting the two sides (A) to size ($3/4$ in. by 7 in. by $12^{1}/_{2}$ in.). The tapered top edge is cut at an angle of 16 degrees on the table or radial-arm saw. Transfer the pattern of the curve to the stock before cutting out with a band or saber saw.

Next, cut the front (part B) to $3/4$ in. by $6^{1}/_{4}$ in. by 14 in., the bottom (part D) to $3/4$ in. by $5^{1}/_{4}$ in. by 14 in., and the back (part C) to $3/4$ in. by 8 in. by 14 in. Two or more narrower boards will probably have to be edge-glued in order to get enough width for part C. Note that a 16-degree bevel is applied to the top edge of parts B and C.

To cut the cove in part F, it's best to start with a wide piece of stock. Clamp a guidestrip to the stock, then rout the cove using a $1/2$ in. core box bit. Now, with the table or radial-arm saw blade set at 16 degrees, rip part F to the width shown.

After cutting the top (E) to size, give all the parts a thorough sanding. Assemble with plastic resin glue and finishing nails, countersunk and filled. Mortise for and mount the $1^{1}/_{2}$ in. by $1^{1}/_{2}$ in. butt hinges. Stain to suit, then finish with three coats of spar varnish.

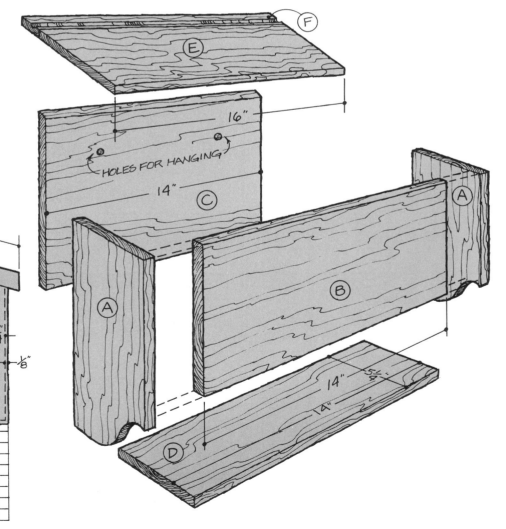

W ith its nicely shaped scroll pattern, this easy-to-build pine wall shelf will make an attractive addition to just about any room in the house.

The back can be made first. Since a 9 in. wide piece of stock is required, it will be necessary to edge-glue two or more narrower boards. To prevent the edges from sliding when clamped, it's a good idea to include two or three 1/4 in. diameter dowel pins in the joint. Apply glue to the edges, then clamp firmly and allow to dry overnight.

Transfer the scroll pattern from the drawing to the stock, then cut out with a band or saber saw. Give the edges a thorough sanding. If you have one, a drum sander will be helpful here. After smoothing the edge, use a router equipped with a 3/8 in. piloted cove bit to apply a cove all around the outside edge.

The shelf can be made next. If necessary, glue up narrower boards, then transfer the grid pattern to the stock. Again, sand the edges and apply the cove detail.

Next, cut the bracket to the shape shown, then lay out and mark the location of the 3/8 in. dowel pins. Give all parts a thorough sanding before staining to suit. When dry, assemble with glue and clamp

Pine Wall Shelf

firmly. Use just a thin coat of glue in order to keep glue squeeze-out to a minimum. Allow to dry overnight. Final finish with two coats of polyurethane varnish, sanding lightly between each coat. Two angled holes drilled through the back and into the shelf provide a convenient means to hang the shelf.

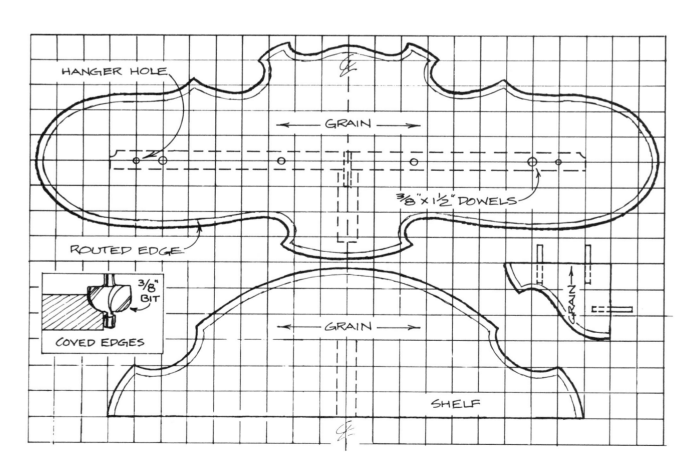

HANGER HOLE

GRAIN

3/8" × 1½" DOWELS

ROUTED EDGE

3/8" BIT

COVED EDGES

GRAIN

GRAIN

SHELF

Bill of Materials			
(all dimensions actual)			
Part	Description	Size	No. Req'd.
A	Top	3/8 x 6 3/8 x 17 3/8	1
B	Bottom	3/8 x 4 5/8 x 17 1/8	1
C	Upper End	3/8 x 1 7/8 x 8 1/4	2
D	Lower End	3/8 x 2 3/8 x 8 1/2	2
E	Frame Side	3/4 x 1 1/8 x 25 1/4	2
F	Frame Top & Bottom	3/4 x 1 1/8 x 17 1/8	2
G	Cleat	3/8 x 3/8	6
H	Mirror	1/8 x 15 7/8 x 24	1
I	Backing	1/8 x 15 7/8 x 24	1
J	Retainer	1/4 in. quarter-round	As Req'd.
K	Spline	1/8 x 2 x 2	4

Chippendale Mirror

This bird's-eye maple mirror is a reproduction of an antique curly maple mirror. For those who might want to make one, there are a number of woods to choose from — cherry, plain maple, birch, mahogany, or even hardwood plywoods. Many of the early mirrors were veneered, but veneering on such thin stock generally ends in warping. This style of mirror was made during the last quarter of the 18th century. The fancy ones are usually called Chippendale. The construction entails some exacting effort but a beginning woodworker should be able to do a good job.

The mirror frame is made first. Parts E and F form the frame. They are cut to width and 1 or 2 in. longer than the finished length. They are sanded and then rabbeted for the mirror (see cross-sectional detail). The rabbets may be prepared on the table saw, shaper, or router. Each corner is mitered, then the parts are clamped for fit and squareness.

Because of the delicate size of the frame, it is recommended that splines be used to reinforce the corners. Unlike most spline miter joints, these won't show when the project is assembled. For this reason it was possible to make the splines wider than normal. Although the cut breaks through the inside edges of the frame parts, the longer miter will result in a stronger joint.

The spline cuts can be made on the table saw, or if necessary they can be done by hand. If you choose to use the table saw, you'll need to make a jig that holds the frame on edge, at a 45-degree angle to the saw table (see detail). Note that the spline groove is 1/8 in. wide and is centered along the thickness of the frame parts. For maximum strength the 1/8 in. thick spline should be made from plywood. The notch on the inside corner is cut out after the spline has been assembled and the glue has dried. It can best be cut out with a sharp chisel, taking care to shave it flush with the edges of the frame rabbets.

The curved shapes (parts A, B, C and D) are made from 3/8 in. thick stock. If you can't purchase 3/8 in. lumber, there are several options. If you have one, a power planer will reduce 3/4 in. stock to 3/8 in. pretty quickly. Or you may be able to have a local millwork shop do it for you. The charge is usually minimal. Both the band saw and the table saw can also be used to resaw thicker stock. However, the table saw is limited to narrow boards, so it will be necessary to edge-glue several resawn pieces in order to get enough width for parts A and B. And, of course, you can always hand plane thicker stock down to 3/8 in. There's not much material involved, so it won't take very long.

After the stock for parts A, B, C and D has been cut to length and width, the curved patterns can be transferred from the grid patterns. Use a band, saber, or jigsaw to cut to shape.

Cut the 3/8 in. by 3/8 in. cleats (part G) for the top (part A), keeping in mind that the cleats do not extend the entire length of the top. They should be cut about 1/2 in. short of each end. Glue the cleats to part A as shown using several brads to secure each cleat in place. When dry, make sure that the edge of the cleat is flush with the edge of part A. If it isn't, use a hand plane to cut a flush joint. This will insure a tight butt joint between parts A and F. The cleats for parts B, C, and D are attached in the same manner.

Parts A, B, C and D can now be joined to the frame. Use glue and brads driven through the cleat into the frame parts. Note that parts A and C, and parts B and D, meet at the corners of the frame. Check to make sure that parts A, B, C and D are flush with the front of the frame. If not it will be necessary to sand them flush.

For the finish, first sand all parts carefully with 220- or 340-grit aluminum oxide paper. A sealing coat of shellac is then applied. This coat should be sanded thoroughly with 220-grit paper. The first coat of varnish is sanded with 340-grit paper, then rubbed down with steel wool. The final coat is dressed with 600-grit wet-or-dry paper, and again rubbed down with steel wool. A good coat of hard paste wax follows.

Single strength mirror glass (part H) is satisfactory. The mirror is backed up with a single piece of $1/8$ in. thick hardboard (Part I). Cut both the mirror and the hardboard backing to fit just inside the frame rabbets. Both these parts are then held in place with $1/4$ in. quarter-round molding (part J). The molding is tacked in place and mitered at the four corners. A pair of eyelets, screwed into the back of the frame, permit it to be hung by a picture frame wire.

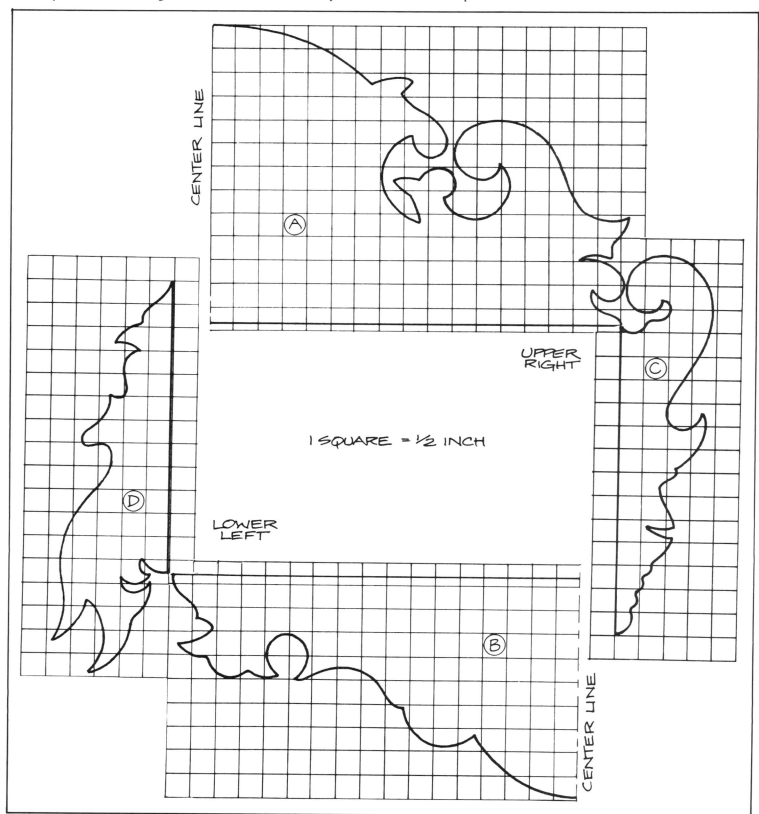

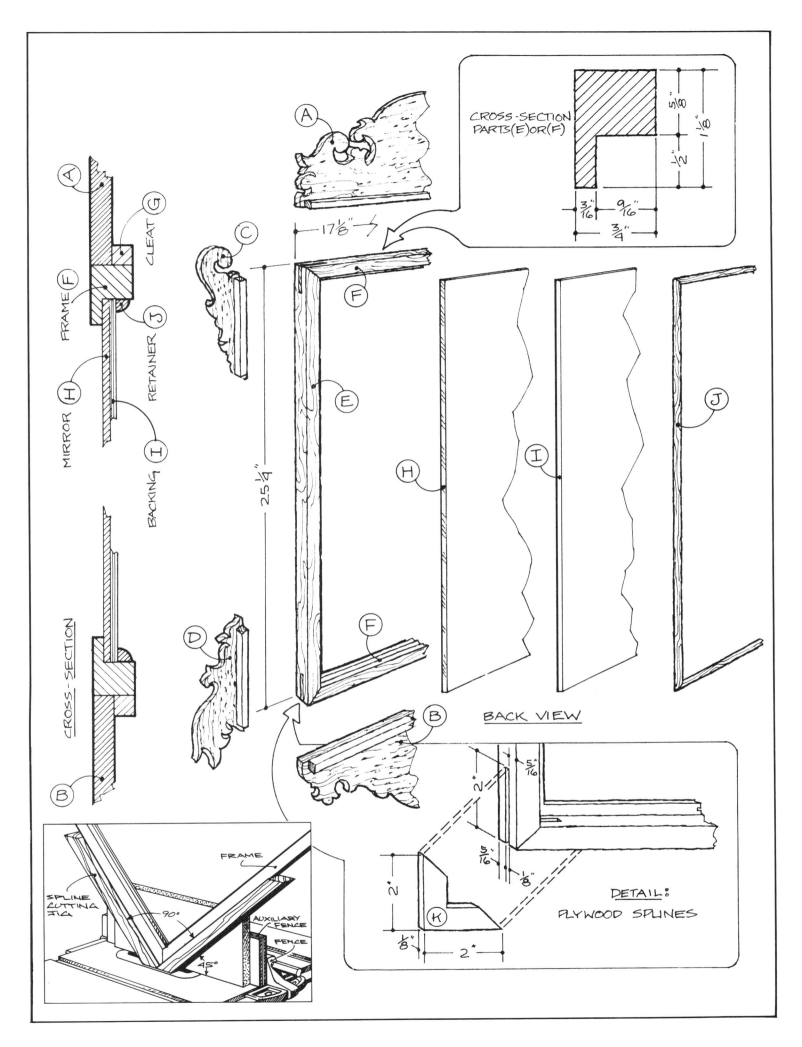

CROSS-SECTION
PARTS (E) OR (F)

5/8"
1/8"
1/2"
3/16" 9/16"
3/4"

A

CROSS-SECTION

A
CLEAT G
FRAME F
J RETAINER
MIRROR H
BACKING I
B

A
17 1/8"
C
F
E
25 1/4"
F
H
I
J

BACK VIEW

D

B

DETAIL:
PLYWOOD SPLINES

5/16"
2"
2"
5/16"
1/8"
K
2"
1/8"
2"

FRAME

SPLINE
CUTTING
JIG
90°
AUXILIARY
FENCE
FENCE
45°

41

Oak Pedestal Table

Massive is probably the best word one can use to describe this oval top table. With $3^1/2$ in. thick feet, a 6 in. diameter pedestal, and a solid $1^3/4$ in. thick top, it can surely be expected to last at least a few generations. The entire table is made from 2 in. nominal thickness ($1^3/4$ in. actual) oak stock, an appropriate wood for a piece like this. The good sized oval top provides room to seat four comfortably.

When dimensioning the members in the rough, we usually leave 1 in. in length and $^1/4$ to $^3/8$ in. in width over finished size. The rough dimensions are used for total board footage and rough cut out. In the case of the table we begin by laying out the top (part F). Try to match the grain to the best possible configuration, keeping in mind that since the top is oval the boards may be reduced in length as they move out from the center.

Another thing to remember is the direction of the annular rings because they determine the direction the board will cup. When you flip the rings so that every other board is the same, the top will remain relatively flat (Fig. 1). When you run all the annular rings the same, they cup in the opposite direction of the rings (Fig. 2).

Once the stock for the top is laid out and cut to rough length, the members of the pedestal (part A) and the feet (parts B and C) are also laid out. In both cases, the thickness is achieved by laminating stock face-to-face. This is a good place to bury the less desirable stock. A nice detail can be achieved when an even number of pieces are used for the lamination. The last parts to be sized are the cleats (parts D and E).

After all stock has been rough cut, it can be surface planed,

jointed and ripped so the edges are parallel. The next step is to glue up all members, starting with the top. To simplify alignment of the boards, it's a good idea to use several $^3/8$ in. diameter by $1^1/2$ in. long dowel pins in each joint; just make sure the dowel pin holes are drilled well within the oval pattern. If you don't, when it comes time to cut the oval shape, you might find a dowel pin showing on the edge of your beautiful top.

Use a yellow (aliphatic resin) glue, but remember that working time is only about 5 minutes. Starting on one end, clamp in one direction (from left to right or vice versa) with an even number of clamps on each side. To avoid staining the wood, make sure that the metal does not come in contact with the glue. Once clamped, check for flatness. Some adjusting may be required. Next to be glued are the two feet. Note that each foot consists of two pieces of $1^3/4$ in. thick by 6 in. wide stock, face-glued to get a total thickness of $3^1/2$ in. On wide surfaces like this, use white glue, which gives longer working time. Also, let them dry longer — the extra width requires more time. A couple of dowel pins in each joint will help keep the two halves in line when clamped. Just be sure to locate them so they won't be exposed when the curved profile is cut out.

If you still have enough clamps, you can glue up stock for the pedestal (A). To keep the boards from shifting, use waxed strips of wood clamped lightly to either end and edges. The face is then clamped from the center out.

By this time the top should be ready to come out of the clamps. The high spots can be flattened with a jointer plane or belt sander. Referring to the drawing, transfer the grid pattern to a template,

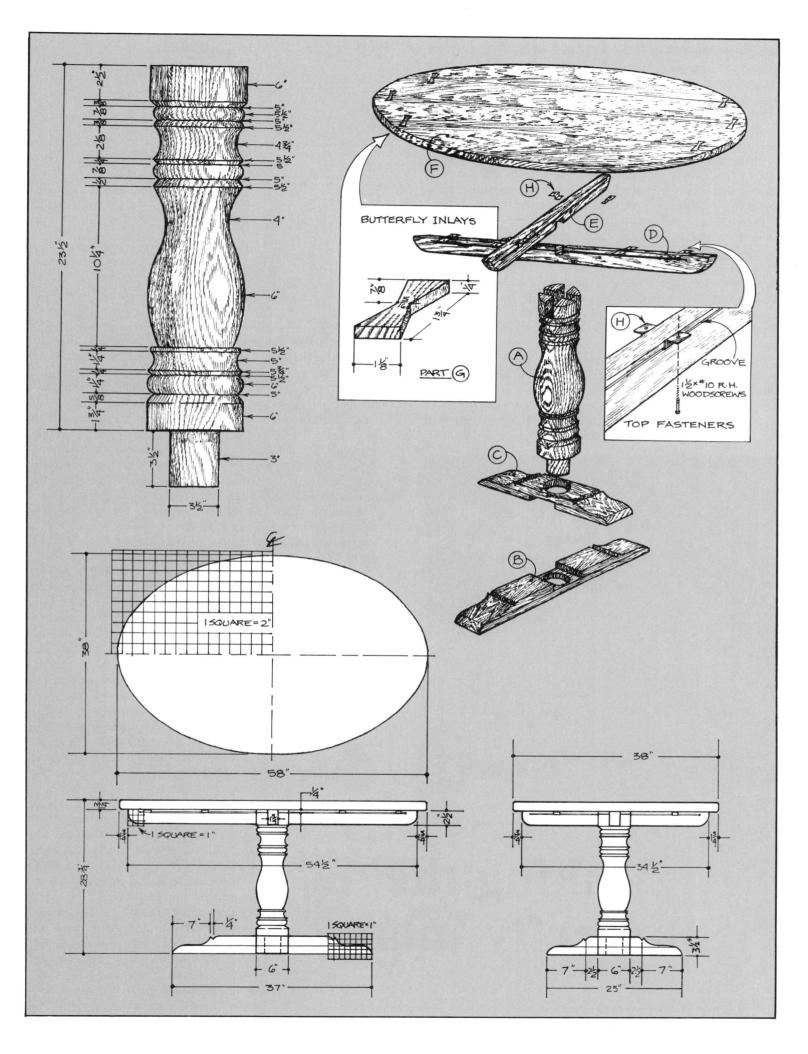

BUTTERFLY INLAYS

PART G

TOP FASTENERS

GROOVE

$1\frac{1}{2}$"x#10 R·H· WOODSCREWS

1 SQUARE = 2"

1 SQUARE = 1"

1 SQUARE = 1"

then use the template to scribe the pattern on the top. Now, with someone helping you to support the top, use a band saw to cut as close to the line as possible. A belt sander is then used to smooth the edge.

Next, square the ends of the pedestal to finished length, then cut the slots for the cleats with a band saw. Also, before turning, you must miter the corners to reduce turning time and tear-out. On larger turnings, such as the pedestal, use a faceplate and dead center. This insures maximum safety along with the ability to remove the pedestal from the lathe at any time without losing the center. The dead center is pre-drilled to $^1/4$ in. for safety.

To turn the pedestal, set up the tool rest as close to the stock as possible and just below center. There are seven basic turning tools used for most lathe work: the gouge for roughing, the $^1/2$ in. and 1 in. round scrapers for scraping and smoothing, the $^1/2$ in. and 1 in. skew chisels for shaping and smoothing, the diamond point, also for scraping and smoothing, and finally, the parting tool for locating depth and cutting material from the lathe. When turning rough, a lower speed and sharp tool will insure a cleaner cut with less tear out. Be sure to use a set of calipers to determine the various diameters. It's also a good idea to make a full-sized hardboard template of the pedestal profile. With the aid of your template, plot out all high and low spots on the wood. With the parting tool, cut on the line to the specific diameter of all the low spots. Then, with your template, choose a cutter that best matches the shape and begin to reduce the form to the shape desired.

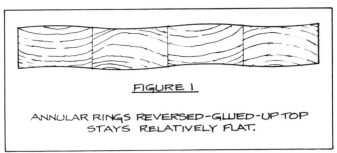

FIGURE 1

ANNULAR RINGS REVERSED-GLUED-UP TOP STAYS RELATIVELY FLAT.

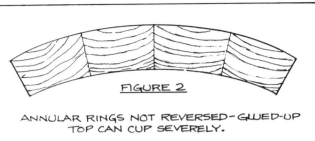

FIGURE 2

ANNULAR RINGS NOT REVERSED-GLUED-UP TOP CAN CUP SEVERELY.

Remember always to leave room for sanding and keep in mind not to heat up the wood too much, as heat will cause small heat checks in the wood.

The next step is to make the feet (B and C) and cleats (D and E). First joint and rip to size, then plot out the lines for the half-lap joints. This may be done on the table saw with either a dado or saw blade. To cut the curved details on the member, first draw the pattern with a template, then cut as close as possible to the line on the band saw. Disk sand the outside curves and hand shape the inside. Next, glue the feet and cleats. When dry, bore the 3 in. diameter tenon hole through parts B and C using a brace and expansion bit. The final step before finishing is the butterfly inlays. These add to both the strength and aesthetics.

We used an oil lacquer finish. Start by applying a good heavy coat of Watco Danish Oil to all surfaces. Rub it out when it becomes tacky, then wait a full day and apply another coat. Wet sand any rough spots with 320- to 400-grit sandpaper and again rub out. The table must then sit for about two weeks. If left in the sun, it will darken more. After about two weeks it can be sprayed, first with about three coats of sealer. The first two coats are not sanded, but the third is. Two coats of a Deft lacquer complete the finishing process.

Use a router or table saw to cut a $^1/8$ in. wide groove for the top fasteners as shown. If not available at your local hardware store, they can be ordered from most mail-order woodworking catalogs (see *Source of Supply Index*). With the top upside down (on a blanket or protective surface), center the base assembly (parts A, B, C, D, and E) on the underside of the top. A dozen top fasteners secure the top to the cleats, completing the project.

Making the Butterfly Inlay

The butterfly inlay, sometimes referred to as a double dovetail or bow tie, provides a useful and decorative way to control checking and splitting. It can be used as an actual joining device or simply as decoration.

Letting one wood into another is known as inlay or intarsia, and the methods of making butterfly inlays are pretty much the same as for other inlay work. The concept of using a butterfly inlay to hold a split together is quite old, but the butterflies were generally used to repair splits by being inlaid on the underside of a slab where they were out of sight. The idea of using them as a decorative device is fairly recent.

More than one butterfly is usually needed for a project, so it's best to prepare

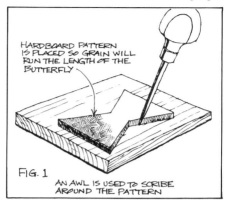

FIG. 1
HARDBOARD PATTERN IS PLACED SO GRAIN WILL RUN THE LENGTH OF THE BUTTERFLY

AN AWL IS USED TO SCRIBE AROUND THE PATTERN

a pattern so that all the butterflies will be alike. A pattern can be cut from hardboard, then laid on the stock and traced around with an awl or knife. A sharp pencil will do, but be careful. The thickness of the pencil lines will make a difference in the fitting of the butterfly.

Be sure to orient the pattern so that the grain runs the length of the butterfly rather than across (Fig. 1). They can be cut using a jigsaw or band saw. Follow slightly outside the pattern line, then clean up to the line with a chisel or file.

If the butterfly and the recess into which it fits have vertical sides, the cutting and fitting must be precise. Even a small error will be noticeable. For this reason, inlays are often made with slightly beveled edges, sloping inward from the top surface. This allows for a very close fit of the butterfly into its recess, like a tapered cork in a bottle neck (Fig. 2). But extra inlay thickness must be allowed and care should

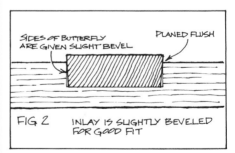

FIG 2   INLAY IS SLIGHTLY BEVELED FOR GOOD FIT

SIDES OF BUTTERFLY ARE GIVEN SLIGHT BEVEL

PLANED FLUSH

be taken to insure that the butterfly will contact the recess bottom without crushing the upper corners. The amount of bevel need only be very slight, about 2 degrees, and this cut is easily done using a jigsaw or band saw with a tilting table.

Butterflies should always be cut thick enough to protrude slightly above the work surface after gluing in place. After the glue has cured, they are then planed flush. The thickness (after planing) can range from 1/4

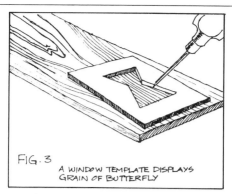

FIG. 3

A WINDOW TEMPLATE DISPLAYS GRAIN OF BUTTERFLY

in. to 1/2 in. or more depending on whether they are to be used for decorative or structural purposes.

Instead of cutting a pattern, you may wish to make a window template (Fig. 3). You can then use the window to see the grain and color of the butterfly stock. Thus unusual grain, figure or color may be selected for decorative work, and flaws can be avoided when the butterflies are used for structural purposes.

Butterflies can go completely through the work but are usually inlaid. When used to firm up a joint or a glued up surface such as a tabletop, or as a decoration, the inlaid piece can be at least 1/4 in. thick. To hold across a check in a thick plank, at least one-half the thickness of the plank will be

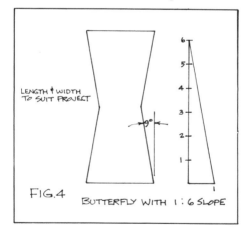

LENGTH & WIDTH TO SUIT PROJECT

9°

FIG. 4   BUTTERFLY WITH 1:6 SLOPE

needed.

The angle of the "wings" will also be determined by the function of the butterfly. A large angle will generally yield a stronger joint (up to 1:5 slope or about 12 degrees). Narrower angles have a more refined appearance (1:8 slope or about 7 degrees). When both appearance and strength are factors, a slope of 1:6, or about 9 degrees can be used (Fig. 4).

A flat-bottomed mortise or recess is most easily cut with a router and template which will cut all but the corners of the wings. These must be cleaned up with a chisel. If you are making many butterflies, the time spent in making the router template will pay for itself.

Use a 1/4 in. straight router bit and a 7/16

in. guide bushing (Figs. 5A and B). The butterfly shaped cutout in the template should be 3/32 in. larger all around than the butterfly pattern. This difference accounts for the thickness of the router bushing walls. Be sure to make the template large enough so it can be easily clamped to the work without interfering with the movement of the router.

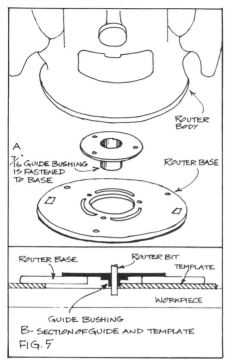

ROUTER BODY

ROUTER BASE

A
7/16 GUIDE BUSHING IS FASTENED TO BASE

ROUTER BASE

ROUTER BIT

TEMPLATE

WORKPIECE

GUIDE BUSHING
B- SECTION OF GUIDE AND TEMPLATE
FIG. 5

Once you've routed along the edges of the recess, it's easy to clean out the center area. The template is then removed, and intersecting end and side lines are scribed to guide the chisel in cleaning out the wing corners.

The butterfly inlay can be used decoratively, incorporating contrasting woods and interesting figure. It can also be used to hide a defect such as a small knot or wormhole, or to hold the seam of a glued-up slab from either the bottom or top side. On monolithic slabs where end checking is always a danger, use a butterfly to prevent further splitting.

If contrasting woods are used, be careful to clean out all the sanding dust. An ebony inset, when sanded flush in an oak surface, will leave black powder in the oak pores. This will mar the appearance if not thoroughly removed.

Few things in life are free and in this case butterflies are no exception. Laying wood cross-grain into the surface may produce expansion problems. However, if the piece is made from dried timbers, sealed properly and not exposed to extreme conditions, a reasonably well fitting inlay, held with yellow glue, will last as long as the piece.

Early American Wall Unit

A wall unit can be put to good use in any room in the house, perhaps explaining why they are always so popular. This one, made of pine, has a distinctive Early American look, a style that continues to appeal to a great many people. The three small drawers come in handy for storing a variety of odds and ends.

Except for the drawer fronts (H), the plywood drawer bottoms (K), and the drawer stops (L), all parts are made from $1/2$ in. thick stock. If you don't have a planer, most millwork shops, for a small charge, will plane down $3/4$ in. thick stock to $1/2$ in. Three six-foot lengths of 1 x 6 stock will provide enough material for the entire project.

Begin by cutting the two sides (parts A) to overall length and width and laying out the location of the three $1/4$ in. by $1/4$ in. dadoes for parts C, E, and F. Using the table or radial-arm saw, the dadoes can be cut using the dado head cutter or by making repeated passes with a regular saw blade. Next, transfer the curved profile from the grid pattern, then cut out with the band or saber saw.

The top shelf (C), the lower shelf (E), and the bottom (F) can now be cut to length and width. The ends must be square, so before cutting to length, check your saw setup. The $1/4$ in. by $1/4$ in. rabbet on each end can be cut using either the dado head cutter or by making repeated passes over the saw blade. Make each cut with care and check for a snug fit in the side dado. Keep in mind that the stock will be reduced in thickness after sanding. In fact, if a lot of sanding is required, it's a good idea to do the heavy sanding before cutting the rabbets. Note that in addition to the end rabbets, part C has a $1/2$ in. wide by $1/4$ in. deep rabbet along the back edge as shown in the side view of the drawing. Also note that the top of part F and the bottom of part E have $1/8$ in. deep by $1/2$ in. wide dadoes to accept the dividers (G). If you use the dado head cutter, a good fit can best be insured by first making a test cut in scrap stock, then checking the cut with the divider stock. Again keep in mind that the divider stock will be reduced in thickness after sanding.

Parts A, C, E, F and G can now be assembled. Give all parts a thorough sanding, taking particular care to smooth the curved edges of the sides (A). We assembled ours by first gluing the divid-

ers to the lower shelf (E) and the bottom (F), using four handscrew clamps to hold everything together. It's important not to use too much glue or else there will be problems with glue squeezing out of the joint. Before these glue joints set up, we immediately glued the two sides (parts A) and the top shelf (part C) using bar clamps to secure them in place. Clamp pads were used to protect the stock. At this point it's important to check for squareness and make any necessary adjustments.

Next, the back (B) can be cut to fit snugly between the two sides. Once satisfied with the fit, the curved profile can be transferred to the stock and cut out with a band or saber saw. The apron (D) can also be cut to fit at this time. With the stock held face side against the table saw miter gauge and the saw blade set for a height of $1^{1}/2$ in., the notch on each end can be cut with two or three passes over the blade. A good fit here is important so make the cuts carefully. Following this, use the dimensions shown to lay out the apron pattern. Use a $3/8$ in. drill bit to cut the seven holes, then cut the curves with the saber saw. Parts B and D can now be sanded and glued in place.

The drawers are made as shown and assembled with glue and finishing nails. Check for a good sliding fit before gluing the drawer stops (L) in place.

Give the entire project a complete final sanding with 220-grit aluminum oxide sandpaper. Any areas of glue squeeze-out should be cleaned up with a sharp chisel. Give all edges and corners a generous rounding-over.

As always, the type of finish is a matter of personal preference. Ours was stained with two coats of Minwax's Golden Oak stain. An inexpensive foam brush makes it easy to apply and it can be tossed out when the job is over. Allow the stain to dry thoroughly. For a clear final finish we applied two coats of polyurethane varnish. Three wooden knobs, stained and varnished, are added to complete the project.

Bill of Materials
(all dimensions actual)

Part	Description	Size	No. Req'd.
A	Side	$1/2$ x $5^{1}/2$ x $16^{3}/4$	2
B	Back	$1/2$ x $4^{3}/8$ x 19	1
C	Top Shelf	$1/2$ x 5 x $19^{1}/2$	1
D	Apron	$1/2$ x $1^{3}/4$ x $19^{1}/2$	1
E	Lower Shelf	$1/2$ x $5^{1}/2$ x $19^{1}/2$	1
F	Bottom	$1/2$ x $5^{1}/2$ x $19^{1}/2$	1
G	Divider	$1/2$ x $5^{1}/2$ $2^{3}/4$	2
H	Drawer Front	$3/4$ x $2^{1}/2$ x 6	3
I	Drawer Side	$1/2$ x $2^{1}/2$ x $4^{5}/8$	6
J	Drawer Back	$1/2$ x 2 x $5^{3}/8$	3
K	Drawer Bottom	$1/4$ x $4^{1}/4$ x $5^{3}/8$	3
L	Drawer Stop	$1/4$ x 1 x 1	6

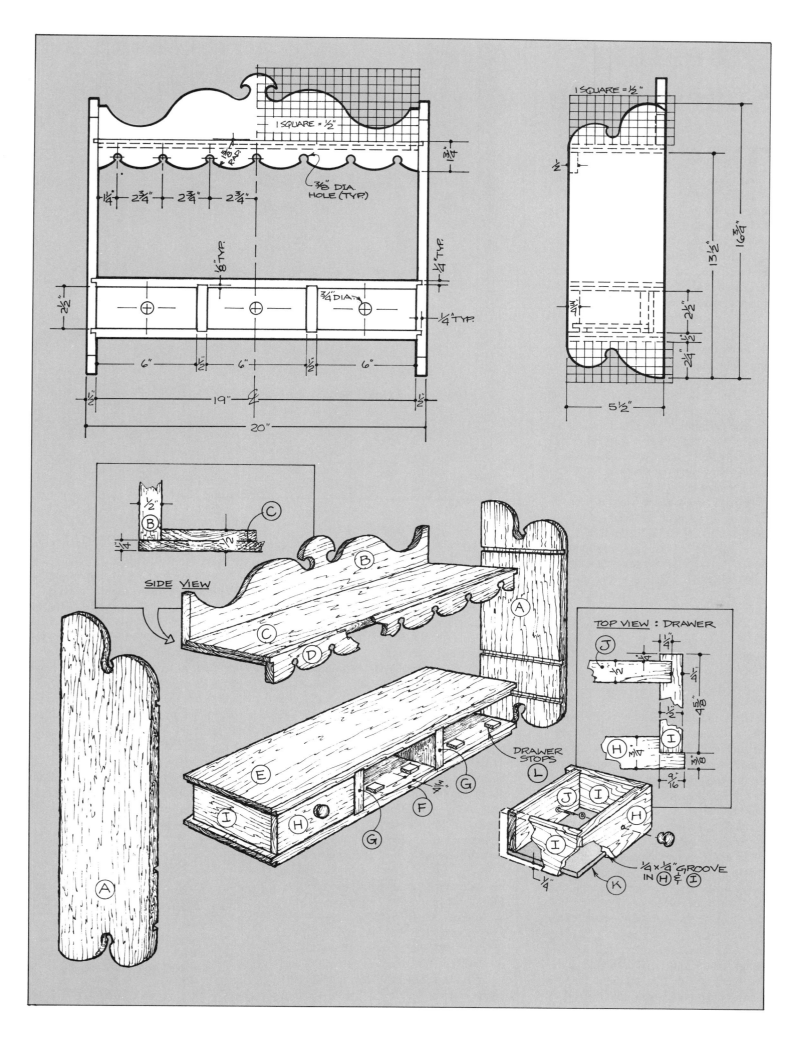

1 SQUARE = ½"

³⁄₈" RAD.

3¾"

3⁄₈" DIA. HOLE (TYP.)

1¼" 2¾" 2¾" 2¾"

⅛" TYP.

¼" TYP.

2½"

¾" DIA.

¼" TYP.

6" 1½" 6" 1½" 6"

1½" 1½"

19"

20"

1 SQUARE = ½"

½"

16¾"

13½"

¾"

2½"

2¼"

5½"

½"

¼"

B

C

½"

SIDE VIEW

A

B

C

D

A

TOP VIEW : DRAWER

J

¼"

¼"

4⅝"

½"

I

H

M/J

3⁄₈"

9⁄₁₆"

E

G

G

F

H

I

H

DRAWER STOPS

L

J

I

H

I

A

K

¼"

¼ x ⅛" GROOVE IN H & I

47

Folding Snack Table

Those who like uncomplicated furniture designs will probably find this piece appealing. It couldn't be much simpler — two frames joined by a pair of hinges along with a round top. To make it easy to store, the top comes off and the two frames fold flat.

We feel a hardwood is most appropriate for a piece like this, so 3/4 in. thick oak was used for all parts. Mahogany and maple also strike us as good choices.

Begin by cutting the four stiles (parts A) to a width of 2 1/2 in. and a length of 19 in. Look for stock that's flat — avoiding any with cup or twist. Using a sharp pencil, lay out and mark the location of the 3/8 in. wide by 2 in. long by 1 5/16 in. deep mortise on each piece. Note that the mortise is slightly deeper than the tenon is long. This allows for a little clearance should there be any excess glue or loose wood chips in the mortise when the joint is assembled later on.

Perhaps the easiest way to cut the mortise is to drill a series of 3/8 in. diameter by 1 5/16 in. deep holes, then clean up the remaining waste material with a sharp chisel. It's important that the holes be square, so use a drill press if you have one. The holes can also be drilled with a portable electric drill or a brace and bit — just keep in mind that care must be taken to insure that the holes will be square.

The mortise can also be cut using a 3/8 in. mortise chisel. Make sure it's sharp, then go to work.

Next, the four rails (parts B) can be made. Cut to a width of 2 1/2 in. and a length of 12 1/2 in. (includes tenons). Again, look for flat stock. Referring to the drawing, lay out and mark the location of the tenon on each piece. The tenons can be cut in a variety of ways, but perhaps the easiest is to use the dado head cutter in the table saw. As shown in the detail drawing, a stopblock is clamped to the rip fence, then the rip fence is adjusted to establish the 1 1/4 in. tenon length. Note the 1 1/4 in. dimension is measured from the block to the *left* tooth of the cutter. With the dado head cutter set to a height of 3/16 in., place the rail against the miter gauge, then butt the end of the rail against the block. With the rail held firmly against the miter gauge, run it through the cutter. Now slide the rail about 1/2 in.

away from the block and make another cut. Continue this until all stock is removed from one tenon cheek. Repeat this process for all eight tenons. Next, set the dado head to a depth of 1/2 in. and use the same technique to cut the 1/2 in. shoulder of the tenon.

The frame (parts A and B) can now be assembled with glue and clamped securely. Check the frames for squareness before setting aside to dry.

The top (part C) is next. To keep the top as flat as possible, it's best to use narrow stock here (our top consists of 10 pieces, each 2 in. wide). Be sure to alternate the direction of the annular rings. Edge-join the boards and clamp firmly. Allow to dry overnight, then scribe the 20 in. diameter circle and cut out with a band saw or saber saw.

Cut the mortise for the two invisible hinges (parts D) as shown. If not available locally, the hinges can be purchased from Woodcraft Supply Corp., 210 Wood County Industrial Park, Parkersburg, WV 26102-1686. Order part no. 06B44. A 1/2 in. drill bit, bored to a depth of 3/16 in. will establish the ends of the mortise. The center socket can be cut with a sharp chisel. The hinges can now be temporar-

ily joined to the frames.

Mark the location of the dowel pin (part E) holes in the frame top rail, then drive a small brad at the center joint of the hole location. Clip the head of the brad so that about 1/8 in. is exposed. With the top (part C) upside down, center the frame on the underside of the top, then press the frames down to punch location holes. All eight holes are then drilled. Use pliers to remove the clipped brads before drilling the eight pin holes.

Remove the hinges, then use a saber saw to apply a generous (about 1 in.) radius to the outside corners of the frame. Give all parts a thorough sanding. Finish with two coats of a penetrating oil, then glue the four pins (E) to the top.

Bill of Materials
(all dimensions actual)

Part	Description	Size	No. Req'd.
A	Stile	3/4 x 2 1/2 x 19	4
B	Rail	3/4 x 2 1/2 x 12 1/2	4
C	Top	20 dia. x 3/4 thick	1
D	Invisible Hinge	Woodcraft 06B44	2
E	Pin	3/8 dia. x 3/4 long	4

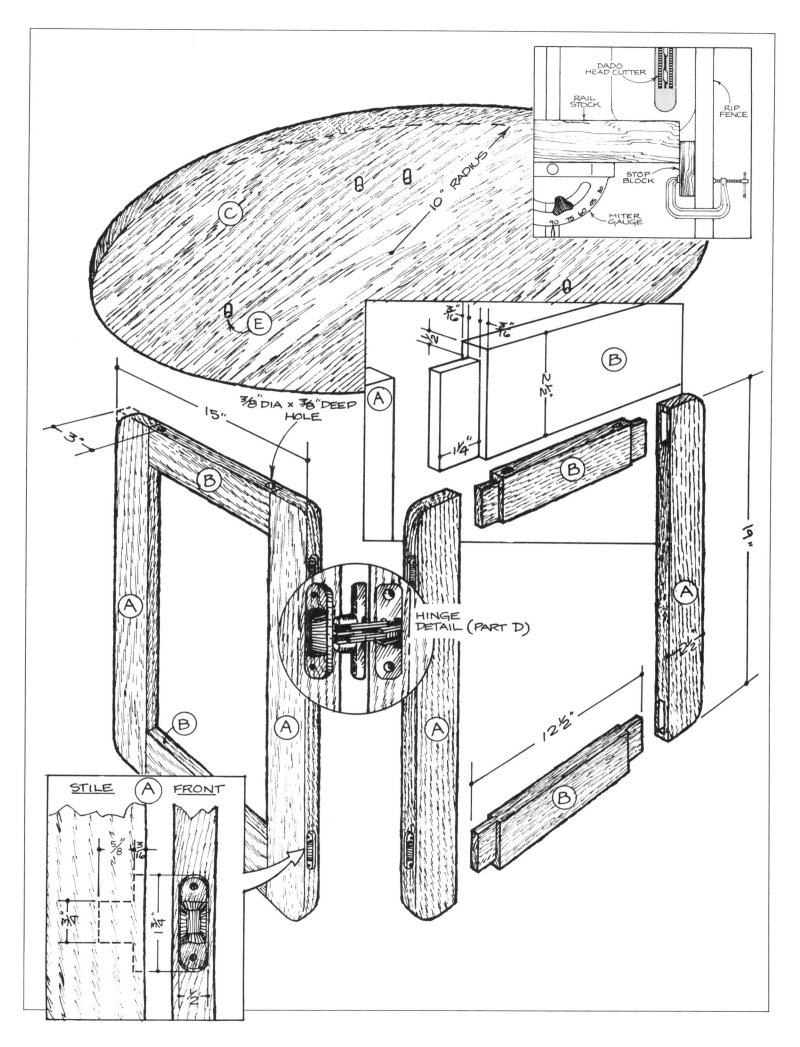

DADO HEAD CUTTER

RAIL STOCK

RIP FENCE

STOP BLOCK

90 75 60 45 30

MITER GAUGE

C

10" RADIUS

E

3⁄16"

3⁄16"

1⁄2"

B

2 1⁄2"

1 1⁄4"

B

A

15"

3"

3⁄8" DIA x 3⁄8" DEEP HOLE

B

A

19"

2 1⁄2"

HINGE DETAIL (PART D)

12 1⁄2"

A

A

B

B

STILE   A   FRONT

5⁄8"

3⁄16"

3⁄4"

3⁄4"

1⁄2"

49

Pine Corner Cupboard

little extra on both length and width. To make it easier to keep the board edges in line when clamping, it's a good idea to include four or five dowel pins in each joint. Since the pins only serve to align the boards it is not necessary to glue them in place. Apply glue to each mating edge, then clamp securely with bar or pipe clamps. When dry, cut to overall lenth and width, keeping in mind that the right back (B) is 3/8 in. narrower than the left back (A).

Continuing work on parts A and B, lay out the location of the five 3/4 in. wide by 1/4 in. deep dadoes. A radial-arm saw equipped with a dado head cutter is probably the best way to cut them. If you don't have a dado head cutter, the same cut can be made by making repeated passes with a regular sawblade. A router can also do the job. Use a guide strip clamped to the stock. The router can also be used to cut the 3/4 in. wide 3/8 in. deep rabbet along the back edge of part A. To complete work on the back parts, use the table saw (with the blade at 45 degrees) in conjunction with the rip fence to cut the bevel on each front edge.

The top (part C) and the five shelves (parts D) are made next. As shown in the cutting diagram, the shelves can be cut from a 6 ft. length of 1 by 12 stock. Take care to cut the 45-degree angles with accuracy. The plate groove can be cut with a router equipped with a 3/8 in. core-box bit. Clamp guidestrips to the stock to guide the router.

The sides (part F) can now be cut to overall width and length. The two 1/4 in. wide by 1/8 in. deep grooves (see cross-section detail) can be cut on the table saw. Set the sawblade to a height of 1/8 in., then adjust the rip-fence to properly locate the blade. Run the stock, face down, along the rip-fence to make each cut.

Next, part E, the rail, and part G, the base, are cut to size. Transfer the grid pattern from the drawing to the stock, then cut out with a band or saber saw.

Cut the two doors (part I) and the four battens (part J) to size. The routed groove in the door is a nice detail and can be made with a router. Using 1/4 in. plywood, make a template to the dimensions shown on the drawing. Center this on the door front and tack in place with four small brads. Be sure to locate the brads so that they will not interfere with the travel of the router. Equip the router with a 1/4 in. diameter straight bit and a 7/16 in. guide bushing. Start the router, then lower the bit into the stock keeping the guide bushing against the template. Now, rout the groove by moving the router in a counterclockwise direction around the template. To get the feel of this step, it's a good idea to make one or two practice cuts on scrap stock.

Now all parts can be given a thorough sanding, taking particular care to remove any deep scratches. Assemble the back parts (A and B) with glue and finishing nails. Before nailing though, it's best to drill pilot holes to minimize any chance of splitting. The five shelves (D) and the top (C) can now be added, again using glue and finishing nails. Parts E, F and G are also glued, but look best if cut nails, which have an antique look, are used. The bed molding can be purchased at most lumberyards. Miter both ends, then glue and clamp in place.

Final sand before staining. We used two coats of Minwax's Early American stain. Following this we applied two coats of their antique oil finish.

Screw the two battens to the back of each door. Attach the doors to parts F with 3 in. "H" hinges. Two 1 in. diameter porcelain knobs complete the project.

Country furniture seems to be especially popular these days, perhaps because the style is characterized by clean lines and sturdy construction. This piece, made of pine, will make a charming addition to a kitchen or dining room. The joinery is basic throughout, so even a beginner should be able to tackle this one with confidence.

The left back (part A) and right back (part B) can be made first. Most lumberyard and building supply centers now carry 3/4 in. pine in wide glued up panels, usually in widths of 18 in. and 24 in. Considering the time they save, it's probably the way to go.

Of course, if you prefer, the back parts can be made by edge-gluing two or more narrow boards. Cut the stock to allow a

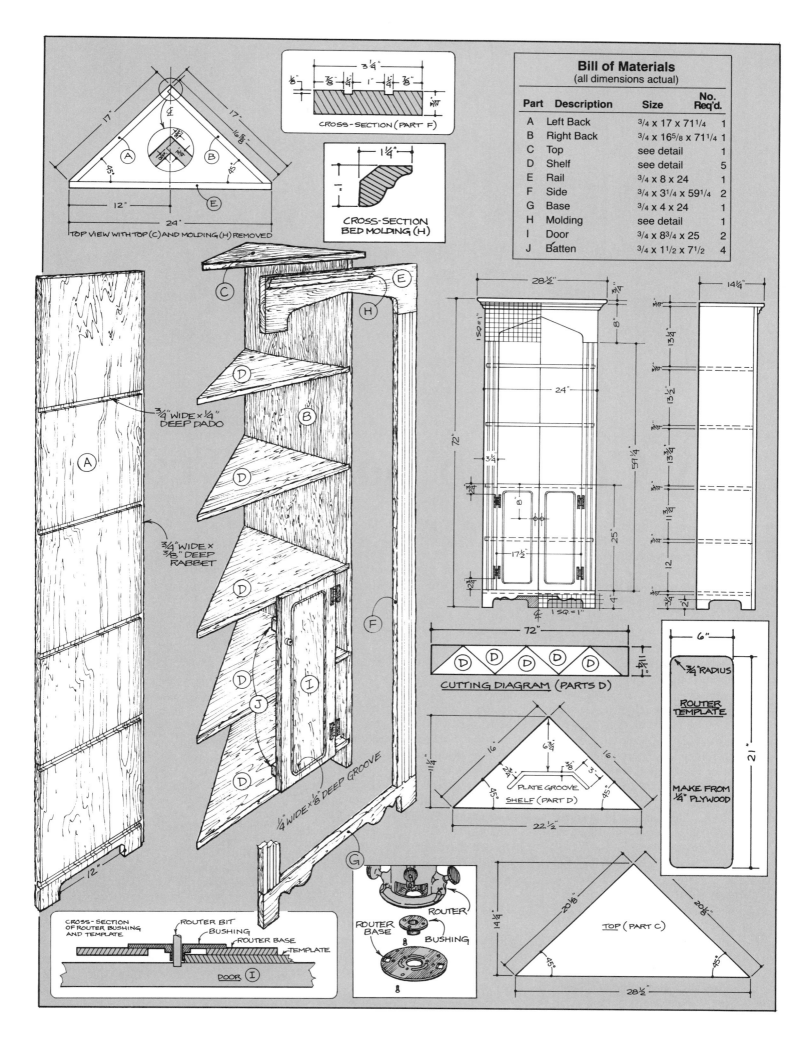

CROSS-SECTION (PART F)

CROSS-SECTION
BED MOLDING (H)

TOP VIEW WITH TOP (C) AND MOLDING (H) REMOVED

Bill of Materials
(all dimensions actual)

Part	Description	Size	No. Req'd.
A	Left Back	3/4 x 17 x 71 1/4	1
B	Right Back	3/4 x 16 5/8 x 71 1/4	1
C	Top	see detail	1
D	Shelf	see detail	5
E	Rail	3/4 x 8 x 24	1
F	Side	3/4 x 3 1/4 x 59 1/4	2
G	Base	3/4 x 4 x 24	1
H	Molding	see detail	1
I	Door	3/4 x 8 3/4 x 25	2
J	Batten	3/4 x 1 1/2 x 7 1/2	4

3/4" WIDE x 1/4" DEEP DADO

3/4" WIDE x 3/8" DEEP RABBET

1/4" WIDE x 1/8" DEEP GROOVE

CUTTING DIAGRAM (PARTS D)

ROUTER TEMPLATE

MAKE FROM 1/4" PLYWOOD

3/4" RADIUS

PLATE GROOVE
SHELF (PART D)

TOP (PART C)

CROSS-SECTION OF ROUTER BUSHING AND TEMPLATE

ROUTER BIT
BUSHING
ROUTER BASE
TEMPLATE

DOOR (I)

ROUTER
ROUTER BASE
BUSHING

Toy Car with Boat & Trailer

Here's a toy that doesn't require a single battery. Instead, it gets its power from another source — a child's imagination. Reasons, it seems, that make a toy like this very worthwhile.

Poplar was used for all parts except the mahogany stripe down the center of the car. Although pine can be used, it's generally better to use hardwoods for toys because, over the years, they will offer better resistance to dents and scratches.

Begin by making the two sides (parts A). Rip $^5/_4$ in. stock ($1^1/_8$ in. actual thickness) to $^7/_8$ in. width, then cut to length. Lay out and mark the location of the wheel-well hole center points, and using a $1^1/_2$ in. Forstner bit, bore the holes to a depth of $^3/_8$ in. Before drilling, clamp a strip of scrap stock along the bottom edge of part A. This will help prevent the wood from splintering as the hole is bored.

Readers who do not have a Forstner bit can use an alternate method to make the body. As shown on the drawing detail, the two outer sections are made from $^3/_8$ in. thick stock while the three inner sections are made from $^1/_2$ in. stock. On the outer sections, lay out the location of the wheel-well hole center points, then use a compass to scribe the curve. Cut out with a band, saber, or jigsaw and sand smooth. The outer and inner sections can

now be glued and clamped.

Cut the stripe (part B) and the center (part C) to size, then glue to parts A. Use several clamps to insure good contact between all glue surfaces. Allow to dry overnight.

To make the top (part D), cut $^3/_4$ in. thick stock to a width of $2^1/_8$ in. and a length of $3^3/_8$ in. To bevel the front and back edge, set the band saw to an angle of about 36 degrees. Take care to keep fingers away from the saw blade. Now, the top can be assembled to the body (parts A, B and C) with glue and clamps.

Carefully locate the center point of the two axles then bore $^5/_{16}$ in. diameter holes through the body.

The car wheels (parts H) can be made to the dimensions shown or purchased from Cherry Tree Toys, P.O. Box 369, Belmont, OH 43718. Order part no. 26. The addition of the bumper (part E) and the hitch (part F) completes the assembly of the car.

The trailer and boat are made as shown on the drawing. The pegs (parts K) and trailer wheels (parts P) can also be purchased from Cherry Tree Toys. Order part no. 2 for the pegs, and part no. 26 for the trailer wheels. The back (part L) is free to pivot on one of the pegs, allowing it to be opened to "unload" the boat. To accomplish this, one peg goes through a

$^1/_4$ in. hole in part L and is glued to part I. The other peg is glued to part L so that $^3/_8$ in. extends through. This then fits into a $^1/_4$ in. hole in part I.

Give all parts a thorough final sanding, rounding all corners and sharp edges. The best non-toxic finish is none at all.

Part	Description	Size	No. Req'd.
\multicolumn{4}{c}{**Bill of Materials** (all dimensions actual)}			

Part	Description	Size	No. Req'd.
		Car	
A	Side	$^7/_8$ x $1^1/_8$ x 7	2
B	Stripe	$^1/_2$ x $^5/_8$ x 7	1
C	Center	$^1/_2$ x $^1/_2$ x $8^3/_8$	1
D	Top	$^3/_4$ x $2^1/_8$ x $3^3/_8$	1
E	Bumper	$^1/_4$ x $^5/_8$ x $2^3/_8$	1
F	Hitch	$^1/_4$ dia. x $1^1/_4$ long	1
G	Car Axle	$^1/_4$ dia. x $2^1/_2$ long	2
H	Car Wheel	$1^1/_4$ dia. x $^3/_8$ thick	4
		Trailer	
I	Base	$^1/_2$ x $1^1/_4$ x 6	2
J	Middle	$^1/_2$ x $^1/_2$ x $7^3/_4$	1
K	Peg	(see Detail)	6
L	Back	$^3/_8$ x $^5/_8$ x 3	1
M	Axle Supports	$^3/_4$ x $^7/_8$ x 3	2
N	Spacer	$^3/_8$ x $^3/_8$ x 3	1
O	Trailer Axle	$^1/_4$ dia. x $3^3/_4$ long	2
P	Trailer Wheel	$^5/_{16}$ thick x 1 dia.	4
		Boat	
Q	Hull	1 x 2 x 6	1
R	Cabin	$^3/_4$ x $1^5/_8$ x $2^5/_8$	1

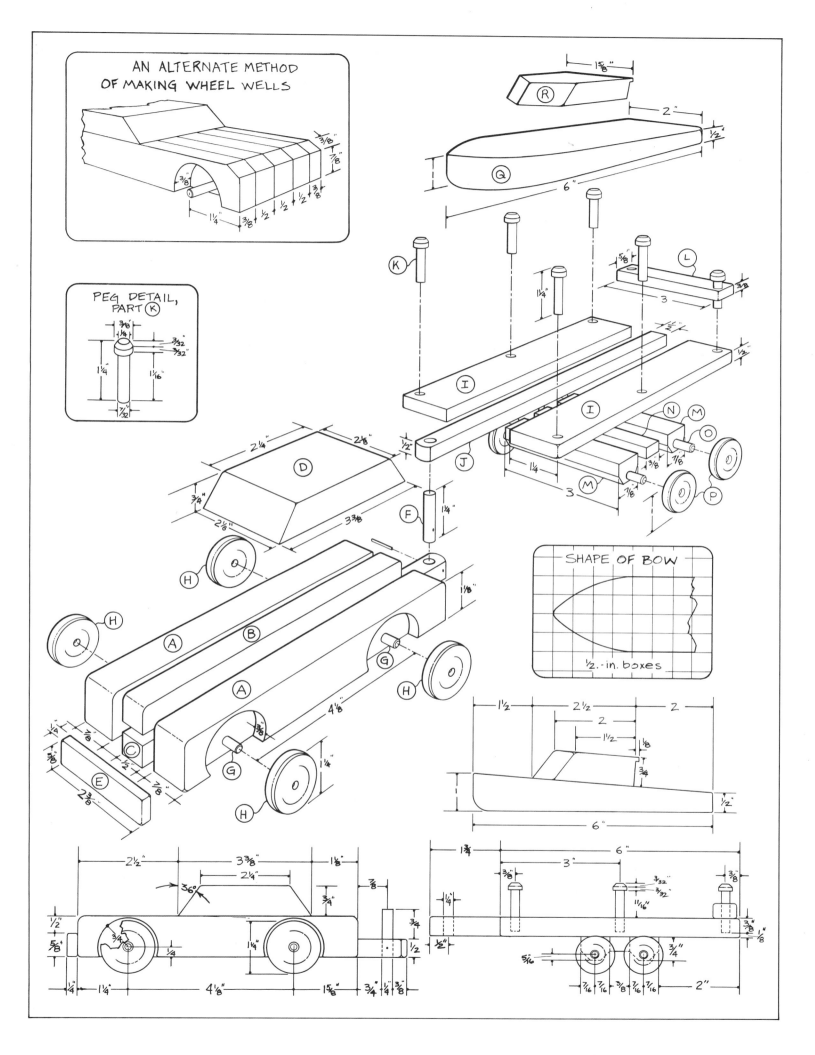

AN ALTERNATE METHOD
OF MAKING WHEEL WELLS

PEG DETAIL,
PART (K)

SHAPE OF BOW

½-in. boxes

Contemporary Serving Tray

When entertaining guests, a serving tray is almost a necessity, not to mention the fact that an attractive tray will complement the food being served. We particularly like this one because it can be made with a minimum of time and materials. Ours was made using mahogany plywood for the bottom, with mahogany solid stock for the frame parts, although just about any type of wood can be used here. However, keep in mind that the bottom does not necessarily have to be plywood. With dozens of veneers on the market, many in exciting colors and configurations, it's always worth considering that option. Use 1/8 in. hardboard and be sure to veneer both sides to equalize stress.

Begin by cutting parts A and B to width but allow a little extra length on each piece. If you don't have 1/2 in. stock, it can be resawn from thicker stock. The 1/4 in. by 1/4 in. groove along each part can be cut with the dado head cutter or by making two or three passes over the regular saw blade.

After cutting the bottom to length and width, the mitered corners on part A can be cut. Then transfer the profile from the grid pattern to part A, and cut out with a saber saw. Assemble all components with glue and clamp firmly.

When dry, give all surfaces a thorough sanding, taking special care to smooth the handles.

Ours was finished with two coats of Watco Danish Oil.

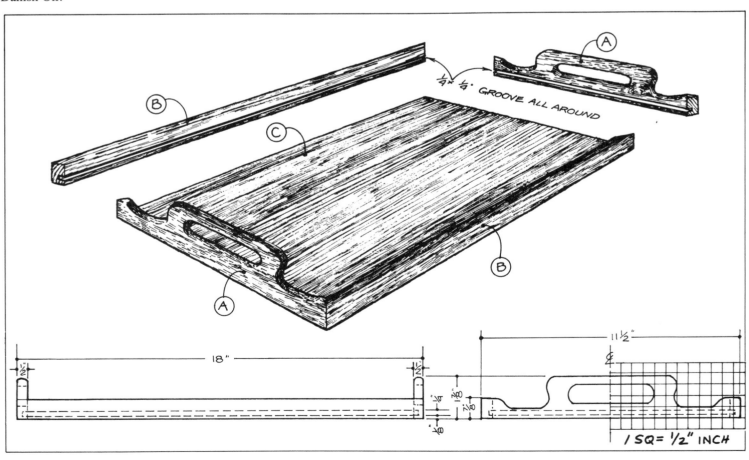

1 SQ = 1/2" INCH

Pine Mirror with Shelf

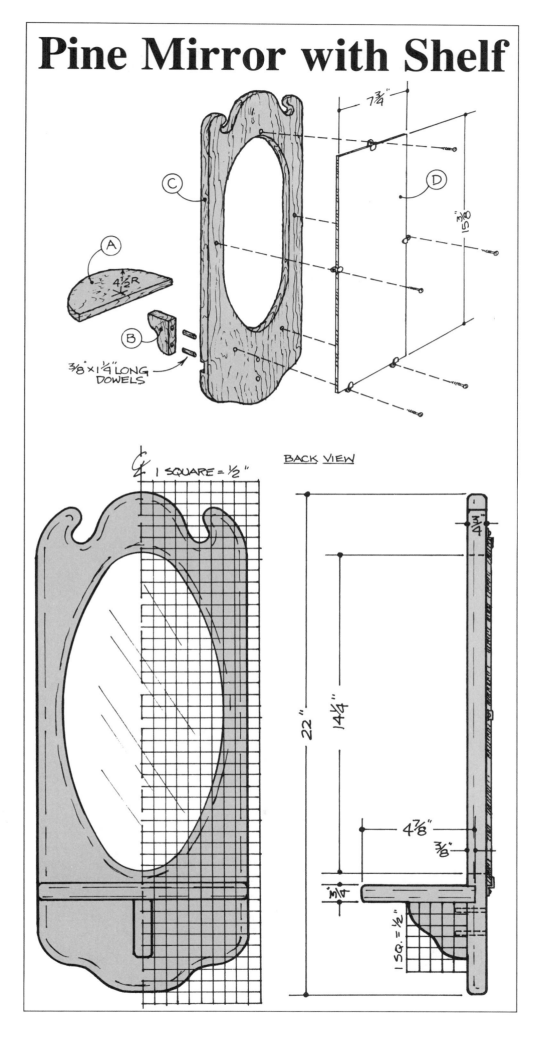

A — 4½R

3/8" × 1¼" LONG DOWELS

C

D

7¾"

15⅜"

BACK VIEW

1 SQUARE = ½"

22"

14¼"

4⅞"

3/8"

3/4"

3/4"

1 SQ. = ½"

A few hours in the workshop are all that's needed to build this eye-catching oval mirror. Ours is made from pine, much in keeping with its Early American style.

The frame (part C) can be made first. Cut 3/4 in. thick stock to a width of 9 in. and a length of 22 in., then mark the location of the 3/8 in. deep by 3/4 in. wide dado for the shelf (part A). The dado can be cut with the dado head cutter or by making repeated passes over the saw blade.

Next, referring to the drawing, transfer the profile from the grid pattern to the stock. To cut out the oval, first drill a 3/8 in. hole in the waste stock, then with this as a starting point, use a saber saw to cut out the opening. The outer profile can be cut out with a band or saber saw.

The shelf (part A) is made from a piece of 3/4 in. thick stock measuring 4⅞ in. wide by 9 in. long. Use a compass to lay out a 4½ in. radius, noting that the radius is centered at a point 3/8 in. from the back edge of part A.

After making part B, all parts can be thoroughly sanded. Part A can now be glued in place and secured with finishing nails. Part B can now be glued and clamped in place. When dry, drill through from the back for 3/8 in. dowels as shown. The mirror (part D) is held in place with five mirror clips as shown.

Stain to suit and finish with two coats of polyurethane.

Carved Eagle

Here's an opportunity to recreate what has been a New England tradition for over a century. This 4 ft. wide American eagle will make a fine addition to a den or family room. It can even be used as a decoration on the outside of your house.

Basswood is a good choice for this piece. It is a "forgiving" wood, and it's so closely grained it carves like soap. If basswood is not available, clear pine makes a good second choice.

To carve the bird from a single solid block would require a considerable amount of time and energy. Instead, build up the areas that need extra thickness by gluing pre-cut shapes (parts B through J) onto the base (part A).

The best approach to beginning the eagle is to sketch the entire piece on tracing paper. From this, tracings of the various laminations can be made. These can then be transferred, using carbon paper, to the lumber.

In order to get enough width, part A will probably have to be edge-glued using two or three boards. If the eagle is to be hung outside, resorcinol, a waterproof glue, will have to be used throughout.

After cutting all pieces to size, glue on the two wing arches (parts B). Note that their outside profile matches part A. A large fishtail gouge will help flow the laminations together.

Transfer the profiles of the neck (part C), the head (part D), the shield (part E), and the banner (parts F, G and H) to part A as shown. The areas of part A that are covered by these parts will not be carved. Now, working on the remaining areas of part A, use the fishtail gouge to make the wings slightly concave. Following this,

all feathers can be established using a V-parting tool for most of the work.

Parts C and D can be glued together and partially carved before being glued to part A. Now glue on the banner (parts F, G and H) and the shield (part E). The claws (parts I and J) are made from maple (or another hardwood) to reduce the risk of splitting, which might happen with a softer wood such as basswood.

It is important that part J butts to part C so the leg continues into the talons (Fig. 1). Also note that the underside of the leg portion of part C is carved away. This can be done before it is glued to part A.

The banner is given a ruffled look by cutting in with a straight chisel at an angle and reducing the background on either side (Fig. 2). This is also necessary where the 1/2 in. thick part G butts to the 1 1/4 in. thick part H (Fig. 3). The striping in the banner is made using a small no. 11 veiner, and the incised stars are done with straight chisels using "V" cuts.

Note that the banner running out of the eagle's mouth goes toward the back of the shield. It will be necessary to butt a small piece of 5/4 in. lumber (part K) to the back of part D. Cut this part K so it fits between and butts to parts E and F. This can be done before parts C and D are glued to part A.

After sanding the entire piece smooth, it should be coated with a heavy-bodied paint sealer. Acrylics will look good on the piece if it's used indoors. If you plan on displaying it outdoors, use enamel paints for durability. This eagle is finished with a rub-on gold leaf, while the banner is painted dark blue, the banner stripe yellow, and the shield red, white and blue.

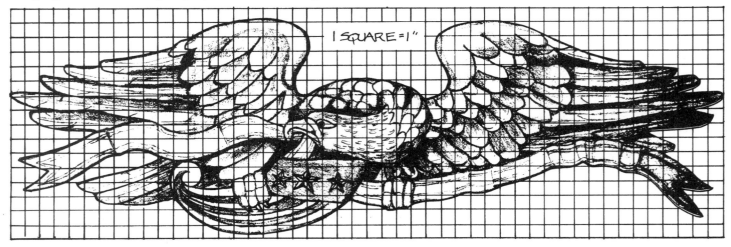

1 SQUARE = 1"

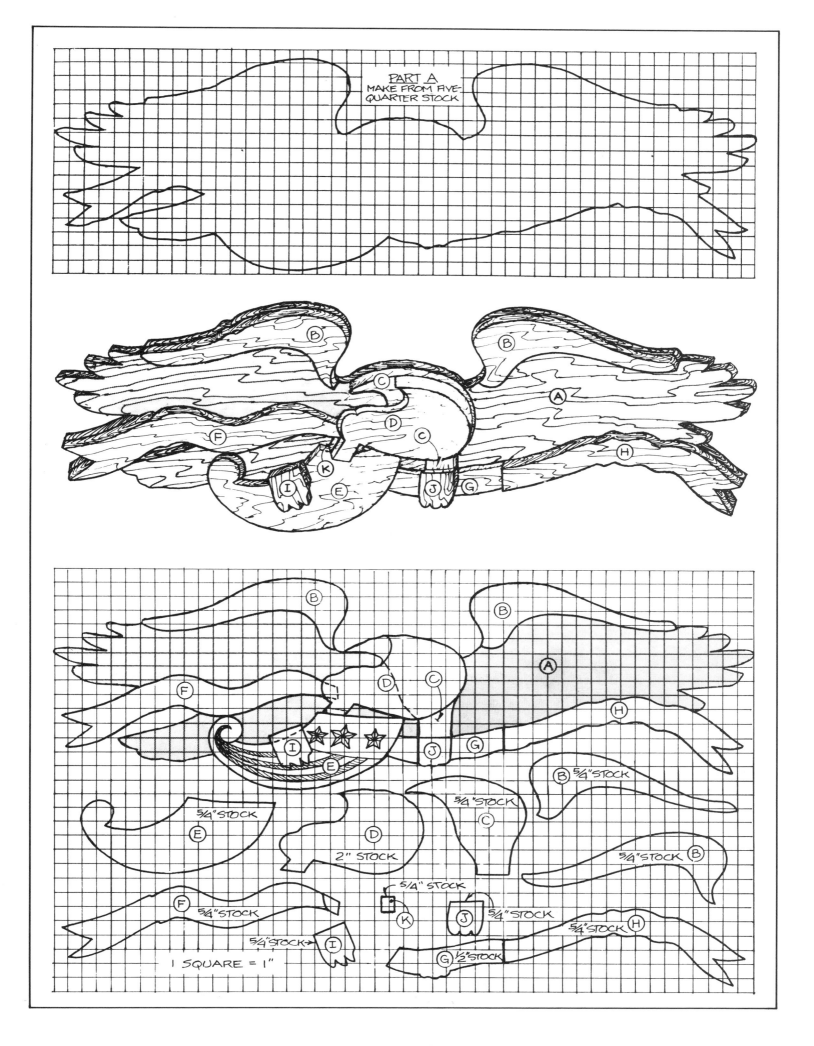

PART A
MAKE FROM FIVE-
QUARTER STOCK

B   5/4"STOCK
5/4"STOCK
C
5/4"STOCK   E
D
2" STOCK
5/4"STOCK   B

5/4" STOCK
F   5/4"STOCK
K   J   5/4"STOCK
5/4"STOCK   I
G   1/2"STOCK   5/4"STOCK   H

1 SQUARE = 1"

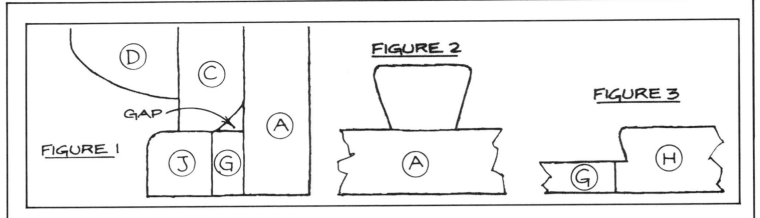

FIGURE 1

FIGURE 2

FIGURE 3

Carving Details

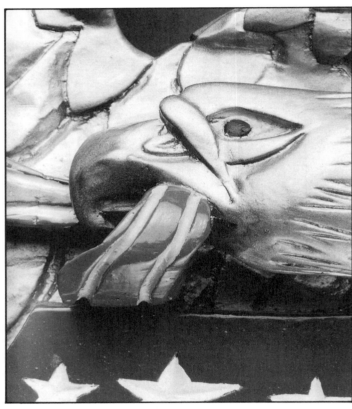

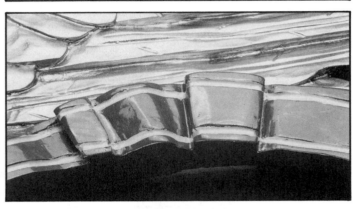

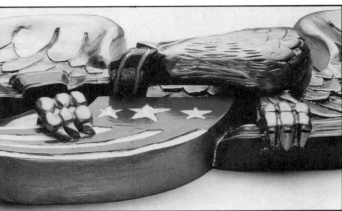

58

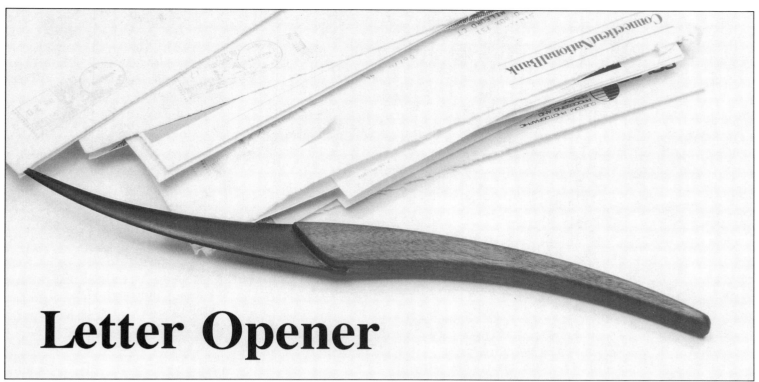

Letter Opener

More than likely your scrap box will yield enough stock to make plenty of these attractive and useful desk accessories. The handle can be made from just about any kind of wood, even pine. For the blade though, use a hard, close-grained wood; maple, birch and beech are some common ones. We used a few somewhat exotic scraps — bubinga for the handle and ebony for the blade.

To make the handle, transfer the profile shown on the grid pattern to ¹/₂ in. thick stock that measures approximately 1¹/₂ in. wide by 7 in. long. Clamp the stock to an auxiliary sliding fence (see drawing), then set the table saw blade to a height of 1 in. and locate the rip fence to cut a ¹/₈ in. wide slot in the handle as shown.

To make the cut, hold the auxiliary fence against the rip fence as the stock is pushed through the blade. And as always, keep fingers away from the blade.

Next, cut out with the band saw or saber saw. Following this use a file and sandpaper to generously round all edges.

To make the blade, resaw stock to a thickness (about ¹/₈ in.) that will permit it to fit snugly in the handle groove. The profile can now be transferred to the stock and cut to shape. For good strength, use aliphatic resin (yellow) glue to join the blade to the handle. A clamp will help insure a good bond. Final sand before sharpening the cutting edge with a file. Two coats of penetrating oil complete the project.

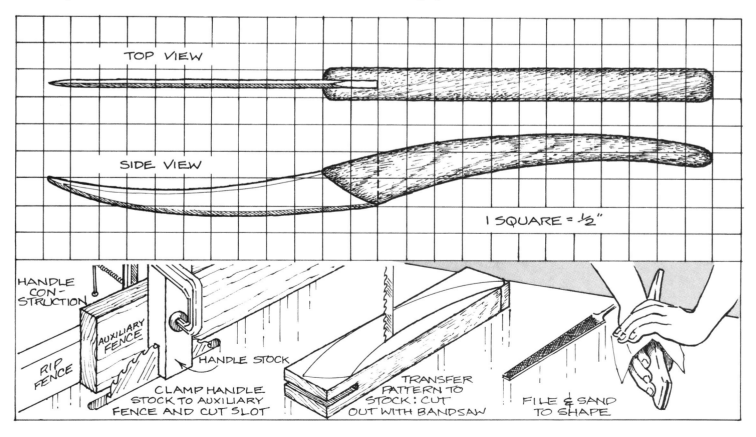

TOP VIEW

SIDE VIEW

1 SQUARE = ½"

HANDLE CON-STRUCTION

AUXILIARY FENCE

RIP FENCE

HANDLE STOCK

CLAMP HANDLE STOCK TO AUXILIARY FENCE AND CUT SLOT

TRANSFER PATTERN TO STOCK; CUT OUT WITH BANDSAW

FILE & SAND TO SHAPE

Drafting Table

This sturdy, attractive table will provide years of service to the draftsman, architect, or artist. To adjust the angle of the top it simply pivots on two wooden pins in the front. It's held open by a pair of adjustable brass-plated stays screwed to the back stile. This hardware makes for quick and easy adjustment of the top and will hold it securely in place.

All parts are made from oak planed to 1 in. thickness, except for the edging (part K), which is $3/16$ in. oak, the top (part I), which is $3/4$ in. particleboard, and the Formica (J).

Begin by cutting the front stile (part A) to a length of $32^1/2$ in. (which allows a little extra length). Referring to the drawing, lay out the location of the two mortises. It's important that they be exactly $24^3/16$ in. apart (as shown). Probably the easiest way to cut the mortise is to drill a series of holes using a $1/2$ in. drill bit. This method removes most of the material. What remains can be cleaned out with a chisel. It's best to make the mortise about $1/16$ in. deeper than the tenon is long (in this case the mortise would be $1^9/16$ in. deep) in order to allow room for any excess glue or wood fibers. If the mortise doesn't have that extra depth and there is excess glue, the joint

won't close properly. Ideally, a drill press should be used to drill the holes because it insures that each hole will be reasonably square to the edge of the stile and parallel to the face. However, if done with care, a hand brace or portable electric drill will do as good a job. Note that the mortises for parts C and D are not the same. The mortise for part C is $2^5/8$ in. long, but the mortise for part D is only $2^1/8$ in. long. After cutting the mortises, part A can be set aside. Don't trim the excess length yet.

The back stile (part B) is next. Cut to a length of 30 in. (allows a little extra length), then lay out and cut the mortises following the procedure just described. Make sure they are spaced exactly $23^1/4$ in. apart. Following this, lay out the location of the $1/2$ in. deep by 3 in. long notch for the back stretcher (E). To use the table saw to cut the notch, set the dado head cutter to a height of $1/2$ in., then hold the stile firmly against the miter gauge (notch edge down) and run it through the cutter. It will take several passes to make the 3 in. width. Part B can now be set aside with part A. Note that the excess length has not been trimmed from part B at this time.

From 3 in. wide stock, cut part C to a length of 23 in. and part D to a length of

15 in. Both dimensions allow extra length. The angled tenon for part C is made first. Using the table saw, set the dado head cutter to make a $1/4$ in. deep cut and set the miter gauge to 16 degrees (see drawing detail).

To cut one cheek, make repeated passes over the dado head (Step 1). Be sure to make the cheek long enough so there will be enough material for the $1^1/2$ in. long tenon. Next, use a try square and a sharp pencil to transfer the shoulder location to the opposite side of the board. Now, transfer the miter gauge to the right hand slot (Step 2). Change the gauge setting as shown, flip the stock, then cut the second cheek. Following this, the cheeks for the angled tenon of part D can be cut using this same technique.

While the dado head is still set up, change the miter gauge to 90 degrees and make the shoulder cut for the opposite (the straight) tenons. Note that the shoulders are 17 in. apart on part C and $10^5/16$ in. apart on part D. Repeated passes will clean up the remaining material to establish the cheeks. To cut the $1/2$ in. shoulder on the tenons, raise the dado head to a height of $1/2$ in., then use the miter gauge (set at 90 degrees) to pass the stock (on edge) over the cutter. Make the cut carefully to insure that it will align with the $1/4$ in. shoulder cuts.

With the miter gauge still at 90 degrees, replace the dado head with the regular saw blade, then trim the two straight tenons to a length of $1^1/2$ in. To trim the angled tenons, set the miter gauge to a 16-degree angle and cut to length.

The straight tenons are now completed. To finish the angled tenons, a back or dovetail saw is used to trim the tenons to fit the mortises.

Parts E and F can now be cut to overall length and width. Use the dado head to cut the $1/2$ in. by 1 in. rabbet on the end of each piece. While the dado is set up, it's also a good time to cut the $1/2$ in. by 3 in. notches on parts B and D.

The frame parts (A, B, C and D) can now be assembled. Apply glue to all mating surfaces and clamp firmly. Once dry, the excess length of parts A and B can be trimmed off and the corners rounded as shown. Next, all parts of the frame can be thoroughly sanded.

Cut the top (part I) to length and width from $3/4$ in. particleboard. Apply Formica (part J) to the underside, trimming the edges flush. Locate the cleats (parts G), then secure through the top with counterbored wood screws as shown.

Temporarily clamp part E to the frame

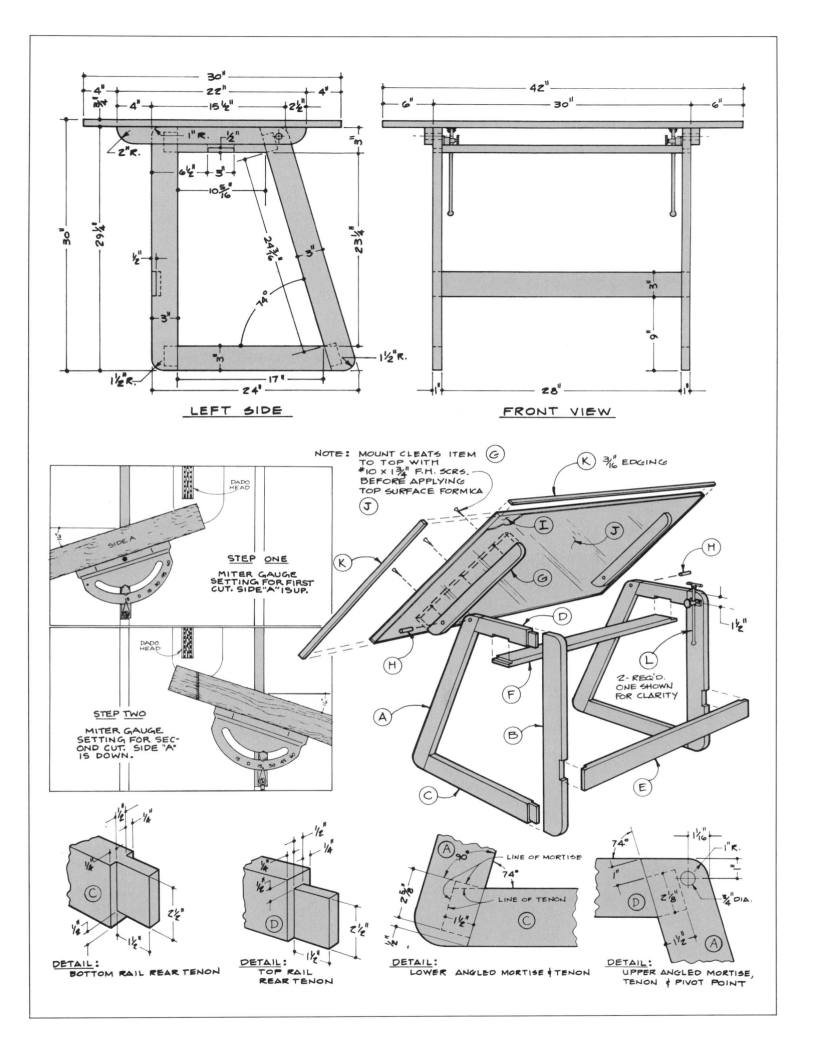

LEFT SIDE

FRONT VIEW

NOTE: MOUNT CLEATS ITEM (G) TO TOP WITH #10 x 1¾" F.H. SCRS. BEFORE APPLYING TOP SURFACE FORMICA (J)

(K) 3/16" EDGING

DADO HEAD

SIDE A

STEP ONE
MITER GAUGE SETTING FOR FIRST CUT. SIDE "A" IS UP.

DADO HEAD

STEP TWO
MITER GAUGE SETTING FOR SECOND CUT. SIDE "A" IS DOWN.

2-REQ'D. ONE SHOWN FOR CLARITY

DETAIL: BOTTOM RAIL REAR TENON

DETAIL: TOP RAIL REAR TENON

DETAIL: LOWER ANGLED MORTISE & TENON

DETAIL: UPPER ANGLED MORTISE, TENON & PIVOT POINT

61

members, then place the top (I) into its proper position on the frame. Use a pair of hand screws (or any type of clamp) to hold parts G to parts D, then remove the screws holding parts G and remove the top. Lay out and mark the location of the holes for the pins (parts H). Use a 3/4 in. spade or Forstner bit to drill the holes completely through both parts. Be sure the holes are square and use a backing block to prevent splintering.

The cleats can now be remounted to the top before applying the top surface Formica. The 3/16 in. thick edging strips are cut to a width of about 1 1/8 in. They are mitered at the corners before gluing and clamping in place. A sharp block plane is used to trim the edging flush with the Formica. If a pencil ledge is desired,

simply glue a 1/4 in. thick by 1 1/4 in. wide strip of oak along the entire front edge.

Next, the pins (H) are glued in place on the frame and allowed to dry. Give all surfaces a complete final sanding.

Assemble the two end frames onto the cleats (G), then glue and clamp parts E and F. Check for squareness. For a clear final finish we used two coats of Watco Danish Oil. The installation of the two adjustable stays (L) completes the project. If not available locally (most lumberyards and hardware stores carry them — ask for casement window adjusters), they can be ordered from Paxton Hardware Co., 7818 Bradshaw Rd., Upper Falls, MD 21156. Order their part no. 5034.

Bill of Materials
(all dimensions actual)

Part	Description	Size	No. Req'd.
A	Front Stile	1 x 3 x 32 1/2 (allows extra)	2
B	Back Stile	1 x 3 x 30 (allows extra)	2
C	Bottom Rail	1 x 3 x 23 (allows extra)	2
D	Top Rail	1 x 3 x 15 (allows extra)	2
E	Back Stretcher	1 x 3 x 30	1
F	Top Stretcher	1 x 3 x 30	1
G	Cleat	1 x 2 x 22	2
H	Pin	3/4 dia. x 2 1/8 long	2
I	Top	3/4 x 29 5/8 x 41 5/8	1
J	Formica		As Req'd
K	Edging	3/16 thick	As Req'd
L	Hardware	12 long	2

Collector's Plate Stand

Here's an attractive way to display a favorite collectors plate. Just about any wood can be used, but cherry or walnut would be especially nice.

Each leg is made from a piece of 3/8 in. thick by 5 1/8 in. wide by 9 in. long stock. If you don't have 3/8 in. stock it can be planed from thicker material.

Transfer the profile from the grid pattern to the stock, then cut out with a band, saber, or jigsaw. Lay out and mark the location of the hinge mortises and the 1/8 in. notches to accept the hinge barrel before cutting them out with a sharp chisel.

Give both legs a complete sanding taking care to make sure the curved edges are well smoothed. The addition of a pair of brass hinges and two coats of polyurethane varnish will complete the project.

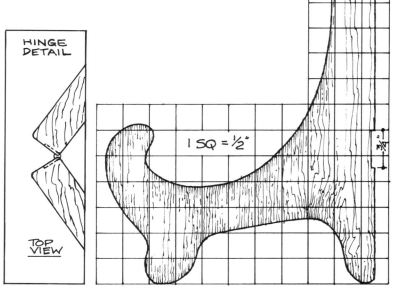

HINGE DETAIL

TOP VIEW

1 SQ = 1/2"

Display Pedestal

This elegant looking hexagonal stand will highlight a favorite house plant, curio, or even a piece of fine sculpture. It's easy to build and will require only a few hours in the workshop. For a piece like this, there's no hard and fast rule that dictates size, so feel free to alter dimensions to suit the piece you plan to display. We used red oak for ours, but just about any wood can be used, even pine.

Our stand measures 10 in. across in the flats which results in a board width of 5¾ in. The boards we used had a length of 23 in. Referring to Fig. 1, set the saw blade at a 30-degree angle and locate the rip fence as shown. Bevel one edge (Step A), then turn the stock and bevel the other edge (Step B). The saw blade must be set at exactly 30 degrees because even a small error will add up to a large gap when you have six joints.

Add glue to all mating surfaces, then assemble and clamp with three web clamps — one at each end and one in the middle. Allow to dry overnight.

To help center the mirror top (B), and to add strength, we glued a ¼ in. plywood inset (C) to the underside of the glass. The inset is cut to fit just inside the box while the mirror is cut to fit the outside of the box. When glued together, a lip is formed which permits the mirror to simply sit on the pedestal. Most glass shops will cut mirror stock to any size and shape. For appearance and safety, be sure to have the edges ground. Also, keep in mind that many adhesives will remove the mirror's silver, so use one that's formulated to use with a mirror. Your local glass shop will probably carry one.

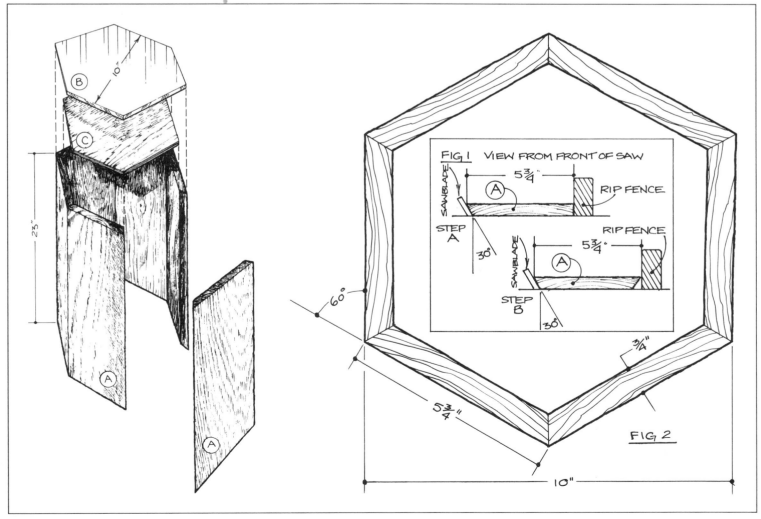

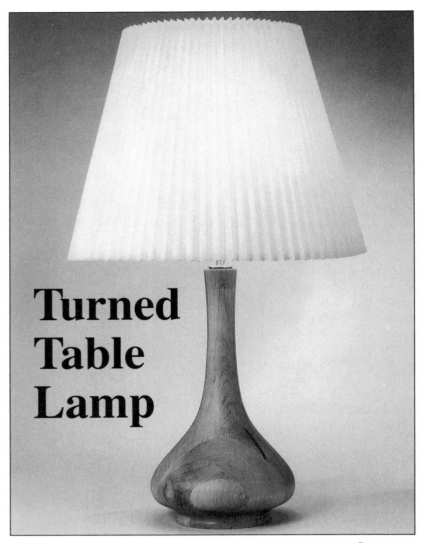

Turned Table Lamp

This graceful turning makes an especially nice lamp base. We used cherry, but maple or walnut will also look handsome.

It's important that the stock be glued up according to the three-step procedure we've given. If it isn't, and the resulting mass is unbalanced, a great deal of vibration and shaking can occur as the stock turns.

Begin by cutting parts A, B, and C to the dimensions shown in the Bill of Materials. Assemble as shown in Step 1, keeping in mind that only parts A and B are glued together. Since the spacer (part C) must be removed after turning (to form a cord hole), it is not glued. Instead, it is given a heavy coat of wax to prevent the glue from sticking. The wax will also make it easier to remove the spacer.

Clamp firmly and allow to dry thoroughly. When dry, joint one of the $2^7/8$ in. wide edges, then use the table saw to rip the same edge on the opposite side. This ripped edge is then jointed. Just keep in mind that after jointing, the assembly should measure $2^7/8$ in. by 3 in., and the spacer should be centered.

Next, glue up parts D and E as shown in Step 2. Follow the procedure just described to joint the $2^7/8$ in. wide edges. After jointing, parts D and E should measure $2^7/8$ in. by $2^3/4$ in.

The two part D and E assemblies can now be glued to the part A, B, and C assembly. Clamp securely, keeping the bottom edges as near to flush as possible. To keep the face edges flush, use a pair of hardwood stickers as shown. Use C-clamps to hold in place. Be sure to wax the stickers to keep them from sticking to the stock.

At this point, to insure a good, flat surface for the faceplate, use the table saw to crosscut the bottom end. Remove only enough material to square the stock.

Parts F and G can now be cut to size and assembled as shown in Step 3. Again use glue and clamps. It's important that all edges be flush, especially the bottom where the faceplate will be attached. Use stickers as necessary to keep everything lined up.

Locate the center point of the bottom, then use a compass to scribe a circle equal to the diameter of your faceplate. (Ours was 6 in.). Use $1^1/2$ in. screws to securely mount the faceplate to the base.

Before attaching the stock to the lathe, it's a good idea to break the edges to minimize tear-out. We used a drawknife, but the band saw, table saw or spokeshave will also do the job.

Next, mount the stock to the lathe using a dead center at the neck portion. The 16 in. length of stock allows $3/4$ in. extra at the top and 2 in. extra at the base. Set the lathe at its slowest speed (ours was about 400 rpm), then use a small ($1/4$ in.) gouge to rough out the stock. A small gouge will keep tear-out to a minimum. Once rounded, a $1/2$ in. or $3/4$ in. gouge can be used to finish roughing out the stock.

Next, determine the overall length of the lamp and use a parting tool to establish this dimension. Working from the parting line at the base, reduce the waste stock to slightly more than the diameter of the faceplate. This step will allow you to undercut the bottom. Use a $1/2$ in. roundnose to scoop out the base approximately $3/16$ in., leaving at least $1^1/2$ in. of the stock diameter intact.

Fine turning is done with a roundnose tool and a lathe speed of 1000 to 2500 rpm. Final sand, then remove from the lathe and cut off the remaining head and tail stock.

With a length of steel rod, drive out the spacer (C). Before part H can be added, all traces of wax must be removed from the area where this block will be glued in place. To remove the wax, use acetone or lacquer thinner followed by a light sanding. Epoxy the glue block in place, then drill a $3/8$ in. diameter hole as shown.

A $3^1/2$ in. length of threaded pipe (I) can now be epoxied to the glue block as shown. The lamp cord is then fed through the $1/4$ in. lamp cord hole in the base and up through the neck and out the threaded pipe. The addition of the lamp hardware and a lamp shade completes the project. Lamp hardware is available from Paxton Hardware, 7818 Bradshaw Road, Upper Falls, MD 21156.

Bill of Materials
(all dimensions actual)

Part	Description	Size	No. Req'd.
A	Turning Stock	$1^1/16$ x $3^1/4$ x 16	2
B	Turning Stock	$3/4$ x $1^1/4$ x 16	2
C	Spacer	$3/4$ x $3/4$ x 16	1
D	Turning Stock	$1^1/16$ x 3 x 9	4
E	Turning Stock	$3/4$ x 3 x 9	2
F	Turning Stock	$1^3/4$ x $8^1/2$ x 9	2
G	Turning Stock	$1^1/16$ x $8^1/2$ x 9	2
H	Glue Block	$3/4$ x $3/4$ x $1^1/4$	1
I	Threaded Pipe	$1/8$ I.P. x $3^1/2$	1
J	Brass Nut	$1/8$ I.P.	2
K	Brass Tubing	$1/2$ O.D. x 2	1
L	Check Ring	$1^3/8$ dia.	1
M	Harp		1
N	Socket		1

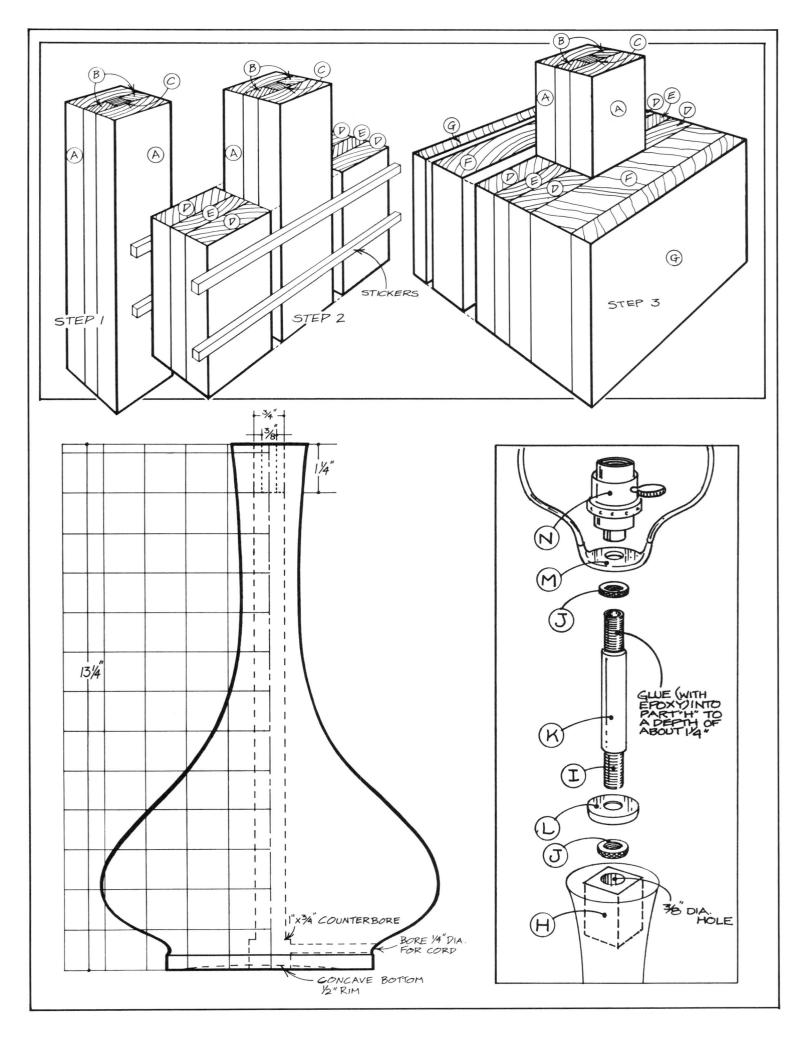

STEP 1

STEP 2

STICKERS

STEP 3

3/4"

3/8"

1 1/4"

13 1/4"

1"x3/4" COUNTERBORE

BORE 1/4"DIA.
FOR CORD

CONCAVE BOTTOM
1/2" RIM

N

M

J

K

GLUE (WITH
EPOXY) INTO
PART "H" TO
A DEPTH OF
ABOUT 1 1/4"

I

L

J

H

3/8" DIA.
HOLE

Record and Tape Cabinet

Music buffs may want to take note of this project. It has two shelves for record albums and three drawers for tape cassettes. With each drawer divided into sixteen rows, and each row holding four cassettes, there's room for over sixty cassettes in each drawer.

Oak plywood was used for parts A, B, C, D, E, H and O, while oak solid stock was used for all other parts.

Begin by cutting enough $^1/8$ in. thick edging stock (part F) to cover all four edges of the sides (parts A) and also the front edges of the top (part B), the upper shelf (part C), the lower shelf (part D), and the bottom (part E). It's best to make the edging wider than necessary, so start with $^5/4$ stock (it actually measures $1^1/16$ in. thick), which can later be trimmed to $^3/4$ in. A piece of stock about 4 in. wide and 43 in. long will provide more than enough edging material for the project.

Cut the two sides (A) to overall length and width, taking care to make sure the edges are square. Glue edging strips to the top and bottom edge of each side and use bar or pipe clamps to secure until dry. The edging may have a tendency to slide when clamped, so before gluing it's a good idea to drive two or three short brads in part A, then clip the heads off so that about $^1/16$ in. is exposed. *Make sure, however, that*

the brads along the bottom edge are located where they won't be hit when the rabbet is cut later on. When dry, remove the clamps and trim the ends of the edging flush with the sides of part A. A block plane can then be used to trim the $1^1/16$ in. wide edging to make it flush with the $^3/4$ in. thick side. Following this, the edging along the sides of part A can be applied and trimmed in the same manner.

The $^3/8$ in. by $^3/8$ in. rabbet along the back edge of part A can best be cut on the table or radial-arm saw using a dado head cutter, but repeated passes with a regular saw blade will also do the job. The same method can be used to cut the $^3/8$ in. by $^3/4$ in. rabbet along the bottom edge and the $^3/8$ by $^3/4$ in. dadoes for the top (part B) and the lower shelf (part D). Note that the $^3/8$ by $^3/4$ in. dado for the upper shelf (part C) does not run the entire width of the side. This joint, called a stopped dado, is best cut using a router guided by a straight length of scrap stock clamped to the side. The corners will be rounded at the point where the router stops, so use a sharp chisel to cut them square.

The top (part B), upper shelf (part C), lower shelf (part D), and bottom (part E) can now be cut to overall length and width, again taking care to make sure the cuts are square. Note that B, C, and D have edging strips along the front edge

only, while E has edging both front and back. Use the methods previously described to apply and trim the edging on all four parts. Following this, use the dado head cutter to make a $^3/8$ in. by $^3/8$ in. rabbet along the back edge of part E (see detail B).

Cut the back rail (part G) to length and width, then use the dado head to make three cuts: a $^3/8$ in. by $^3/8$ in. rabbet on each end, a $^3/8$ in. by $^3/8$ in. rabbet along the bottom edge, and a $^3/8$ in. by $^3/4$ in. groove to accept part B (see detail D).

The carcase (parts A through G) can now be assembled. Before starting, though, give all parts a thorough sanding, finishing with 220-grit sandpaper. Assemble with glue and pipe or bar clamps, then check for squareness. You'll probably find it will be helpful to have an extra pair of hands to help with this step. And use clamp pads to protect the stock. It's important that the case be square, so make adjustments, if necessary, before the glue starts to set up. A few finishing nails can be used to help secure parts E and G to the case. Allow to dry overnight.

Once dry, the clamps can be removed. Measure for the back (part H), then cut to size. Give both sides a thorough sanding before joining it to the case with glue and finishing nails.

The door (parts I, J, K, and Q) is made next. Cut the door stile (part I) to length and width, then use a dado head to cut the $^1/2$ in. deep by $^3/4$ in. wide grooves for parts J. Note that at the top of the door this groove is cut at a point $2^1/4$ in. from the top end, while at the bottom it forms a rabbet. Next, cut the $^1/4$ in. wide by $^3/8$ in. deep groove to accept the smoked Plexiglas front (Q). This cut is best made using the router in conjunction with a $^1/4$ in.

Bill of Materials (all dimensions actual)			
Part	Description	Size	No. Req'd.
A	Side	$^3/4$ x $16^3/4$ x $41^3/4$	2
B	Top	$^3/4$ x $16^1/2$ x $21^1/4$	1
C	Upper Shelf	$^3/4$ x $12^1/8$ x $21^1/4$	1
D	Lower Shelf	$^3/4$ x $16^1/2$ x $21^1/4$	1
E	Bottom	$^3/4$ x $16^7/8$ x $21^1/4$	1
F	Edging	$^1/8$ x $^3/4$	As Req'd
G	Back Rail	$^3/4$ x 5 x $21^1/4$	1
H	Back	$^3/8$ x $21^1/4$ x 37	1
I	Door Stile	$^3/4$ x $1^1/4$ x 42	2
J	Door Ends	$^3/4$ x $1^1/4$ x $21^1/2$	2
K	Door Rail	$^3/4$ x 2 x $21^1/2$	2
L	Drawer Front	$^3/4$ x $2^3/4$ x $20^3/8$	3
M	Drawer Sides	$^1/2$ x $2^3/4$ x $15^3/4$	6
N	Drawer Back	$^1/2$ x $2^3/4$ x $18^7/8$	3
O	Drawer Bottom	$^1/4$ x $15^1/4$ x $18^3/4$	3
P	Drawer Slides	No. 237-005	3 pr.
Q	Plexiglas	$^1/4$ thick	1
R	Casters		4

diameter straight bit and an edge guide. Note that this groove is located ¹/₄ in. from the front edge of part I. You can also use the router (equipped with a ³/₈ in. diameter straight bit and edge guide) to cut the ¹/₂ in. deep by ³/₈ in. wide notch for part K. Use a chisel to square the rounded corners. To finish work on part I, lay out a 1¹/₄ in. radius on the top end, then cut out with a band or saber saw.

Parts J and K can now be cut to size. Note that part J has a ¹/₄ in. wide by ³/₈ in. deep groove to accept the smoked glass (Q). To cut this groove, use the same router setup as was used to cut the groove in part I.

Final sand all door parts, then cut the

¹/₄ in. Plexiglas to size. Dry fit (without glue) parts I, J, and K, then bore three holes for countersunk wood screws through part K into part J as shown in detail A. At the bottom joint bore the holes through part J into part K.

Assemble the door parts as shown. Use glue and clamp securely. However, do not glue the joint between parts J and K at the door bottom. This joint is held together only by the counterbored wood screws. Therefore part K can be removed to replace the glass should it break or scratch. After clamping the door parts, check to make sure the door is square. Make adjustments if necessary.

Cut and assemble the drawer parts as

shown. Note that dadoes in the drawer sides accept ¹/₈ in. thick hardboard dividers. The 16 in. full-extension drawer slides (P) can be purchased from the mail-order company Woodworker's Supply of New Mexico, 5604 Alameda Place NE, Albuquerque, NM 87113. Order part number 237-005. Mounting instructions are included with the drawer slides.

Give the entire project one more sanding using 220-grit paper. Final finish is a matter of personal taste. The one shown was finished with two coats of Watco Danish Oil. The addition of a brass piano hinge and a magnetic catch completes the project. If desired, four casters (R) can be added to make the unit portable.

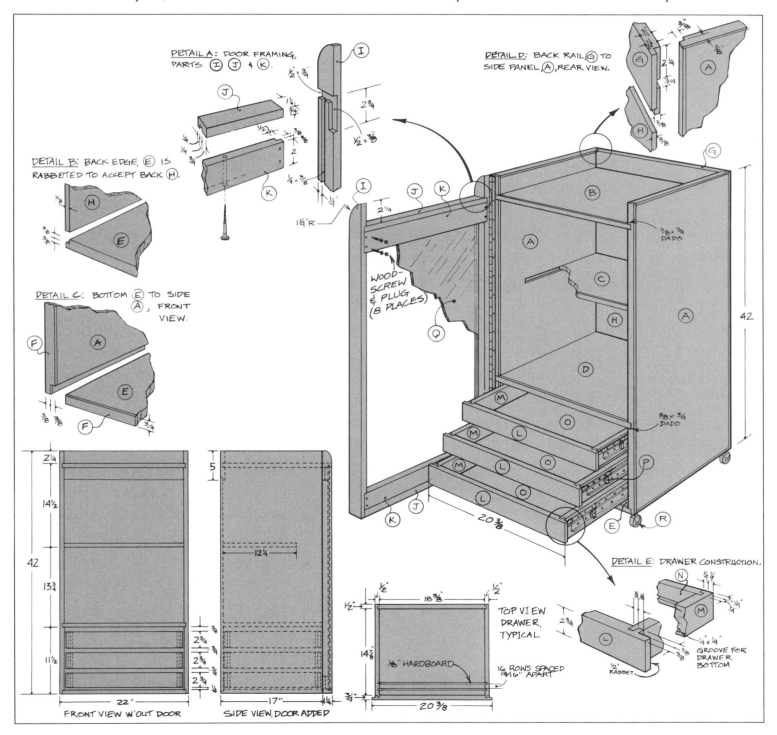

Chinese Tea Table

If you have a chance to visit the Portland, Oregon, Art Museum, be sure to take in the permanent display of 15th-century Mandarin wood furniture. You will appreciate the skill of these woodworkers of centuries past, and also the beautiful simplicity of the lines. No overly ornate reproductions these; they present a clean freshness that can only be approached in modern times by Scandinavian design. They are not, however, devoid of decorative touches sensitively applied.

Mahogany solid stock was used for all parts, although maple or cherry would also be good choices. Construction of the table is best performed in a specific order. Start with the four legs (Part A), made from the 3 by 3 stock. Cut the four pieces to length first. If you can, joint the ends of the legs immediately with a disk sander, because they will be more difficult to smooth later. Next, use a router or drill press, in conjunction with a dovetail bit, to cut the dovetail grooves. It is important to do this before the bandsawing, because afterwards the legs will not have easily

available flat surfaces to rest the work upon. Cut the grooves on two adjoining sides of each leg, centered 1 3/8 in. from the common corner. Make them 1/2 in. deep, and extend the cut from the end of the leg down exactly 1 in., measured at the center of the bit.

Next, mark the sides of the legs that have dovetails on them, and make up a template for the leg profiles. Note carefully the relation of the pattern to the dovetail groove. A circle gauge with a 2 1/2 in. diameter cutout will be helpful for drawing the curves on the template. Transfer the pattern from the template to the workpieces and use a band saw to cut the drawn pattern, leaving a small margin for sanding later.

At this point, the legs can be given a thorough sanding. A drum sander, if you have one, will be helpful when sanding the inside curves.

Next, lay out and mark the location of mortises for the stretcher (part G). A sharp 1/4 in. chisel will cut each mortise in short order.

When all the legs are complete, the

next step is to make the aprons (Part B). Cut four 16 in. lengths of 1 by 2 stock, and then rip them to 3/4 in. thick by 1 1/4 in. wide. The next operation is to form the dovetails on the ends. These should be cut 1/2 in. into the ends, at a width that produces a tight joint with the table legs. (Don't expect these aprons to fit flush with the top of the legs). The 1/2 in. depth of these dovetails is also critical. The fitting to the top frame is dependent upon the correct length of the aprons.

Since the stretchers (Part G) are mated to the cutout surfaces of the legs, and since the leg cutout and sanding process provides only imprecise depth control, it is best to individually fit these parts. This is done by assembling (without glue) the table, and placing the aprons with their dovetails into the grooves in the legs. The raw cut edge of the rails should be on top and will remain higher than the leg tops by 1/4 in. when correctly placed. Number the legs and sides so that you can recreate this same parts relationship later.

After carefully squaring the table, measure the distance on each side from leg to leg at the mortise point. This is the length that the stretchers need to be made.

Once the tenons are formed, the stretchers may be marked according to the pattern and bandsawed to shape. Again, a drum sander will speed the task of smoothing if you remember to turn with the grain and not into it.

Once the legs, aprons and stretchers have been made, the table is ready for assembly of the first portion. This two-step assembly makes the critical fitting of the top frame easier, since that way it will be mated to a solid form. Begin by final sanding all of the finished pieces up to now, then take a practice run (without glue) at the assembly of the base.

The sequence is as follows: assemble the stretchers (G) into each of the legs (A), then add the aprons (B). Keep in mind that the top edge of the aprons will be 1/4 in. above the top of the legs.

Once in this configuration, clamping the assembly is done with a single band clamp placed around the outsides of the

Bill of Materials (all dimensions actual)			
Part	Description	Size	No. Req'd.
A	Leg	2 1/2 x 2 1/2 x 15 3/4	4
B	Apron	3/4 x 1 1/4 x 16	4
C	Rail Trim	1/2 x 3/4 x 15	4
D	Top Frame	3/4 x 2 1/2 x 20	4
E	Web Support	1/2 x 3/4 x 5 1/4	4
F	Web Frame	1/2 x 3/4 x 7 1/2	4
G	Stretcher	3/4 x 1 1/2 x 17 1/2	4
H	Glass Top	1/4 x 15 3/8 x 15 3/8	1

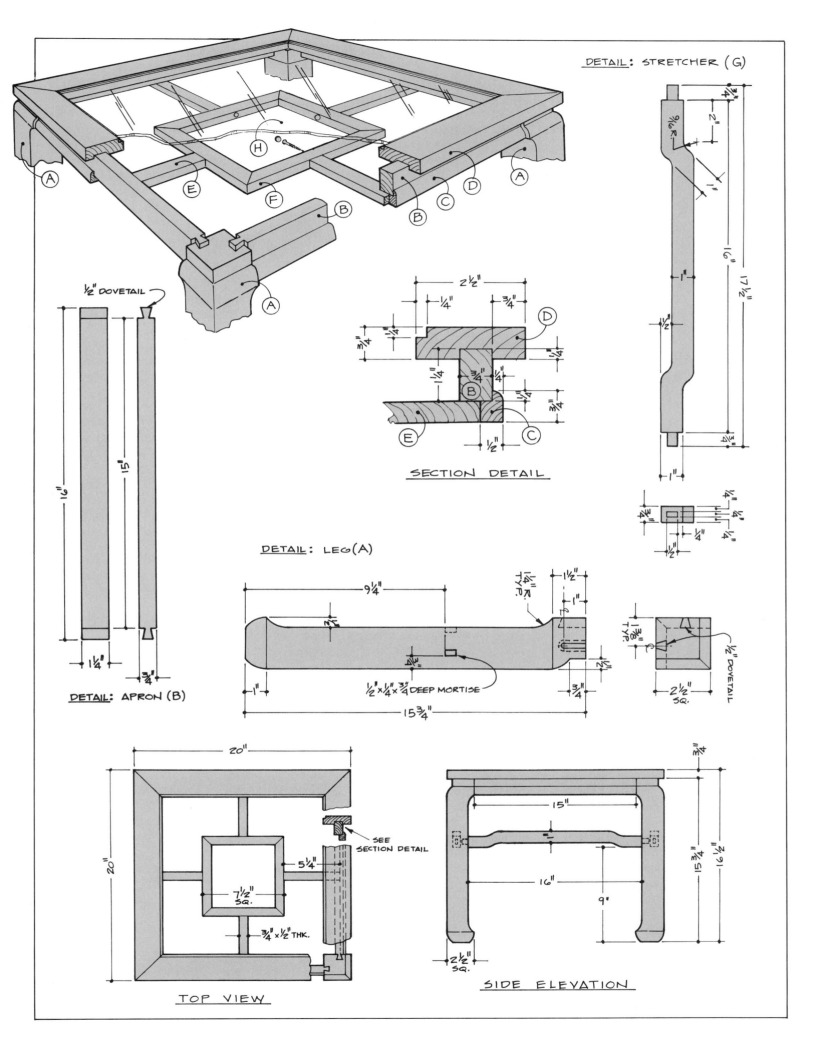

DETAIL: STRETCHER (G)

½" DOVETAIL

SECTION DETAIL

DETAIL: APRON (B)

DETAIL: LEG (A)

½" x ¼" x ¾" DEEP MORTISE

½" DOVETAIL

2½" SQ.

TOP VIEW

20"

20"

7½" SQ.

5¼"

¾" x ½" THK.

SEE SECTION DETAIL

SIDE ELEVATION

15"

16"

9"

15¾"

16½"

¾"

2½" SQ.

Webwork is glued to underside of aprons.

legs at a height between the aprons and stretchers. Once the clamp is tightened the assembly will take on a rigidity that will allow squaring the legs.

When the practice run is perfected, the base is ready for gluing. Glue each joint generously as it is being assembled, and finish the assembly quickly but without haste. Clamp the assembly and then square everything well.

The final structural assembly is the top frame (Part D), which holds the glass as well as providing structural rigidity. This top frame is made from the 1 by 3 stock. Cut the stock to slightly more than 20 in. and examine each piece for the face with the best appearance. Mark the opposite faces.

In each marked face, cut a groove $3/4$ in. wide and $1/4$ in. deep, set $3/4$ in. from one edge (and therefore 1 in. from the other edge). A dado blade makes the job a matter of a single pass, but repeated saw cuts may be performed to get the same effect, provided that the bottom of the groove is checked for smoothness — take care to make sure each cut is to full depth.

After cutting the grooves, turn the pieces over and mark the top edge farthest from the groove (over the 1 in. surface left after grooving). This edge is then cut to form a $1/4$ in. by $1/4$ in. rabbet. If you use a table saw to form the rabbet, carefully sand it smooth on both sides and make sure the corner is square.

The next step is to cut the miter ends of the prepared stock. These are cut with the rabbet edge on the inside and therefore shorter than the other edge, which should be cut to just over 20 in. After cutting all four pieces, place them on the table loosely, like pieces of a picture frame, with the bottom groove mated to the aprons.

Since the pieces were cut a little long, the top frame may not all fit into place. This trial assembly provides the opportunity to measure exactly how much needs to be trimmed to make everything fit. Make some test cuts in scrap to make sure your miter gauge is set to 45 degrees.

The top frame members can now be glued to the aprons. Assemble all four members, making sure the miter joints fit well, then use C-clamps to clamp the top frame members to the aprons. Be sure to apply glue to the mitered ends of the top frame parts.

The remainder of the table assembly is trim work; the structural part of the table is done. All the trim utilizes stock $1/2$ in. by $3/4$ in.

From some of the stock just made, measure and cut four pieces just over 15 in. These will form the rail trim (Part C). Cut a $1/4$ in. by $1/4$ in. rabbet the length of one edge of each piece. Across the narrow face of the pieces, the other edge needs to be rounded. A router may be used, but a sanding block is more than sufficient. Final sand the four trim rails and check them for length against each of the aprons. The rabbet is built to receive the exposed bottom edge of the aprons (see Section Detail). If necessary, adjust the length of the trim rail and then put some glue in the rabbets and glue them in place, clamping them with wooden cabinet-maker's clamps.

The remaining stock is used to make the webwork pattern. Carefully cut four lengths to exactly $5\frac{1}{4}$ in. Miter cut four more lengths so that the long side is exactly $7\frac{1}{2}$ in. If a disk sander is available, cut all eight pieces a little long and joint the cuts to make the correct length.

Glue and assemble parts F of the webwork, clamping with miter clamps if available. Otherwise use any clamping arrangement that provides a finished webwork that is flat. If necessary, this may be done in stages rather than all at once. Let the glue dry completely before proceeding, because the webwork is not inherently strong, and insufficient curing will only make the assembly more fragile.

To prepare the table for attachment of the webwork, lay it top down on a cloth-covered level surface. On the exposed bottom surface of the aprons, mark the exact center of each length. Then, place parallel lines across the grain on the aprons $3/8$ in. to either side of the center mark. These lines demarcate the placement of the web supports (E). The Section Detail shows the relationship of the apron, the trim rail, the top frame and the

web supports. Note that parts E are joined to parts F with small countersunk and plugged wood screws.

Place a layer of glue within the marked area of the aprons and lay the webwork, best face down towards the top frame, on the glued areas. Adjust position (if necessary) until all four ends of the webwork fall within their marked areas. Clamp firmly and allow to dry.

Use a sanding block to preserve the flatness of the surfaces. If necessary, sand the appropriate edge near each joint to make the miter joint exactly on the corner. The outside edges of the top frame may be rounded slightly ($1/16$ in. radius) to remove sharp corners; if this is done, you might want to similarly treat the vertical edges of the legs and the bottom edge of the rail trim. When complete, the glass will protect the webwork, but while sanding and finishing, remember that it is not a structural part and is subject to damage should, for example, a heavy tool fall upon it. Before finishing, the areas around all joints should be touched up with finish grade sandpaper to remove glue traces on the surfaces.

At this point, construction of the table is complete, and the only pieces that still require finish sanding are the rail trim and the top frame. Finish sand these parts now, making sure that the top frame joints are perfectly smooth. You can get the $1/4$ in. thick plate glass at most glass shops. Be sure to have them grind the edges smooth.

A clear penetrating oil finish looks best on a piece like this. Three coats of Watco Danish Oil were applied, each being allowed to soak in for about five minutes before wiping off the excess.

After final sanding, a clear penetrating oil is added to provide an attractive finish.

Old World Weather Forecaster

The weather house type of weather forecaster is a very old traditional type that was popular in Europe, especially Germany. Changes in the weather cause a gut string to twist. The string is attached to small figures of a man and a woman. If the woman is outside of the house, the weather will be fair; when the man comes out, stormy weather is predicted. If you like to carve and are interested in the weather, this is a very enjoyable project.

Start by cutting the front (A) and the back (B) out of a ³/₄ in. thick board. Mahogany or walnut will work well for this project. The outlines of both pieces are identical. Once the outline of the back is cut it is complete, but the front requires further work. Cut the two arched doors in the front with a coping saw, band saw or jigsaw. Use a router with a ¹/₈ in. radius cove bit that has a pilot to cut the cove around the doors. Next use a 1¹/₂ in. spade or Forstner bit to start the hole for the sun carving (K). Stop drilling when the hole is ¹/₄ in. deep. Switch to a 1¹/₄ in. bit and finish drilling the hole through the

front. This hole is necessary to attach part (J) to part (N) when the house is complete. Using the two drill diameters will form a lip around the hole that will hold the sun carving.

Now cut out the base (C). Use a power carving tool or a router to cut out the recess for the pivot arm (F) and the two semi-circular slots. Use the router and a ¹/₄ in. radius cove bit to make the decorative cove around the front and both ends. Don't cut a cove along the back.

The sides (D) and the top (E) are ¹/₄ in. thick. You can resaw a piece of ³/₄ in. thick wood to make them. Since the angle at the peak of the roof is 90 degrees, a standard 45-degree miter is used to join the two roof pieces (E). Cut a 45-degree angle at the top of both sides (D) where it will join with part E.

Attach the front and back to the base with flathead screws (P) and glue. Countersink the screw heads into the base and be sure to drill pilot holes. The wood is likely to split if you don't, especially on the front where there is only a small section of wood next to the door to screw

into. Next glue and clamp the sides (D) in place. The sides are flush with the back and they overhang slightly on the front.

When the glue has cured on the sides, trim the angle on the top of them to conform exactly to the angle of the front and back, then glue the roof pieces in place. The best way to clamp the roof pieces is with a web clamp, but you can also position small C-clamps or spring clamps in the door openings and in the hole for the sun carving.

Next, drill a ¹/₄ in. hole through the base and center divider of the front at the position indicated on the plan. Stop the hole when you see the drill enter the hole for the sun carving. Drill another ¹/₄ in. hole through the peak of the roof to match up with the hole drilled through the base. It will be easier to start the hole if you first flatten the peak of the roof in the area where the hole should go by filing it with the flat edge of a triangular file. It's all right if there is a slight amount of misalignment between the two holes because the gut string (J) is flexible and can compensate for some error.

Cut out the chimney (L) and drill a 1/4 in. hole through its center. You can get the angle cut in the bottom of the chimney to fit the angle of the roof perfectly by folding a piece of fine sandpaper over the peak of the roof with the cutting side facing up. Hold the chimney in place on top of the sandpaper and slide it back and forth across the peak until the sandpaper is cutting evenly across both faces of the cutout in the chimney.

At this point, apply a walnut colored Danish oil finish to the house and set it aside while you work on the figures.

The two figures (H and I) are carved from a lightweight wood such as pine or balsa. The weather-sensing gut string doesn't have too much turning power, so if the figures are too heavy they will make the forecaster less sensitive. Use a jack-knife or small carving chisels to carve the figures. Start with a block 1 in. by 1 in. by 8 in. for each figure. The extra length gives you a good handle to hold onto while you work. When the figures are complete, carve a 1/4 in. diameter pedestal below their feet that will fit into the slot in the base. After carving the pedestal, use a fine-tooth saw to cut the figures off from the handles. Apply a clear finish to the figures.

The pivot dowel (G) fits into a blind hole drilled in the center of the pivot arm (F). Check to see that the dowel fits loosely into the hole drilled for it in the base of the house; if it binds, you may have to sand it down to a smaller diameter.

The heart of this weather forecaster is a section of gut violin string (J). Buy a "D" violin string at a music store. The cheaper the better as long as it's real gut. More expensive strings are made to resist weather related changes so they won't go out of tune. If not available locally, a "D" violin string can be ordered from Folkcraft Instruments, P.O. Box 807, Winsted, CT 06098. One string will give you enough gut to build several forecasters. The string will be wrapped with a covering of steel wire and a layer of thread wrapped under that. You must remove both of these layers to expose the bare gut underneath. Cut a section of the string, slightly longer than needed, with wire cutters and unwrap the steel and thread. Moisten a clean piece of cotton with rubbing alcohol and use it to wipe off the gut. This will remove any oils that are on the gut that would prevent it from responding to weather changes. Drill a 1/16 in. diameter hole about 1/2 in. deep in the top of the pivot dowel (G). Apply a small amount of glue to the end of the gut

string and insert it into the hole.

When the glue has cured, you are ready to test the gut. Hold the free end of the gut string and let the pivot dowel and pivot arm dangle freely below it. Move the gut close to a flow of steam escaping from a teapot. The pivot arm should turn. The direction that it turned is the indication of stormy weather. Mark that end of the pivot arm for later reference. If the arm didn't move, try cleaning the gut again with alcohol. If it still won't react, you will have to get another piece of gut.

Position the pivot dowel in its hole in the base; the gut string should be visible in the hole that the sun carving fits into. Make certain that the ends of the figures

will fit freely into the semi-circular slots in the base. Glue the male figure to the side of the pivot arm that you previously marked as the stormy side. Glue the female figure to the opposite end of the pivot arm. Before the glue sets, rotate the arm to make sure that the figures don't bind anywhere along the slots.

The setting knob (M) is made from a small section of 5/8 in. diameter dowel. Drill a blind hole in one end to accept a dowel, and glue the setting knob dowel (N) into the hole. Round the edges of the knob with sandpaper and stain the knob to match the rest of the house. Drill a 1/16 in. diameter by 1/2 in. deep hole into the end of part N. Insert the setting knob assembly into the chimney. You should be able to see the end of part N inside of the hole for the sun carving. The string's length should be adjusted so it will suspend the pivot arm just below the surface of the base when it is fitted into part N. Apply a small amount of glue to the end of the gut string and insert it into the hole drilled in part N. You may need to use tweezers to do this.

After the glue is cured, place the house upright and turn the setting knob back and forth to see that the figures move freely in their slots. If everything functions smoothly, install the sun carving (K) to cover the access hole. If you make the carving carefully, you can get a snug enough fit so you won't need any glue; that way you can remove the carving if you ever need to replace the gut. Finish the carving to match the rest of the house and press it into place.

Cover the bottom of the base with a piece of felt (O). The felt covers the pivot arm recess and prevents the house from scratching any furniture it is placed on.

To use the forecaster, place it near a window or door where it will be most likely to get some outside air. Observe what the weather is like outside and set the forecaster by turning the setting knob. If it is stormy, turn the knob until the man is part of the way out of the door. If it is fair, turn the knob the other direction until the woman is part way out of her door. Leave the forecaster set this way for several days and observe the changes. After you have observed the movement of the figures over a period of weather change, you can make further adjustment. For example, if the initial setting was made during stormy weather, the woman should come out as the weather clears. If the man moves back some but not enough for the woman to come out, the initial setting was too far toward the stormy side. Turn the knob back a little so that the woman is slightly out of the door. After a few such adjustments, you will have the forecaster set so that the first indication of a storm will cause the woman to go inside and the man to come out. You can judge the relative strength of a storm or the length of a fair spell by how far the figures move out of the door.

Bill of Materials
(all dimensions actual)

Part	Description	Size	No. Req'd.
A	Front	3/4 x 5 x 5 3/8	1
B	Back	3/4 x 5 x 5 3/8	1
C	Base	3/4 x 3 1/4 x 6 1/2	1
D	Side	1/4 x 2 1/4 x 2 15/16	2
E	Roof	1/4 x 2 3/8 x 4 1/2	2
F	Pivot Arm	3/16 x 1/2 x 3 1/4	1
G	Pivot Dowel	1/4 dia. x 2 3/16	1
H	Man	See Detail	1
I	Woman	See Detail	1
J	Gut Violin String	"D"	1
K	Sun Carving	See Detail	1
L	Chimney	3/4 x 3/4 x 1	1
M	Setting Knob	5/8 dia. x 3/8 thick	1
N	Setting Dowel	1/4 dia. x 2 3/16	1
O	Felt Bottom	As Req'd	1
P	Flathead Screws		4

Toy Tractor with Cart

When you consider that many commercially made toys last no longer than a few weeks, it's refreshing to think that a sturdy toy like this is likely to last several generations. Poplar, which is reasonably priced, yet hard enough to stand up to rough service, was used for most parts. The cart bottom (R) is 1/4 in. mahogany plywood and the front wheels (O) and cart wheels (W) are maple.

From five-quarter stock (which actually measures 1 1/16 in. thick), cut the hood (A) to a width of 1 1/4 in. and a length of 4 in. Referring to the drawing, mark the location of the holes for the muffler (I) and the radiator cap (J), then use a 1/4 in. diameter drill bit to bore each hole.

The body (B) is also made from 5/4 stock. Cut to a width of 1 1/4 in. and a length of 6 3/4 in., then lay out and mark the location of the 5/8 in. deep by 3/4 in. wide dadoes for parts C and D. The dadoes can be cut on either the table or radial-arm saw. A 3/4 in. dado-head cutter will cut each dado with one pass, but repeated passes with a regular saw blade will also do the job.

The front and rear axle supports (parts C and D) are made from 1 in. nominal stock (which actually measures 3/4 in. thick). Cut to the length and width shown, then lay out and mark the location of the axle holes. Drill a 7/16 in. diameter hole through part C and a 5/16 in. diameter hole through part D. If you have one, use a drill press here because it insures that the holes will be reasonably square. However, if done with care, a hand brace or portable electric drill will do as good a job.

Parts A, B, C, and D can now be assembled. Before gluing part A to part B, drive a couple of short brads in part B, then clip the heads off so that about 1/8 in. is exposed. This will keep the two parts from sliding when clamped. Use a non-toxic glue (such as Elmer's Glue-All®) and clamp firmly. Allow to dry overnight.

Parts I and J can be turned to the dimensions shown or, if you don't have a lathe, similar pins can be ordered from the company Meisel Hardware Specialties, P.O. Box 70, Mound, MN 55364. Glue in place as shown in the drawing. The steering wheel (F) can be cut using a 3/4 in. hole saw or ordered from Meisel. Parts E, G, and H are made as shown and glued in place. Two 1/8 in. diameter dowels will add strength to the joint between parts E and H. Note that the steering post (G) is not glued into the hood (A) but rather left free to turn. The seat (H) prevents it from coming out all the way.

The rear wheels (N) are best made using the lathe, although if done carefully, they can be cut on the band or saber saw and sanded smooth. The front wheels (O) can be made in the same manner or purchased from Meisel.

The parts for the cart are cut to the dimensions shown in the Bill of Materials. Assemble parts P and Q with glue and clamps then set aside to dry. If necessary use clipped brads to keep the parts in line.

Assemble parts R, S, and T with glue and clamps. When dry, this unit can be assembled to parts P and Q.

The axle supports (U) can now be cut to the dimensions shown in the detail. After drilling the 5/16 in. axle hole, part U can be glued and clamped to the bottom of the cart. The cart wheels (W) can be turned to the dimensions shown or purchased from Woodworks.

Give all parts a thorough sanding taking care to round all sharp edges. Final sand using 220-grit sandpaper. The best non-toxic finish is no finish at all.

Bill of Materials
(all dimensions actual)

Part	Description	Size	No. Req'd.
Tractor			
A	Hood	1 1/16 x 1 1/4 x 4	1
B	Body	1 1/16 x 1 1/4 x 6 3/4	1
C	Rear Axle Support	3/4 x 1 1/4 x 3	1
D	Front Axle Support	3/4 x 1 3/4 x 2	1
E	Seat Back	1/4 x 1 x 1 1/4	1
F	Steering Wheel	3/4 dia. x 3/16 thick	1
G	Steering Post	3/16 dia. x 1 1/2 long	1
H	Seat	1/2 x 1 x 5/8	1
I	Muffler	see detail	1
J	Radiator Cap	see detail	1
K	Hitch	1/4 dia. x 1 1/4 long	1
L	Rear Axle	3/8 dia. x 4 7/8 long	1
M	Front Axle	1/4 dia. x 3 3/8 long	1
N	Rear Wheel	3 dia. x 3/4 thick	2
O	Front Wheel	2 dia. x 1/2 thick	2
Cart			
P	Center Frame	1/2 x 3/4 x 9	1
Q	End Frame	1/2 x 3/4 x 5	2
R	Bottom	1/4 x 3 1/4 x 7	1
S	Side	3/8 x 1 5/8 x 7	2
T	End	1/2 x 1 5/8 x 2 1/2	2
U	Axle Support	see detail	2
V	Cart Axle	1/4 dia. x 3 1/2	2
W	Cart Wheel	1 1/4 dia. x 3/8 thick	4

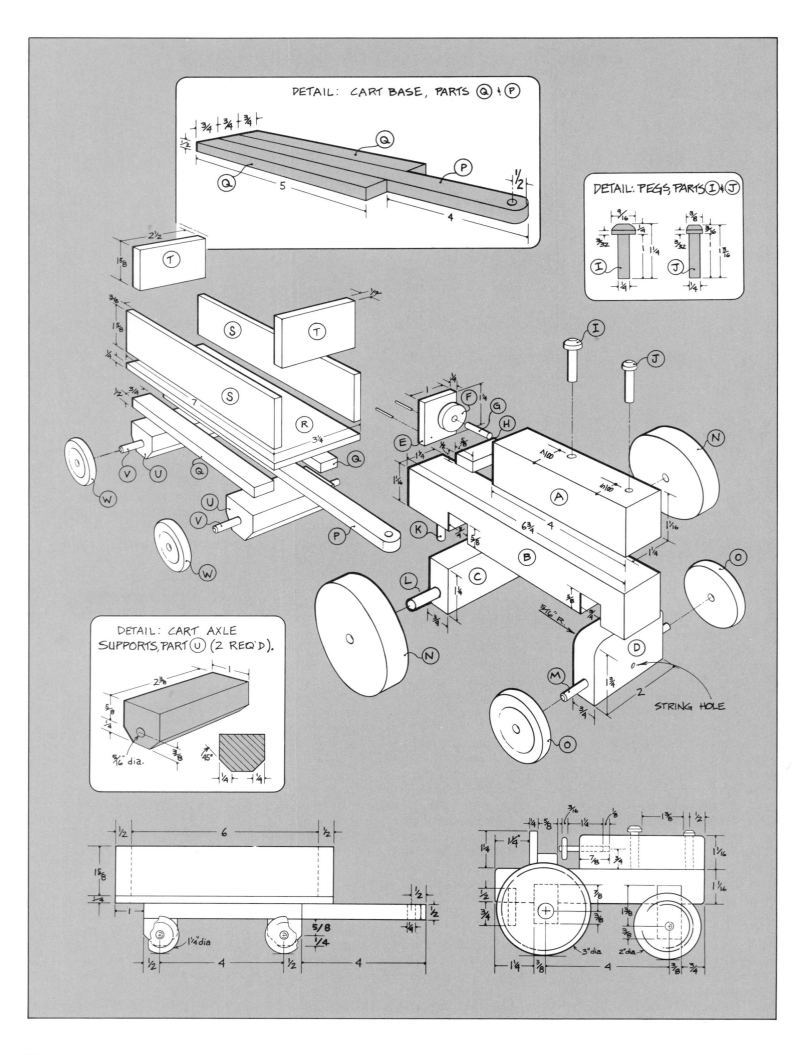

DETAIL: CART BASE, PARTS Q & P

DETAIL: PEGS, PARTS I & J

DETAIL: CART AXLE
SUPPORTS, PART U (2 REQ'D).

STRING HOLE

Fret Sawn Planter

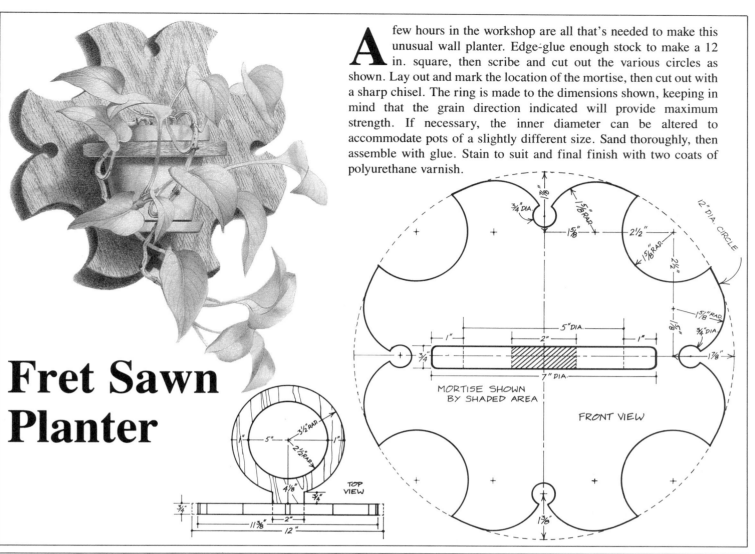

A few hours in the workshop are all that's needed to make this unusual wall planter. Edge-glue enough stock to make a 12 in. square, then scribe and cut out the various circles as shown. Lay out and mark the location of the mortise, then cut out with a sharp chisel. The ring is made to the dimensions shown, keeping in mind that the grain direction indicated will provide maximum strength. If necessary, the inner diameter can be altered to accommodate pots of a slightly different size. Sand thoroughly, then assemble with glue. Stain to suit and final finish with two coats of polyurethane varnish.

MORTISE SHOWN BY SHADED AREA

FRONT VIEW

TOP VIEW

Salt Box Planter

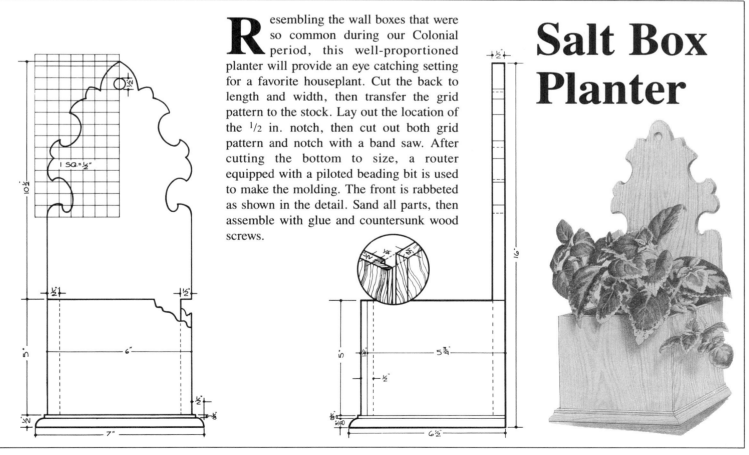

Resembling the wall boxes that were so common during our Colonial period, this well-proportioned planter will provide an eye catching setting for a favorite houseplant. Cut the back to length and width, then transfer the grid pattern to the stock. Lay out the location of the 1/2 in. notch, then cut out both grid pattern and notch with a band saw. After cutting the bottom to size, a router equipped with a piloted beading bit is used to make the molding. The front is rabbeted as shown in the detail. Sand all parts, then assemble with glue and countersunk wood screws.

1 SQ.= 1/2"

Shaker Desk

W e discovered this lovely example of a Shaker writing desk at a local cabinetmaker's shop. While not an exact reproduction, the overall design is very nearly the same as the Shaker original.

Cherry was used for this piece, a wood commonly chosen by the Shakers. The drawer sides, back, and bottom are made of pine, although maple could also be used here.

The four legs (A) can be made first. From 2 in. stock (which actually measures $1^3/4$ in.), rip each leg to a width of $1^3/4$ in. Although the overall length of the legs is $27^1/8$ in., it's best to initially cut them slightly oversized, then trim them to final length later on.

Lay out and mark the location of the apron mortises on each leg. To cut each mortise, use a drill press equipped with a $3/8$ in. diameter bit and drill a series of holes. This will remove most of the material and what remains can be cleaned up with a sharp chisel. Be sure to cut the mortise about $1/16$ in. deeper than the

tenon length. This extra depth will allow room for any excess glue that may be in the joint when it is later assembled. If the joint does not have room for excess glue, it becomes just about impossible to make it close.

At this time, also cut the small mortises for the drawer frame (parts D and E) tenons. These can best be cut with a chisel.

Referring to the drawing, note that each leg is tapered down to 1 in. on two sides. The taper starts at a point just below the apron (B), $5^1/4$ in. from the top of the leg. If you have a tapering jig for your table or radial-arm saw, this is a good time to use it, although a good sharp hand plane will also do the job in little time.

The two side aprons (B) and the back apron (C) can be made next. Cut to the length and width shown in the Bill of Materials, making sure to include the tenon length. Although the tenons can be cut by hand using a back saw, we generally prefer to use a table saw equipped with a dado head cutter. Set the dado head to a height (about $3/16$ in.) that will provide a snug fitting tenon when

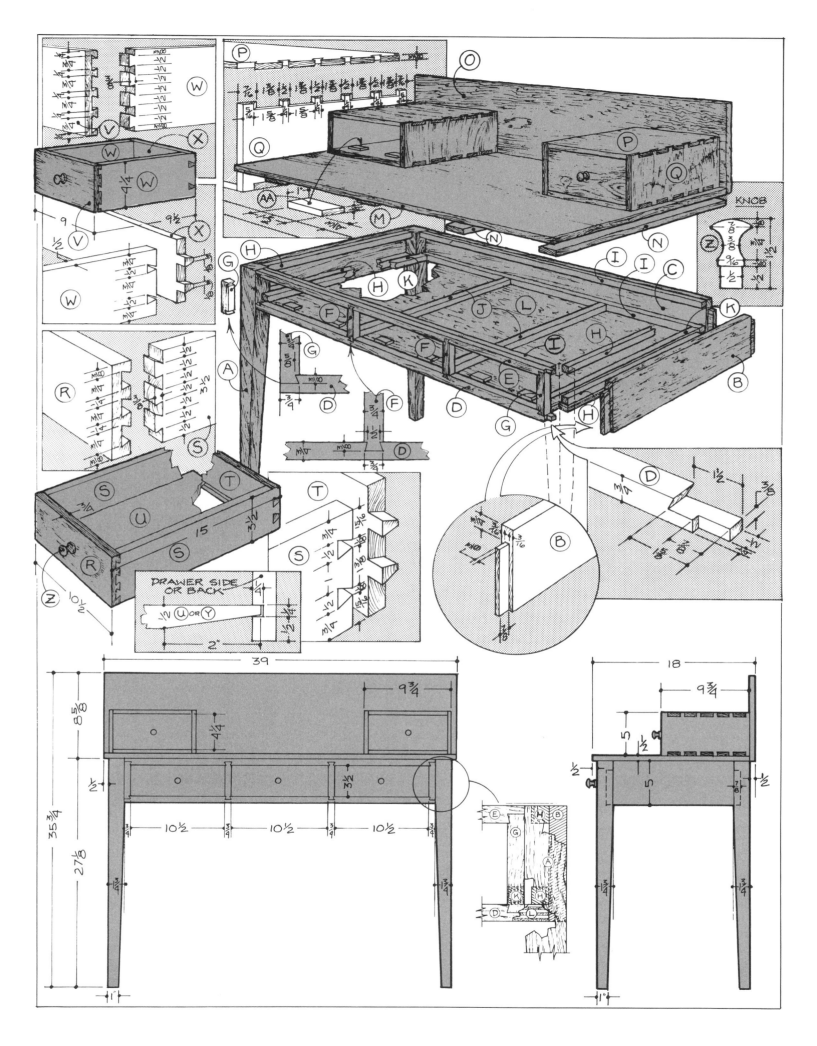

KNOB

DRAWER SIDE OR BACK

both cheeks are cut, then use the miter gauge to pass the stock over the cutter. Make some test cuts on scrap stock before starting.

Cut the inner and outer dividers (parts F and G) to overall length from $3/4$ in. square stock. Use a sharp hard pencil to lay out the dovetail profile, then use a dovetail or fine-toothed back saw to cut out. For best results, cut just on the outside of the line, then use a sharp chisel to pare the material exactly to the line.

Next, make the upper and lower drawer frame (parts D and E). Cut to overall length from $3/4$ in. square stock, then lay out the location of the dovetail pins. To insure accuracy, use the divider dovetails as templates. And to avoid confusion later on, label each divider dovetail and its corresponding pin on the drawer frames. Once marked, use a dovetail saw and chisel to remove the pin material. Cut just inside the line and use the chisel to pare to an exact fit.

Before assembly, give the legs, aprons, drawer frame members and dividers a thorough sanding. Be sure to remove any unsightly planer marks that tend to give a washboard effect to the stock.

Assemble each side apron (B) to a pair of legs as shown. Apply glue to the apron tenon, then assemble the leg and clamp with a bar or pipe clamp. Use scrap stock as clamp pads to prevent marring the legs. Check for squareness before setting aside to dry.

The inner and outer dividers (F and G) can now be glued to the upper and lower drawer frames (D and E). Use glue and clamp lightly. When dry, this frame unit and the back apron (C) can then be joined to the two previously glued sub-assemblies consisting of the side apron and legs. Again, use bar or pipe clamps and check for squareness before setting aside to dry.

Now the side apron and long apron cleats (H and I) can be cut to length from $3/4$ in. square stock. Properly cut, they should fit snugly inside the legs. To permit the cleats to be screwed and glued to the aprons, drill and countersink each one for $3/4$ in. by no. 8 flathead wood screws.

The lower cleats serve as a means for the

bottom (L) to be attached. They can now be secured in place, keeping in mind that they are located $3/4$ in. from the bottom edge of the apron (see drawing).

The upper cleats provide a means for attaching the top (M) and need to be predrilled and countersunk before assembly. To permit expansion and contraction of the top, these holes should be slotted.

The bottom (L) can now be cut to size from $3/4$ in. thick birch plywood. Note that it will have to be notched at the corners in order to fit around the legs. With the desk base unit upside down, drop the bottom in place, then drill and countersink holes for $1^{1}/4$ in. by no. 8 flathead wood screws.

Next, cut the inner and outer drawer guides (parts J and K) to length so they fit snugly between the dividers and the back apron cleat. Secure to the bottom (L) with roundhead wood screws and washers. It's best to make the drawer guide holes slightly slotted so they can be adjusted later on when the drawers are added.

Part M, the top, is made from $1/2$ in. thick stock. If you can't get $1/2$ in. stock, most millwork shops will plane down $3/4$ in. material. Or, if you have a band saw, you can resaw narrow stock to $1/2$ in. thickness.

Cut the top boards a bit on the long side (about 40 in.) before edge joining. Since the edges have a tendency to slip over each other when clamp pressure is applied, it's a good idea to add two or three $1/4$ in. diameter dowel pins to each edge joint. Apply glue to all mating surfaces (the dowel pins don't need any) then clamp firmly with bar or pipe clamps. Following this, the back (O) can be made in the same manner.

The battens (part N) serve to stiffen the top and prevent warping. They are cut to fit just inside of parts I, but are attached only to the top. Four slotted holes (to allow expansion and contraction of the top) are drilled in each batten to take $7/8$ in. by no. 8 roundhead wood screws and washers.

The dovetailed drawer boxes (parts P and Q) are made from $3/8$ in. thick stock as shown. Once the dovetails are cut, the boxes are assembled as shown. Again, use glue and clamp firmly. Check for squareness before setting aside to dry.

Both the top (M) and the back (O) can now be thoroughly sanded. Work through 220-grit to insure a smooth surface.

The base can now be attached to the top. Place the top upside down on a blanket or other protective surface, then locate the base in its proper position. With the bottom (L) removed, mark the location of the holes in cleats. Remove the base and drill pilot holes for 1 in. by no. 8 flathead wood screws. Attach the base, then add the bottom (L).

The drawer boxes (parts P and Q) are not glued to the top. Instead, angled screws are driven through the bottom of the box and into the top. Two are driven at the front of the box and two at the back. The back (O) is also screwed in place.

After the drawers are made, the entire project can be final sanded. Note that the bottom edge of drawer backs (T) and (X) must be notched to fit over the drawer stops (AA). Lightly round all corners. Check drawers for a good sliding fit and adjust as necessary. Three coats of Watco Danish Oil complete the project.

Bill of Materials
(all dimensions actual)

Part	Description	Size	No. Req'd.
A	Leg	$1^{3}/4$ x $1^{3}/4$ x $27^{1}/8$	4
B	Side Apron	$3/4$ x 5 x $15^{1}/4$*	2
C	Back Apron	$3/4$ x 5 x $36^{1}/4$*	1
D	Lower Drawer Frame	$3/4$ x $3/4$ x $36^{1}/4$*	1
E	Upper Drawer Frame	$3/4$ x $3/4$ x $36^{1}/4$*	1
F	Inner Divider	$3/4$ x $3/4$ x $4^{1}/4$**	2
G	Outer Divider	$3/4$ x $3/4$ x $4^{1}/4$**	2
H	Side Apron Cleat	$3/4$ x $3/4$ x $13^{1}/2$	4
I	Long Apron Cleat	$3/4$ x $3/4$ x $34^{1}/2$	3
J	Inner Drawer Guide	$3/4$ x $3/4$ x $14^{3}/4$	2
K	Outer Drawer Guide	$3/4$ x $3/4$ x $14^{3}/4$	2
L	Bottom	$3/4$ x $15^{1}/2$ x $36^{1}/2$	1
M	Top	$1/2$ x $17^{1}/2$ x 39	1
N	Batten	$1/2$ x 2 x 14	4
O	Back	$1/2$ x $8^{5}/8$ x 39	1
P	Box Top & Bottom	$3/8$ x $9^{3}/4$ x $9^{3}/4$	4
Q	Box Side	$3/8$ x $9^{3}/4$ x 5	4
R	Base Drawer Front	$3/4$ x $3^{1}/2$ x $10^{1}/2$	3
S	Base Drawer Side	$1/2$ x $3^{1}/2$ x $14^{5}/8$	6
T	Base Drawer Back	$1/2$ x $3^{1}/2$ x $10^{1}/2$	3
U	Base Drawer Bottom	$1/2$ x $9^{7}/8$ x $14^{1}/8$	3
V	Box Drawer Front	$3/4$ x $4^{1}/4$ x 9	2
W	Box Drawer Side	$1/2$ x $4^{1}/4$ x $9^{1}/8$	4
X	Box Drawer Back	$1/2$ x $4^{1}/4$ x 9	2
Y	Box Drawer Bottom	$1/2$ x $8^{3}/8$ x $8^{5}/8$	2
Z	Drawer Knob	See Detail	5
AA	Drawer Stop	$1/4$ x 1 x $1^{1}/2$	10

* includes tenon
** includes dovetails

Laminated Turned Bowl

T urned bowls are always popular and we expect that this one, with its graceful profile, will be no exception.

Basically, the turning block is made up of six $1^1/4$ in. thick octagonal layers (A through F, Fig. 3), each layer a different size. The eight segments that form each octagon are separated by veneer spacers. All six octagons are then glued in a stack, largest on the bottom, smallest on the top. The turning block is ready for turning after the addition of a glue block and faceplate.

The veneer spacers serve as a visual highlight and, to be effective, the color must contrast with that of the wood segments. Our segments are made from walnut (which is dark), with maple (which is light) for the veneer spacers.

Begin by making layer A, the largest octagon (see Detail A-A). Cut $1^1/4$ in. thick stock to a width of $1^7/8$ in. and a length of about 40 in. This length allows for a few extra segments to be cut.

To improve safety and accuracy, we devised a simple jig (see Fig. 1 and Detail B-B) to use when making the mitered cuts. It consists of a short (about 20 in.) auxiliary fence (Part X) with a strip of 220-grit sandpaper rubber cemented to the front face. Screwed to the auxiliary fence is a stopblock (Part Y), mitered at $22^1/2$ degrees on one end. The stopblock is located $4^9/16$ in. from the blade for all layer A segments. The clamp block (Part Z) is used to secure the stock to the jig, and it's held in place with a C-clamp. Ideally, the stopblock (Y) should be about $1/32$ in. narrower than the stock to be cut. This results in a good clamping action when the C-clamp is attached.

Once properly set up, you need only push the miter gauge through the blade. The jig will securely hold the segment while the remaining stock is cut free. Your hands are kept safely away from the blade.

The same jig is used for layers B through E, however it will be necessary to relocate the stopblock (Y) for each layer. The proper location is shown in Detail B-B.

It's important to note that to cut an accurate octagon, the miter gauge must be set at exactly $22^1/2$ degrees. A deviation of as little as $1/2$ degree can cause a gap in the joints. Before cutting any walnut, it's best to check the accuracy of your gauge by making one or two test octagons out of scrap stock.

Unlike the other layers, the segments for layer F are 3 in. wide and shaped in the form of a triangle. Rather than make another jig, we feel it's easier to individually measure, mark and cut each piece. Just be sure to cut the stock with enough extra length so that your fingers are a safe distance from the blade on the last cut.

Once cut, the segments for each layer

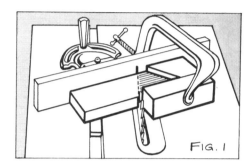

FIG. 1

can be glued together with the veneer spacers sandwiched in between (Fig. 2). Apply glue to all mating surfaces and clamp firmly with the web clamp. It's important that the veneer be flush with the outside of the octagon and overhang the inside as shown. To keep the octagon flat, it's best to glue it up on a flat surface. Use wax paper to prevent sticking.

Since the six octagons will be stack glued together, it's important that each one be flat. A glue board makes this easy

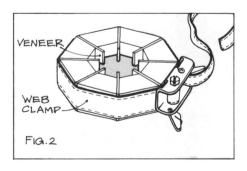

VENEER

WEB CLAMP

FIG. 2

to do. To make one, cut a piece of $1/2$ in. or $3/4$ in. thick particleboard to 24 in. square, then use rubber cement to glue four pieces of standard size 80-grit sandpaper to the board. Butt the edges together to form a smooth surface. To flatten the stock, first remove any excess glue with a sharp chisel, then simply lay the octagon on the board and move it back and forth, applying light pressure. The surface will be flattened in short order.

The octagons can now be glued together (Fig. 3). Their proper orientation is shown in Detail A-A. We found it easiest to glue two layers at a time, temporarily tacking several brads in place to keep the octagons from sliding over each other. Once dry, the three resulting sub-assemblies are glued and clamped in the same manner (Fig. 4).

Note that a 1¼ in. thick glueblock is glued to layer F, with a piece of paper (brown grocery bag type works well) sandwiched in between. The paper will make it easy to remove the glue block later on.

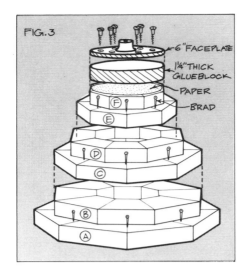

FIG. 3

6" FACEPLATE
1¼" THICK GLUEBLOCK
PAPER
BRAD

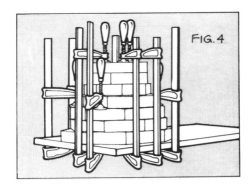

FIG. 4

The 6 in. faceplate can now be added. Take care to locate it exactly at the center of the turning block, otherwise the mass will be unbalanced and you'll be faced with considerable shaking and vibration as the stock turns. To cut down on some

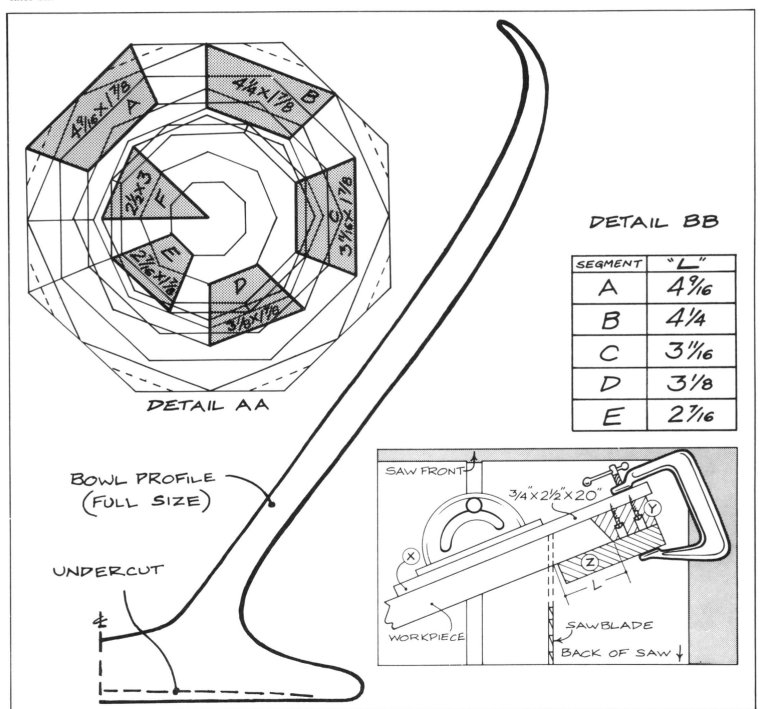

DETAIL AA

BOWL PROFILE (FULL SIZE)

UNDERCUT

DETAIL BB

SEGMENT	"L"
A	4⁹⁄₁₆
B	4¼
C	3¹¹⁄₁₆
D	3⅛
E	2⁷⁄₁₆

SAW FRONT

¾" X 2½" X 20"

WORKPIECE

SAWBLADE

BACK OF SAW

FACEPLATE
GLUE BLOCK

FIG. 5

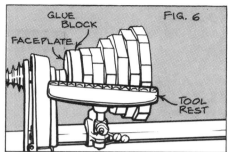

GLUE BLOCK
FACEPLATE
FIG. 6
TOOL REST

of the mass, we used the band saw to trim the corners off of layer A (Fig. 5). The cut line we followed is shown in detail A-A.

Secure the turning block to the lathe (Fig. 6). The tool rest is fixed roughly parallel to the angle of the block and about 1/8 in. below the horizontal center line. Set the lathe at its slowest speed (ours was about 600 rpm).

The full-size profile of the bowl is shown in section. Use a 3/4 in. gouge to reduce the outside of the turning block to rough form (Fig. 7). Once roughed out, switch to a 1/2 in. gouge to further reduce and smooth the shape (Fig. 8).

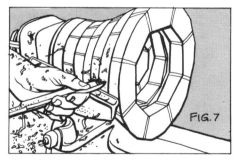

FIG. 7

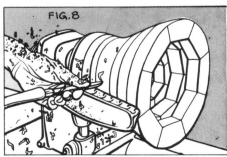

FIG. 8

The lathe speed is now increased to about 1,000 rpm and a 1/2 in. round nose is used to shape the outside of the bowl to its final profile (Fig. 9). However, don't shape the profile of the base at this time.

To turn the inside of the bowl, the tool

rest must be relocated and the lathe speed changed to about 600 rpm (Fig. 10). As before, it should be roughly parallel to the angle of the turning block and about 1/8 in. below the horizontal center line.

FIG. 9

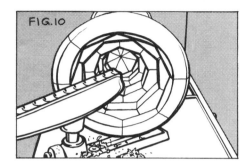

FIG. 10

Use a 1/2 in. gouge to begin removing material from the inside of the bowl (Fig. 11). At a point about one-half way into the bowl, we found that the gouge began to grab, so we switched to a 1/2 in. round nose (Fig. 12). This tool was used to turn the entire inside surface to its final profile.

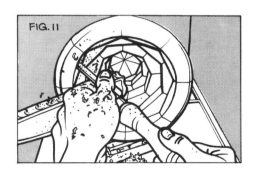

FIG. 11

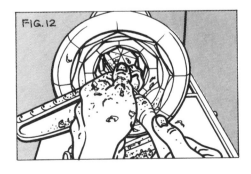

FIG. 12

profile.

Reposition the tool rest to the outside of the bowl. It should be as close as possible to the base of the bowl. A 1/2 in. round nose is used to finish shaping the base.

Finish sand all inside and outside surfaces (Fig. 13). Start with 80-grit, then

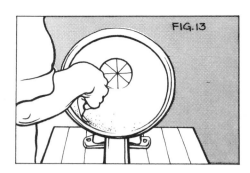

FIG. 13

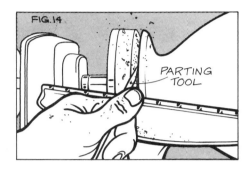

FIG. 14

PARTING TOOL

finish with 100, 120 and 150.

Use a parting tool to partially cut into the base at the paper line. The parting cut should stop at a point that leaves the stock measuring about 1 1/2 in. in diameter (Fig. 14). At this point, it's a good idea to slightly undercut the base of the bowl. The undercut will help the bowl to sit flat

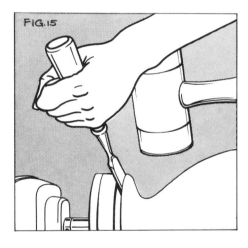

FIG. 15

on slightly uneven surfaces.

The bowl can now be removed from the lathe. A sharp chisel blow at the paper joint will knock it free (Fig. 15). Sand the bottom to smooth out the undercut.

If the bowl is to be used for food items, it's best to use a non-toxic finish. Woodcraft Supply Corp., 210 Wood County Industrial Park, P.O. Box 1686, Parkersburg, WV 26102-1686 sells one that's approved by the U.S. Food and Drug Administration. It's called Salad Bowl Finish. Several coats will provide an attractive look.

Oriental Table

This Oriental Table has similarities in design to the Huang-Hua-Li variety of Chinese end stands and dates back to the Ming Dynasty of the 16th and 17th centuries. The concave surfaces bring a play of light and dark, and the scroll brackets enrich the design. Rosewood is the traditional wood, although we used mahogany to make this one. Cherry or any other close-grained hardwood that will finish dark will also give excellent results.

There's a variety of ways that this project can be made. If you have a shaper,

you'll no doubt want to use that versatile machine. However, since many woodworkers do not own shapers, this article will describe how to make the table using a molding-head cutter in conjunction with a table saw. The molding-head keeps costs to a minimum.

Cut all four legs to 2 in. square. It's best to cut them a little longer than 29 in.; they can be trimmed to exact length later. To cut the corners, we used a Sears molding-head and a $1/4$ in. quarter-round cutter (Sears No. 9-2351), although a router equipped with a bearing-guided $1/4$

in. quarter-round bit can also be used. Before starting you'll need a plywood insert for the table saw. The metal one that comes with the saw cannot be used with the molding-head and must be removed. Trace the outline of your present insert onto a piece of scrap plywood of the appropriate thickness: $1/4$ in. thick for a Sears 10 in. saw, $1/2$ in. thick for a 10 in. Rockwell Unisaw. Cut the pattern and fit it to the saw. Mount the three cutters to the molding-head and mount it on your saw. Lower the cutters below the table, then add the new plywood insert and rotate the cutter by hand to make sure it is below the plywood. (This should be done with the power off and the cord disconnected).

While holding down the insert with a stick, start the saw and raise the cutter very slowly. Continue raising the cutter until it is slightly above the desired height, then lower it slightly to back it off the plywood. Make a test cut and adjust if necessary. A new insert should be made for each cutter to minimize chipping out.

Often when using the molding-head, part or most of the cutter must be buried in the fence. This necessitates an auxiliary wood fence. Straight, square stock should be chosen, as long and high as the metal fence and $1/2$ in. thick. Clamp it to the saw fence and screw it in place with two no. 12 by 2 in. flathead wood screws. The wooden fence should then be moved into approximate position with the cutter lowered below the table. The spinning cutter should then be slowly raised with the fence locked in place. Again, the cutter should take a slightly heavy cut before being backed off. For the first cut with the quarter-round cutter, set it for flush round; cut the two back corners of the rails (B) and the inside corner of each leg (A).

Maintaining the fence in the same position, raise the cutter $1/4$ in. to make the double cuts on the other three sides of the legs. Before cutting, it's best to test on a piece of scrap to see if the cut is correct. Run the piece through on one corner and then reverse the piece end-for-end and cut the same corner. Adjust if necessary and cut the remaining three sides of the legs.

Drop the cutter back to make the partial cuts on the front edges of the rails (B).

The mortises are cut in the sides of the legs (A) before the cove cuts are made on the outer faces. Lay out the mortises with a sharp pencil and a square or a marking gauge. Mortise with a hollow chisel in the drill press, or use a regular bit and clean out with a chisel. Note that the fretwork mortises are $1/16$ in. deeper than the

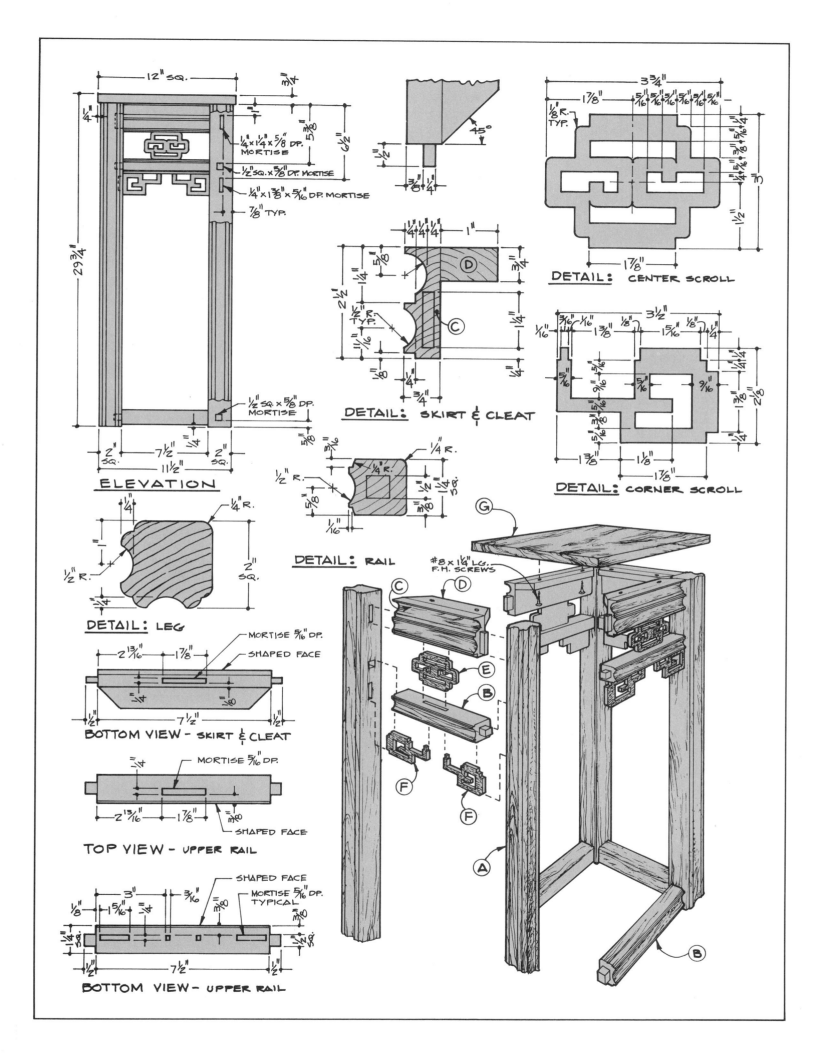

12" SQ.

29¾"

11½"
2" SQ.   7½"   2" SQ.

¼" × 1¼" × ⅝" DP. MORTISE
½" SQ. × ⅝" DP. MORTISE
¼" × 1⅜" × ⁵⁄₁₆" DP. MORTISE
⅞" TYP.

½" SQ. × ⅝" DP. MORTISE

ELEVATION

45°

½"
⅜" ¼"

DETAIL: SKIRT & CLEAT

3¾"
1⅞"

1⅛" R. TYP.

DETAIL: CENTER SCROLL

3½"

DETAIL: CORNER SCROLL

¼" R.
½" R.
2" SQ.

DETAIL: LEG

½" R.
¼" R.

DETAIL: RAIL

2¹³⁄₁₆"   1⅞"
MORTISE ⁵⁄₁₆" DP.
SHAPED FACE
7½"

BOTTOM VIEW – SKIRT & CLEAT

2¹³⁄₁₆"   1⅞"
MORTISE ⁵⁄₁₆" DP.
SHAPED FACE

TOP VIEW – UPPER RAIL

3"   ³⁄₁₆"
1⁵⁄₁₆"
SHAPED FACE
MORTISE ⁵⁄₁₆" DP. TYPICAL
7½"

BOTTOM VIEW – UPPER RAIL

G
#8 × 1¼" LG. F.H. SCREWS
C
D
E
B
F
F
A
B

Bill of Materials
(all dimensions actual)

Part	Description	Size	No. Req'd.
A	Leg	2 x 2 x 29	4
B	Rail	1¼ x 1¼ x 8½	8
C	Skirt	¾ x 2½ x 8½	4
D	Cleat	¾ x 1 x 7½	4
E	Center Scroll	¼ x 3 x 3¾	4
F	Corner Scroll	¼ x 2⅛ x 3½	8
G	Top	¾ x 12 x 12	1

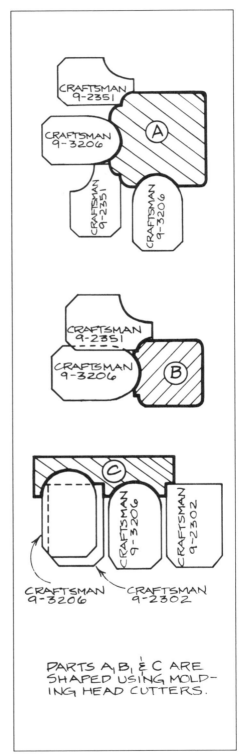

PARTS A, B, & C ARE SHAPED USING MOLDING HEAD CUTTERS.

corresponding tenons, and that the rail and skirt mortises are ⅛ in. deeper than the corresponding tenons.

To make the ½ in. radius cove cuts, mount the fluting cutters (Sears no. 9-3206 1 in. flute) in the molding-head. Cut the flutes on the legs (A), the rails (B), and the skirts (C), changing the fence and cutter height as needed. Note that the cutter height for the rail flutes can be no more than 1/16 in.

The remaining cuts in the skirts (C) can be made with a molding cutter (Sears no. 9-2302) or a dado blade.

Once all the molding cuts have been made, cut the rails, legs, and skirts to exact length. Referring to the drawing, use the dado blade on the table saw to cut tenons on each end.

Cut the top (G) to size from a wide board or glued-up stock. Also, you can use a ¾ in. mahogany plywood and edge it with mahogany. If solid wood is chosen, slot the screw holes in the cleats (D) to compensate for expansion. Plywood need only be glued and screwed in place.

The scrolled pieces (E and F) are made

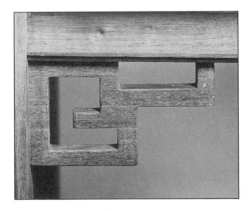

from ¼ in. thick stock. This can be resawn on the table saw.

Make a copy of the pattern and rubber cement it to your stock. A scroll saw, power fret saw, fret saw or coping saw may be used to make these cuts. Drill a ⅛ in. hole in each of the cutouts for saw blade entry. Using a fine (no. 5 or 7) blade, enter the blade through the hole and mount to the saw.

After all cutouts have been made, cut the outside pattern. Clamp the pieces in a wooden vise or handscrew and even out all cuts with small files and sandpaper.

The pieces should be clamped so that the part to be filed is just above the vise or hand screw and is being held securely. Don't try to file too far away from the vise or these delicate pieces may break. Round over all edges to soften their appearance.

After you have made all the scrolled pieces, dry fit each side of the table, making any adjustments necessary. Don't force the scrolled pieces into their place. They are more likely to break than go in.

After checking for fit, final sand each

piece. (Don't forget to mark mating pieces so that you will be able to get them all back together in the same orientation). To sand the flutes, wrap sandpaper around a ⅞ in. dowel. You can also round over the edge of a piece of scrap that is ¾ in. thick with a ⅜ in. round-over bit in the router. Apply felt over this and then wrap your sandpaper over the felt.

When sanding the corners and edges, don't round them too much. This piece gains visual strength from the angularity of its design. Once sanding is complete, you may begin gluing up. Start with one entire side. Assemble the skirt (C) with rail (B) and the three scrolled pieces. Insert this assembly into one leg (A) and add the bottom rail (B). These can be glued on a flat surface without strain. Move the second leg into position and gently insert the tenons into their mortises. Don't force them. The scroll pieces may need some jockeying around and, if you drive the assembly together with a clamp, they may break. Check the whole assembly for squareness and clamp together once the pieces are all the way home and square.

After gluing up two sides, assemble the intermediate sides and glue up the entire piece (less the top). Lay on a flat surface and check for squareness.

When dry, chip off excess glue and add the top. Again, if you are using solid stock, screw down one edge of the board and then screw down the other edge in slotted holes.

To get a nice finish, apply Watco Oil liberally over the entire piece. Wait 10 minutes and dry off excess with a rag. (Oil soaked rags are a fire hazard, so dispose of them carefully). Wait one day and repeat. Wait until thoroughly dry (3-4 days) and then wax using Butcher's wax or your favorite brand. However, don't use spray-on waxes because they contain water and will raise the grain. Butcher's wax contains pine oil, which gives it a nice smell. Wait overnight and buff to a high shine.

Early American Spoon Rack

This rack will provide a lovely setting for your favorite spoon collection. Ours, with its Early American styling, is made from pine, although cherry would also be a good choice.

If you don't have 1/2 in. thick stock, most millwork shops will plane down 3/4 in. material. Also, you can resaw narrow stock on the table saw, then edge-glue it to get enough width for the front (A) and the back (B). Or you can get it the way our forefathers did by going to work on thicker stock with a well sharpened hand plane.

The front (A) can be made first. Cut to a width of about 4 3/4 in. and a length of about 18 1/2 in. These dimensions will be trimmed later on. Transfer the profile of the top edge to the stock, then cut out with a band or saber saw.

The back (B) measures 18 in. wide, so it will be necessary to edge-glue two or more narrower boards. Apply glue to all mating edges, then clamp firmly with bar or pipe clamps. To keep the edges from sliding out of alignment, it's helpful to clamp two pairs of cleats (made from scrap stock) across the width of the board. To prevent sticking, use wax paper between the cleats and the stock. Once dry, remove the clamps, then transfer the curved profile of the top. Cut out with a band or saber saw.

Once the sides (C) have been made, the spoon holders (parts E and F) can be cut to length and width. Mark the location of each spoon, then bore a 1/2 in. diameter hole as shown. The hole should be centered along the 1 in. width. The notches can then be cut out with a dovetail or back saw. Readers should keep in mind, though, that some spoon designs may require slightly different cutouts.

Give all parts a thorough sanding, taking particular care to smooth the curved edges. Assemble as shown. Use glue and finishing nails, countersunk and filled. Final sand before staining to suit. Several coats of a good penetrating oil, such as Deftco, will provide an attractive final finish.

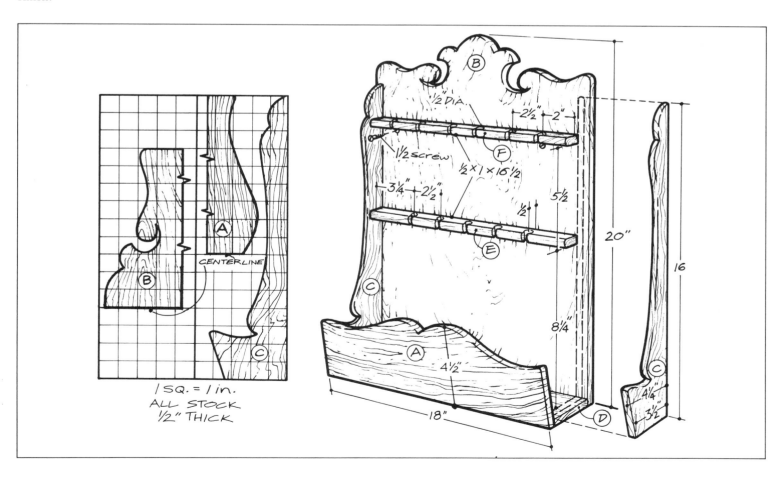

Band Saw Box

There doesn't seem to be an end to the various ways that small wooden boxes can be designed and constructed. Often called fancy boxes, they've become a popular item at gift shops and craft fairs. We particularly like this one because its straightforward design makes it surprisingly easy to build.

Our box measures about 7³/₄ in. long by 4 in. high by 4³/₄ in. deep, however there is no hard and fast rule that dictates the best size. The size that is best will depend on its intended use and, of course, the personal taste of the woodworker.

There's no limit to the way these boxes can be used. A medium-size box, like ours, is ideal for jewelry, while a smaller one might hold sewing needles, business cards, pocket change, or even toothpicks. Sometimes a box serves as a decorative piece and holds nothing.

One nice feature of this design is that the "core" cut from the box blank (see Step 4) can be used to make a second box, and the core from that box will make even another box. Thus, several boxes, all in descending size, can be made from the initial box blank. Little scrap stock re-

sults.

Since these are generally considered fancy boxes, they look best if made with one of the so-called elegant or exotic woods. We used a walnut body and a crotch walnut lid. A few of the many other possibilities include cherry, mahogany, teak, bubinga and rosewood.

Begin by cutting stock for the blank. Three pieces are required to make our box, each measuring 1¹/₄ in. thick by 3¹/₂ in. wide by 8¹/₄ in. long. The 8¹/₄ in. dimension allows extra length that will later be trimmed. Once cut, glue the three pieces together (edges up) using your bench top as a flat surface (Fig. 1). Clamp

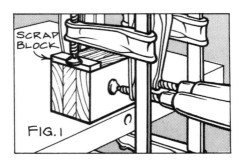

lightly across the edges with a scrap block to prevent shifting, then use additional clamps to apply pressure on the face. Remember to wax both the scrap blocks and your bench top to avoid sticking. Allow to dry for at least one hour before removing all clamps. Following this, use the table saw to trim each end while cutting to a final length of 7³/₄ in.

Before going any further, it's a good idea to flatten any unevenness along the edges of the blank. A hand plane will work well here — just keep in mind that the plane must remain parallel to the edges.

Lay out and mark a ¹/₂ in. guideline around the perimeter of the box. This establishes the thickness of the sides and base. Now use a drill press to bore a ¹/₂ in. diameter hole in the lower corners of the blank (Fig. 2). The outside diameter of the hole should just touch the guidelines. Use a scrap block under the blank to avoid tear out.

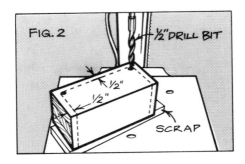

Two steps are required to remove the core. The first step is done on the table saw (Fig. 3).

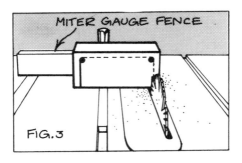

When cutting heavy stock like this, we've found that the table saw blade often tends to wobble resulting in an uneven cut. To minimize the problem, it's best to make two cuts, the first one ¹/₁₆ in. to ¹/₈ in. on the waste side of the line, the second one right on the line. The blade is set to a height of 2⁵/₈ in. for all cuts.

The band saw is used to make the remaining cut (Fig. 4). To save time, we made a freehand cut along the guideline. However, if you plan to make a number of boxes, it would be helpful to set up an auxiliary rip fence.

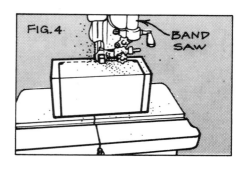

FIG. 4 · BAND SAW

Due to the nature of the table saw and band saw, some tear out may occur. If this happens, it will be necessary to sand both sides. A sanding board, which is easy to make, can be put to use here. Cut a piece of $3/8$ in. or $3/4$ in. particleboard to 24 in. square, then use rubber cement to glue four pieces of standard size 100-grit sandpaper to the board. Butt the edges to form a smooth surface (Fig. 5).

The two $1/2$ in. thick sides can now be

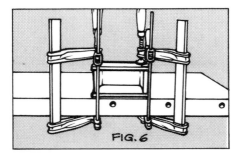

FIG. 5

cut to length and width. It's best to cut them a little on the long side to allow for later trimming. If you don't have $1/2$ in. thick stock, it can be resawed on the table saw from thicker material. After resawing, use a block plane to remove the saw

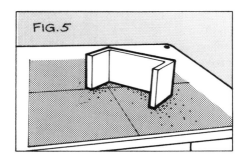

FIG. 6

marks and flatten the stock. Once completed, the sides are glued and clamped in place (Fig. 6). Be sure to keep the top and bottom edge aligned with the sides.

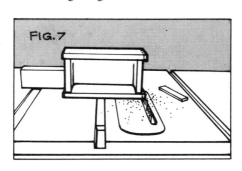

FIG. 7

When dry, the extra length allowed for the sides can be trimmed on the table saw (Fig. 7). It's best not to trim flush; instead

FIG. 8

leave a $1/32$ in. to $1/16$ in. lip to be cleaned up on the sanding board. The router equipped with a laminate trimmer bit can also be used. The trimmer bit will

FIG. 9 · ROUTER TABLE · TOP

automatically leave a $1/32$ in. lip. The sanding board is now used to clean up the top, bottom and ends of the box (Fig. 8).

The lid can now be cut to size. Ours measured $1\,1/16$ in. thick by $4\,3/4$ in. wide by $7\,3/4$ in. long. Using a router table and a $3/4$ in. diameter straight bit, cut a $1/2$ in.

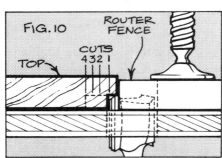

FIG. 10 · ROUTER FENCE · CUTS 4 3 2 1 · TOP

deep rabbet at a point $9/16$ in. from the edge of all four sides (Figs. 9 and 10). As shown in Fig. 10, the cut is done in four steps. The height of the bit never changes, only the depth of the cut which is regulated by the location of the fence.

Next, the box is flocked to give the

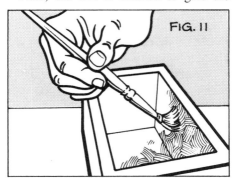

FIG. 11

FIG. 12

interior a velvet-like surface. Flocking is a powder-like material that is sold in a variety of colors at most craft shops. It's easy to do and results in an attractive look.

Select an oil-based paint that roughly matches the color of the flocking. Then apply the paint to the interior of the box (Fig. 11). Allow to dry. Apply a second coat of paint, then sprinkle a small amount of the flocking into the box (Fig. 12). Cover the box with an oversized piece of wood and shake thoroughly to spread the flocking evenly over the paint. Allow to dry and remove any excess flocking.

A chamfered edge can now be applied to both the top and base. We used a router

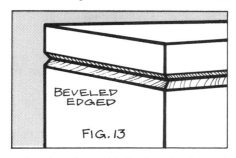

BEVELED EDGED

FIG. 13

and a bearing-guided chamfer bit, although a hand plane or hand sanding will also give good results (Fig. 13). The chamfer not only provides a nice detail, it makes it easier to remove the lid.

Final sand the box on the sanding board to at least 220-grit. The sanding board will keep the edges crisp. Apply a coat of penetrating oil to the box and wet sand with 400-grit paper. Wipe off the excess and allow to dry. Apply additional coats until the finish has been built up to your satisfaction. A coat of paste wax completes the project.

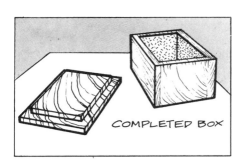

COMPLETED BOX

Toy Pumper Firetruck

Young firefighters will enjoy playing with this toy. It's a sturdy replica of a "pumper" firetruck, complete with a pair of ladders for second story rescues.

Just about any type of wood can be used, although we chose poplar because it's reasonably priced yet hard enough to stand up to pretty rough service. If you're looking for maximum durability, though, maple is the best choice of the commonly available woods.

The frame (part A) is made first. Cut to overall length and width from 1/2 in. thick stock, then lay out and mark the location of the front and back wheel cutouts. These cutouts are best made using a dado head cutter in conjunction with a table saw.

Hold the stock against the miter gauge (edge down), then pass the stock through the dado head cutter. A 3/4 in. wide cutter will require three or four passes to form the 2 1/4 in. wide cutouts.

The cab parts (B, D, and E) are made next. Cut to length and width from 5/4 stock, keeping in mind the grain direction as shown. Note that part D has four "headlight" holes while part E has a single hole for the warning light (W).

Parts C, the front fenders, are also made from 5/4 stock. Rip to a width of 1/2 in., then scribe the radius as shown. Cut out with a band or saber saw.

The pump panel parts (G, H and I) can

now be cut to size. The 1/4 in. thick stock for part I can best be obtained by resawing 3/4 in. thick material. Holes for the hose connectors (parts X and Y) are drilled as shown.

The reel rack assembly consists of parts J, K, L and M. The hose reel (part L) is made from 3/4 in. diameter dowel stock cut to a 1 in. length. A 1/4 in. diameter hole is drilled through the center of each one.

Next, parts Q, R, and S are cut to length and width as shown. Together, these parts form the tank assembly. Note that part S is located at each end of the assembly.

The remainder of the parts are cut to the sizes specified in the Bill of Materials. The wheels (parts DD) can be made as shown or ordered via mail-order from Constantine's, 2050 Eastchester Road, Bronx, NY 10461. Their part no. WW11 has a 2 in. diameter and 1/4 in. axle hole.

Before assembly, give all parts a thorough sanding, however, don't round any edges or corners yet. Since toys should be well smoothed, it's best to use 220-grit for the final sanding.

Assemble all parts as shown on the drawing. Use glue and clamp securely. When building toys, it's best to use a non-toxic glue such as Elmer's Glue-All. Final sand all surfaces, taking special care to round all sharp edges and corners. The best non-toxic finish is none at all.

Bill of Materials
(all dimensions actual)

Part	Description	Size	No. Req'd.
A	Frame	1/2 x 4 x 13 3/4	1
B	Lower Cab	1 1/16 x 3 x 4 1/2	1
C	Front Fender	1/2 x 1 1/16 x 4 1/2	2
D	Center Cab	1 1/16 x 4 x 4 1/2	1
E	Upper Cab	1 1/16 x 4 x 4 1/2	1
F	Divider	1 1/16 x 2 x 1 3/4	1
G	Pump Panel End	1/2 x 2 1/4 x 2 1/4	2
H	Pump Panel Side	1/2 x 2 1/4 x 3	2
I	Pump Panel Top	1/4 x 2 1/4 x 4	1
J	Reel Rack Side	3/8 x 3/4 x 3 1/2	2
K	Reel Rack End	1/2 x 3/4 x 1 1/8	2
L	Hose Reel	3/4 Dia. x 1 long	2
M	Hose Reel Axle	3/16 Dia. x 1 5/8 long	2
N	Rear Fender	1 1/16 x 1 1/4 x 5	2
O	Ladder Rack	3/4 x 3/4 x 4 3/4	2
P	Support	1/4 x 1 3/4 x 4 3/4	2
Q	Tank Side	1/4 x 2 x 4 3/4	2
R	Tank Top	1/4 x 1 7/8 x 4 3/4	1
S	Tank End	1/2 x 2 x 1 3/8	2
T	Rear Bumper	1/2 x 1/2 x 4	1
U	Ladder Side	5/16 x 3/8 x 5 1/4	4
V	Ladder Rung	1/8 Dia. x 1 long	20
W	Warning Light	1/2 Dia. x 1 long	1
X	Hose Connector	3/16 Dia. x 3/4 long	4
Y	Hose Connector	3/8 Dia. x 3/4 long	2
Z	Front Bumper	1/2 x 1 1/16 x 4 1/4	1
AA	Axle	1/4 Dia. x 4 1/4 long	2
BB	Front Axle Holder	see detail	1
CC	Rear Axle Holder	see detail	1
DD	Wheel	2 Dia. x 1/2 thick	6

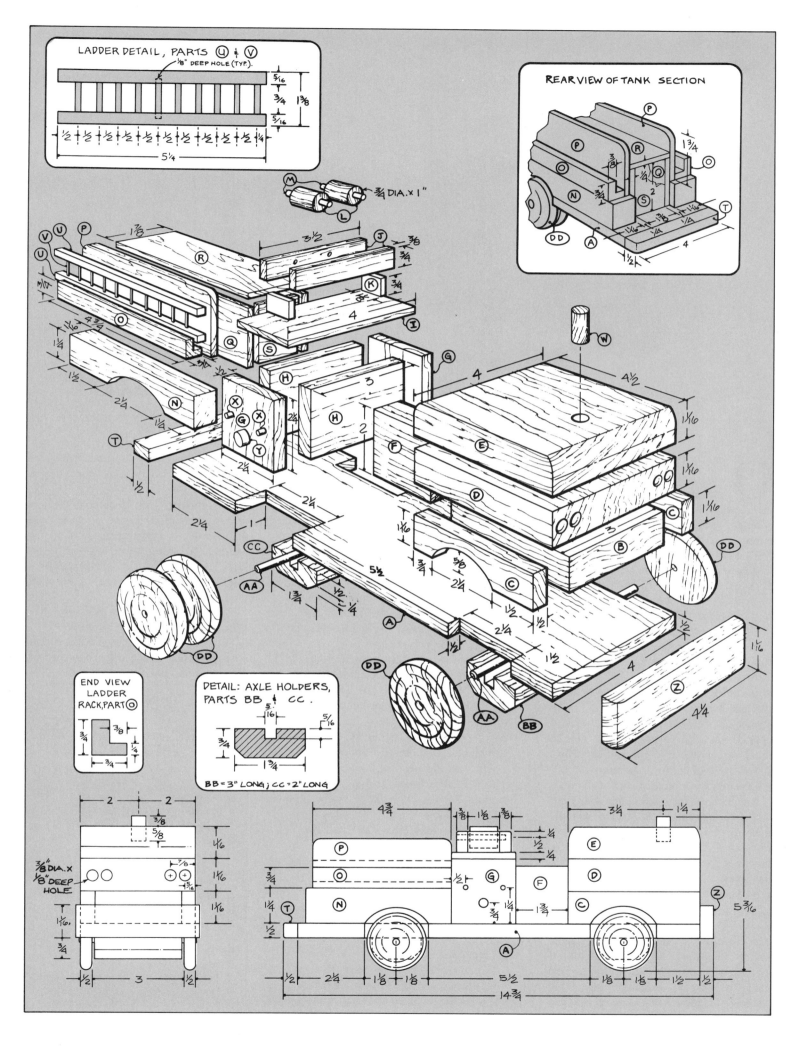

LADDER DETAIL, PARTS U & V

1/8" DEEP HOLE (TYP.)

5/16
3/4
1 3/8
5/16

1/2 1/2 1/2 1/2 1/2 1/2 1/2 1/2 1/2 1/2 1/4

5 1/4

3/4 DIA. X 1"

REAR VIEW OF TANK SECTION

END VIEW LADDER RACK, PART O

3/8
3/4
1/4
3/4

DETAIL: AXLE HOLDERS, PARTS BB & CC.

5/16
5/16
3/4
1 3/4

BB = 3" LONG; CC = 2" LONG

3/8 DIA. X 1/8" DEEP HOLE

Toy Airplane

Of all civilian aircraft, the Piper Cub is probably the most widely known. Over the years, its simple, safe flying qualities have made it popular with a great many weekend pilots.

This toy is a scaled-down version of that famous plane, with general proportions that are roughly the same. We suspect kids will have as much fun buzzing around with this toy as grownups do with the real thing.

Readers will be pleased to learn that it can be made with a minimum of materials — and it requires only a few hours in the workshop. We used poplar because it's not exceptionally expensive, yet it stands up to wear reasonably well. Of course, pine can be used, but it will be more susceptible to dents and scratches. If you are looking for maximum durability, use maple or birch stock for all parts.

The fuselage (part A) can be made first. Cut five-quarter stock (which actually measures $1^1/16$ in. thick) to a width of $1^1/4$ in. and a length of 7 in. Transfer the profile of the fuselage from the drawing to the stock, then cut out with a band or saber saw.

Next, the cabin (part B) is made. To get the $1/2$ in. thick stock that's needed, it's best to resaw thicker stock on the table saw or band saw. Once cut to a width of $1^1/4$ in., the bevel on each end is formed using a dovetail or back saw. Two shallow "window" holes are then added as shown.

The wing (part C) is made from $1/4$ in. stock, so again it will be necessary to resaw thicker stock on the table saw or band saw. After resawing, the wing can be cut to overall length and width. The wing ends are then generously rounded as shown.

On a piece of $1/4$ in. thick stock, lay out the shape of the stabilizer (part D) as detailed in the drawing. Cut to shape with a jigsaw or, if done by hand, with a dovetail or backsaw. The rudder (part E) is made in the same manner.

The landing gear assembly (parts H, I, J, K, L and N) can now be cut to the sizes shown. With the wheels (part K) readers have the option of ordering them from Toys and Joys, P.O. Box 628, Lynden, WA 98264. A peg similar to part N can also be ordered from Toys and Joys.

After cutting and shaping the propeller (part M), all parts can be given a complete sanding. Sand through 220 grit to insure a smooth surface.

Use a non-toxic glue (such as Elmer's Glue-All) for all assembly. Begin by joining the cabin (B) to the fuselage (A). Clamp securely and allow to dry.

The stabilizer (D) and rudder (E) can now be added, again using clamps. When dry, bore holes for pins G, P and Q, then add the pins and sand flush. Also add the tail rest (part O).

Landing gear assembly parts H, I, and J are glued together as shown. When dry, this assembly is glued and clamped to the underside of the fuselage. The turned peg

(N) adds strength to the joint. Following this, the wheels (K) and axle (L) are added.

The propeller (M) is secured to the nose with a sheet metal screw. To make sure that the screw stays in place, it's a good idea to add a drop of epoxy glue to the screw hole. Note that a small washer is installed between the fuselage and the propeller.

Now glue and clamp the wing (C). When dry, add the wing pins (F).

Final sand all surfaces, taking special care to round all sharp edges and corners. The best non-toxic finish is none at all.

Bill of Materials
(all dimensions actual)

Part	Description	Size	No. Req'd.
A	Fuselage	$1^1/16$ x $1^1/4$ x 7	1
B	Cabin	$1/2$ x $1^1/4$ x $2^1/4$	1
C	Wing	$1/4$ x $1^3/8$ x 10	1
D	Stabilizer	$1/4$ x $3/4$ x 4	1
E	Rudder	$1/4$ x $1^3/8$ x 3	1
F	Wing Pin	$1/8$ dia. x $5/8$ long	2
G	Stabilizer Pin	$1/16$ dia. x $5/8$ long	2
H	Landing Gear Base	$5/16$ x $3/4$ x 2	1
I	Landing Gear Support	$3/8$ x $3/8$ x $3/4$	2
J	Landing Gear End	$3/8$ x $3/4$ x $1^1/8$	2
K	Wheel	$5/16$ thick x 1 dia.	2
L	Axle	$3/16$ dia. x $3^1/2$ long	1
M	Propeller	$1/4$ x $1/4$ x $2^1/4$	1
N	Peg	See Detail	1
O	Tail Rest	$3/16$ dia. x $5/8$ long	1
P	Pin	$3/16$ dia. x $3/4$ long	1
Q	Pin	$1/16$ dia. x $3/4$ long	1

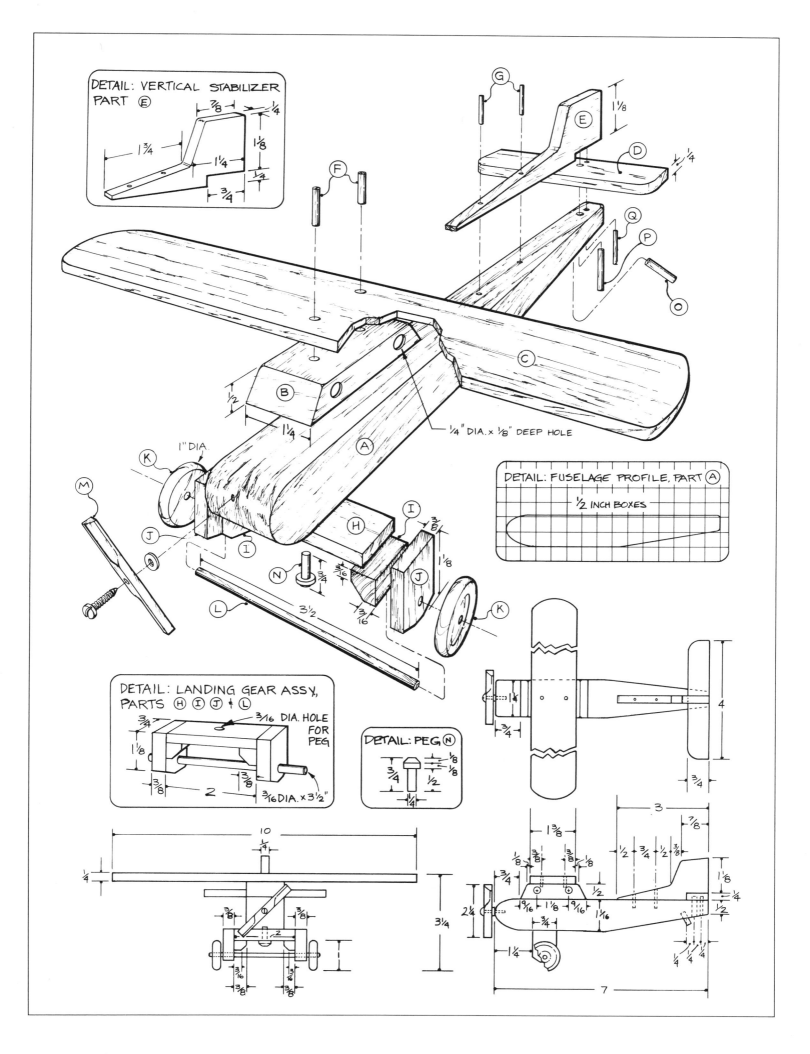

DETAIL: VERTICAL STABILIZER PART E

DETAIL: FUSELAGE PROFILE, PART A
½ INCH BOXES

DETAIL: LANDING GEAR ASSY, PARTS H I J & L
3/16 DIA. HOLE FOR PEG
3/16 DIA. x 3½"

DETAIL: PEG N

¼" DIA. x ⅛" DEEP HOLE

1" DIA.

Magazine Rack

A weekend in the workshop is all that's needed to complete this project. With its Early American styling, pine is a good choice, particularly since it's relatively inexpensive. We used ³/₄ in. thick stock throughout.

Begin by cutting the two sides (D) to overall length and width from ³/₄ in. thick stock. If necessary, edge-join stock to get the 6 in. width.

Referring to the drawing, lay out and mark the location of the ³/₄ in. wide by ³/₈ in. deep dado for the bottom (E). To cut the dado, use the table saw equipped with a dado head cutter or use a regular saw blade and make repeated passes.

Since the dadoes for the dividers (Parts A, B and C) must be stopped at the bottom dado, it's best to use a router for this operation. Equip the router with a straight bit. If you have a ³/₄ in. diameter bit, each cut can be made with one fence setting, although you'll need at least three depth adjustments to get the ³/₈ in. depth. Smaller bits will take more passes and the edge-guide will need to be relocated after each pass. To cut the dadoes, clamp the edge guide to the stock, then hold the router against the guide as you make the cut. A piece of scrap stock that has a straightedge will make a good edge guide. Be sure to stop the cut at the point it meets the bottom dado.

Next, transfer the profile from the drawing to the sides, then cut out with a band or saber saw. This completes preliminary work on the sides.

The dividers (parts A, B and C) can now be cut to overall length and width as shown. Transfer the grid pattern to the stock and cut out with a band or saber saw.

After cutting the bottom to size (³/₄ x 6 x 24 in.), all parts can be given a complete sanding. Give special attention to the curved edges, as these should be well smoothed with no rough areas.

Assemble as shown. Use glue and wood screws to join the sides (D) to the dividers (A, B and C) and the bottom (E). Countersink the wood screws, then plug with wood plugs.

Final sand all parts. Give the corners and edges a good rounding to simulate years of wear, and sand the wood plugs flush with the surface.

Apply stain to suit (we used Minwax's Early American), then apply two coats of polyurethane varnish as a final clear finish.

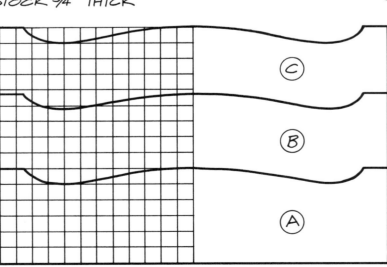

³/₄" WIDE + ³/₈" DEEP DADO FOR DIVIDERS

1 SQ. = 1 in.
ALL STOCK ³/₄" THICK

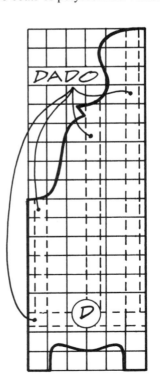

DADO

Bootjack

Boots seem to be as popular as ever today, in spite of the fact that getting one off almost always results in an annoying struggle. We suspect that, in one form or another, this simple tool has been around nearly as long as the boot itself. Our version, made of ash, can be built in just a few hours in the workshop — time well spent if you own a pair of troublesome boots.

To make the base you'll need a piece of $3/4$ in. thick stock measuring $5 1/4$ in. wide by 15 in. long. Transfer the grid pattern, then cut out with a band or saber saw. The stand is made as shown, then glued to the base using a pair of $3/8$ in. by $3/4$ in. long dowel pins. Sand thoroughly, rounding all edges, then apply two coats of polyurethane varnish to complete the project.

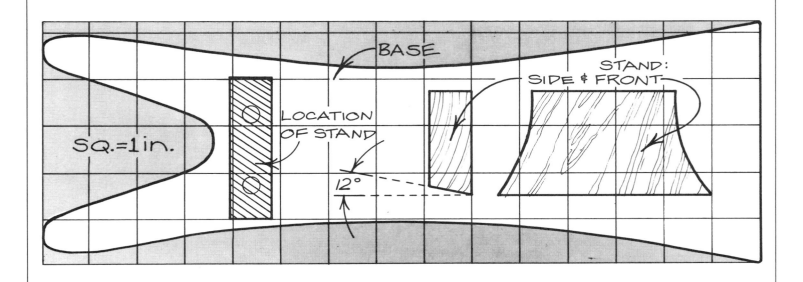

BASE

STAND: SIDE & FRONT

SQ.=1in.

LOCATION OF STAND

12°

parts D, are made next. All box units are made from ³/₄ in. thick plywood. Cut parts C to 7¹/₄ in. wide by 5¹/₂ in. long, and parts D to 8³/₄ in. wide by 8¹/₈ in. long.

Note that the corners of each box unit are mitered at 45 degrees. Set up the table saw or radial-arm saw to make this cut, then make a few test cuts on scrap stock to check the accuracy of the angle. If the setup looks satisfactory, cut the miters on the corners as shown.

The mitered corners have a ¹/₈ in. thick hardboard spline added to increase strength (see detail of corner construction). Cut the grooves for the splines, then cut the splines from ¹/₈ in. thick hardboard.

Next, at a point ¹/₄ in. from the edge, cut a ¹/₄ in. wide by ¹/₄ in. deep groove for the panels (parts E and F). Note that on the small boxes the panel will be located at the top; on the large boxes the panel will be located on the bottom.

Now, dry assemble the boxes with the splines and panels in place. Use masking tape to secure the joints so that the boxes are rigid.

The boxes can now be cut at a 17-degree angle as shown. Using the table saw, set the miter gauge to 17 degrees and raise the blade to its maximum height. Pass the box over the blade, then flip the piece, reverse the miter gauge, and make the same cut on the opposite side. The box is too wide to be separated by the two cuts, so you'll need to complete the cut using a dovetail saw. Once cut, use a sanding block to carefully smooth and flatten the area cut by the dovetail saw.

The various edging stock can now be cut. You'll need about 4¹/₂ ft. of ³/₈ in. thick by 1³/₄ in. wide oak (parts G) for each end of the vertical members (parts A and B), about 11 ft. of ⁵/₁₆ in. thick by 1³/₄ in. wide walnut (parts H) for the front and back of the vertical members, about 24 ft. of ³/₈ in. thick by 1 in. wide oak (parts I) for the edges of the small and large boxes, and about 8 ft. of ³/₈ in. by ³/₈ in. walnut (parts J) for the box corner edging. The part I is 1 in. wide to allow for coverage where it butts to the angled box ends.

Next, set the saw blade to an angle of 17 degrees and trim the vertical ends and center (parts A and B) to final length. The oak edging (parts G) can now be glued to each end.

Once dry, use a hand plane or router equipped with a laminate trimmer to trim the part G edging flush all around. Parts A and B can now be ripped to final width (make sure the ends of the edging are trimmed flush before ripping, otherwise the stock won't butt against the rip fence). After ripping, the walnut edging (parts H) can be glued and trimmed in the same manner.

Remove the masking tape and disassemble the boxes. Add glue to the spline joints, then re-assemble and clamp. The panels (parts E and F) must be included, however there's no need to glue them in place. If you have them, web clamps are ideal for this type of clamping job, although masking tape can also be used to pull the joints closed.

Bill of Materials
(all dimensions actual)

Part	Description	Size	No. Req'd.
A	Vertical End	1¹/₂ x 7³/₈ x 24	2
B	Vertical Center	1¹/₂ x 7³/₈ x 12	1
C	Small Box Sides	³/₄ x 7¹/₄ x 5¹/₂	8
D	Large Box Sides	³/₄ x 8³/₄ x 8¹/₈	8
E	Small Box Panel	¹/₄ x 6¹/₈ x 6¹/₈*	2
F	Large Box Panel	¹/₄ x 7⁵/₈ x 7⁵/₈*	2
G	Oak Edging	³/₈ x 1¹/₂	As Req'd
H	Walnut Edging	⁵/₁₆ x 1¹/₂	As Req'd
I	Oak Box Edging	³/₈ x 1	As Req'd
J	Box Corner Edging	¹/₄ x ¹/₄	As Req'd
K	Fixture Panel	¹/₂ x 6¹/₄ x 6¹/₄	2
L	Bezel	See Detail	2
M	Light Fixture		2

* Panel sized a little smaller than actual groove-to-groove distance.

Lighted Wall Planter

O ak plywood is combined with oak and walnut edging, to create this exceptionally handsome piece. It needs no additional superlatives from us — we'll simply let the photograph speak for itself.

The ends (parts A) and the center (part B) are made first. Note that both parts consist of two pieces of ³/₄ in. thick oak plywood face glued together. Most local lumberyards will order oak plywood for you if it's not carried in stock.

Cut each piece of plywood to approximately ¹/₄ in. over the length and width shown in the Bill of Materials. Apply a thin coat of glue to the mating surfaces, then clamp securely using clamp pads to protect the oak surfaces.

The two small box units, parts C, and the two large box units,

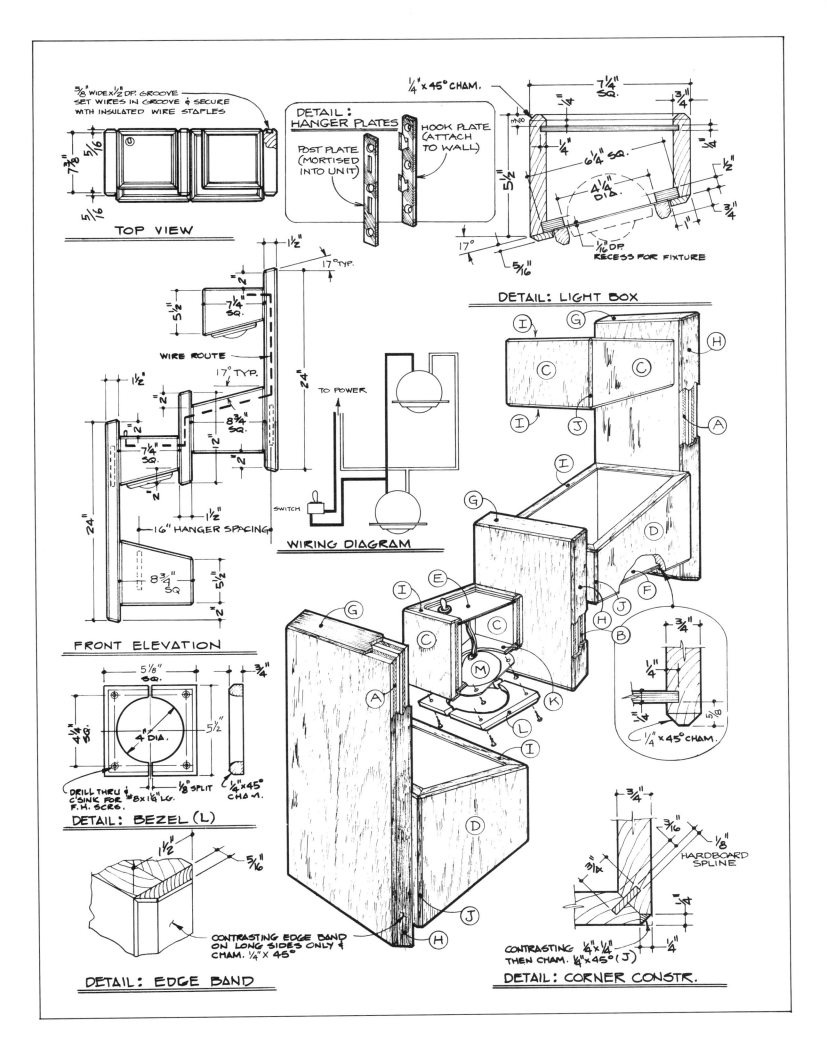

5/8" WIDE × 1/2" DP. GROOVE SET WIRES IN GROOVE & SECURE WITH INSULATED WIRE STAPLES

7 3/8"
5/16
5/16
5/16

TOP VIEW

1/4" × 45° CHAM.

DETAIL: HANGER PLATES

HOOK PLATE (ATTACH TO WALL)

POST PLATE (MORTISED INTO UNIT)

7 1/4" SQ.
3/4"
1/4
5 1/2"
1/4
6 1/4" SQ.
4 1/4" DIA.
1/2"
3/4"
1"
17°
5/16"
1/16" DP. RECESS FOR FIXTURE

DETAIL: LIGHT BOX

1 1/2"
17° TYP.
7 1/4" SQ.
5 1/2"
2"
2"
24"
WIRE ROUTE
17° TYP.
1 1/2"
2"
8 3/4" SQ.
2"
7 1/4" SQ.
2"
24"
1 1/2"
16" HANGER SPACING
8 3/4" SQ.
5 1/2"
2"

TO POWER
SWITCH

WIRING DIAGRAM

FRONT ELEVATION

5 1/8" SQ.
3/4"
4 1/4" SQ.
5 1/2"
4" DIA.
1/8" SPLIT
1/4" × 45° CHAM.

DRILL THRU & C'SINK FOR #8 × 1 1/4" LG. F.H. SCRG.

DETAIL: BEZEL (L)

1 1/2"
5/16"

CONTRASTING EDGE BAND ON LONG SIDES ONLY & CHAM. 1/4" × 45°

DETAIL: EDGE BAND

3/4"
1/4"
1/4"
5/8"
1/4" × 45° CHAM.

3/4"
3/16"
1/8"
HARDBOARD SPLINE
3/4"
1/4"

CONTRASTING 1/4" × 1/4" THEN CHAM. 1/4" × 45° (J)

DETAIL: CORNER CONSTR.

97

clamped, the brads will keep them from slipping out of position.

Once dry, a $^1/_2$ in. deep by $^5/_8$ in. wide groove is cut along the back side for the wiring. The path of the cut is shown on the drawing. A $^5/_8$ in. diameter straight router bit will cut the groove in short order. You'll also need to drill a $^3/_8$ in. hole through the back of both small boxes for the wires to go through, and a $^1/_2$ in. hole in the lower small box panel for the toggle switch.

We've included a diagram to show the wiring layout. Take your time and do a neat and careful job. Sloppy wiring causes fires. If you're not experienced in electrical work, have a licenced electrician do it for you.

Eyeball style light fixtures are available at just about any electrical store. Note that the edges of the fixture must be trimmed to fit inside the box. The addition of a pair of 50 watt "GRO-Lights" helps keep the plants healthy.

Although the planter can be wired to a plug which inserts into a standard wall outlet, we chose to wire ours through the wall to a junction box. This method eliminates having a cord that shows. If

Next, cut the $^1/_4$ in. by $^1/_4$ in. groove for the box corner edging (parts J). Use a router or a table saw equipped with a dado head cutter to form this groove, then glue the corner edging in place. Once dry, trim the edging flush with a hand plane or laminate trimmer bit.

A $^1/_2$ in. deep rabbet can now be cut on the angled edge of the small boxes (see Detail: Light Box). If you have a router table, it can be put to good use here, although you'll have to change the location of the fence as you cut around the box. The rabbet width is wider on the front and back than on the two sides. Another option is to use a sharp chisel to chop out the rabbet.

The fixture panel (part K) is next. Cut a piece of $^1/_2$ in. thick hardwood plywood to fit just inside the rabbet. A piece $6^1/_4$ in. square should be just about right. Once fit, use a compass to scribe a $4^1/_4$ in. diameter circle in the center of the piece, then cut out using a hole cutter or saber saw. Following this, use a router equipped with a trammel-point guide and a rabbet bit to cut a $^1/_{16}$ in. deep recess all around for the light fixture. The fixture panel can now be glued in place.

The oak box edging (I) is now added to the boxes. Carefully miter each corner at 45 degrees, then glue in place. A few small finishing nails can be used to temporarily hold the edging as it dries.

The bezel (part L) is made to the dimensions shown in the detail. Use a hole cutter or saber saw to make the 4 in. diameter hole. You'll probably find that it's less likely to split if you cut the hole in oversized stock, then trim it to $5^1/_8$ in. by $5^1/_2$ in. square. You can also cut the hole by faceplate turning the bezel on a lathe.

Once the hole has been cut, split the piece in two using the table saw, then drill and countersink for wood screws as shown.

A router equipped with a $^1/_4$ in. piloted chamfering bit is used to apply a $^1/_4$ in. chamfer to all edges shown on the drawing. All parts can then be given a thorough sanding.

Assemble the parts as shown. Use glue and clamp securely. It will be helpful to drive several small brads, then clip the heads off so that about $^1/_8$ in. is exposed. When the parts are assembled and

you use the latter method, check local codes as they may require that this be done by a licenced electrician.

This project is fairly heavy, so it's important that a sturdy fastening system be used to hang it on a wall. We chose bed fasteners sold by The Wise Company, 6503 St. Claude Ave., Arabi, LA 70032. Their part no. B12 contains four post plates and four hook plates.

Mortise the post plates into the project, 16 in. on center as shown. A secondary mortise will have to be added so that the hooks can fit in place. The hook plates can then be secured to the wall studs, 16 in. on center.

Final sand all parts. For a clear finish we applied several coats of Waterlox, a penetrating oil that offers excellent moisture protection.

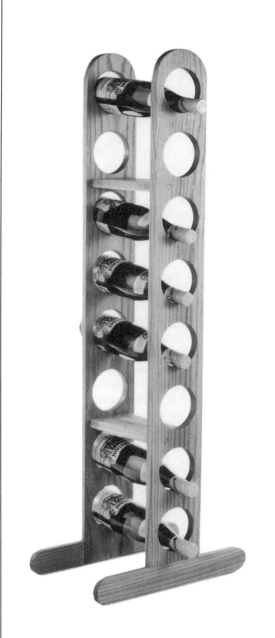

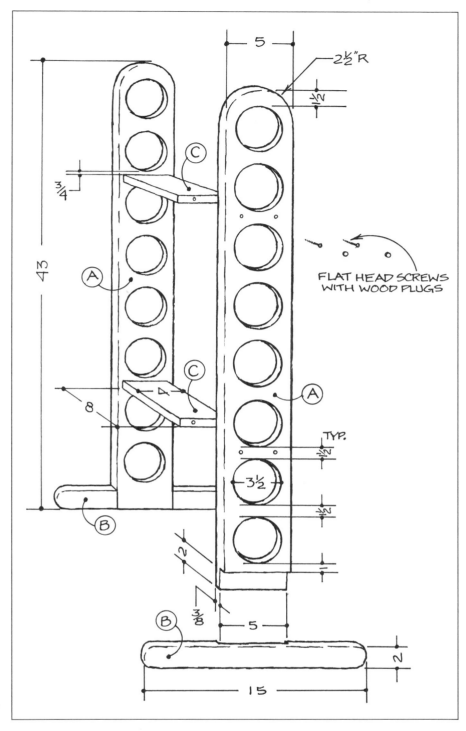

Wine Rack

Over the years we've seen a lot of interesting wine rack designs, but we think this one is especially unique. With a tall, slender profile, it fits nicely in any location where space is at a premium.

We used ³/₄ in. thick oak for all parts, an appropriate wood for a piece like this. Cherry, we think, would be another good choice.

Begin by cutting the two sides (parts A) to overall length and width. Referring to the drawing, lay out and mark the center line location of the eight holes. The holes can be cut with either a 3¹/₂ in. diameter hole saw, an adjustable circle cutter, or a saber saw. The top edge is rounded with a band or saber saw.

The ³/₈ in. deep by 2 in. wide rabbet on the bottom of the sides is best cut using the dado head cutter on the table saw or radial-arm saw, although repeated passes with a regular saw blade will also do the job.

Cut the two feet (parts B) 2 in. wide by 15 in. long, then lay out the location of the half-lap. Again, use the dado head cutter to make the ³/₈ in. deep groove.

Use glue and clamps to join the feet to the sides, then cut the stretchers (parts C) to length and width.

To look best, this piece needs to have its edges well rounded. A router equipped with a piloted ¹/₄ in. rounding-over bit will make the job easy. Be sure to do all edges, including the inside of the holes and those on the stretchers.

Sand all surfaces, then assemble the stretchers to the sides with wood screws, countersunk and plugged, as shown. Sand the plugs flush with the surface, then final finish with two coats of Watco penetrating oil. Allow to dry, then rub down with a soft cloth.

Early American
Wall Secretary

Early American furniture continues to enjoy a great deal of popularity in this country. This piece, made from pine, certainly has all the flavor and the charm of that style.

It's a piece that can be put to use almost anywhere in the house, but we think it can be particularly handy near a telephone since the front folds down to form a writing surface.

The two sides (parts A) can be made first. If you can't get $9^1/4$ in. wide stock you'll have to edge-glue a couple of narrower boards in order to get the needed width. Apply glue to both mating surfaces, then use bar or pipe clamps to clamp together. Allow to dry overnight.

Cut both sides to overall length and width, then lay out and mark the location of the dadoes for the top (part B), upper shelf (part C), middle shelf (part D), and the bottom (part E). The dadoes for parts B and C are $3/8$ in. deep by $3/4$ in. wide and go completely across the board. The dado for part E is also $3/8$ in. deep by $3/4$ in. wide, but it is stopped at a point $1^3/4$ in. from the front edge. The dado for part D is $3/8$ in. deep by $1/4$ in. wide and is stopped at a point $1^1/2$ in. from the front edge.

The dadoes are best cut using the dado-head cutter in conjunction with the table saw, although a router can also do the job. It's a good idea to cut the dadoes slightly less than the thickness of the mating board. Then, when the mating board is later sanded, the fit should be just right.

Next, use a router equipped with a $1/4$ in. piloted rabbet bit to cut the $3/8$ in. by $1/4$ in. rabbet along the inside back edge. Note that the rabbet stops at the dadoes for parts C and E.

Now, the grid pattern for the side panels can be transferred from the drawing. A band or saber saw will cut it to shape in short order.

Parts B, C, D and E can now be cut to overall length and width. All are $3/4$ in. thick stock except for the $1/2$ in. thick part D. A router with a $1/4$ in. straight bit will cut the $1/4$ in. by $1/4$ in. stopped dadoes (for parts H) in the bottom of part C and the top of part D. The tenons on each end of parts D and H and the dadoes in parts H for the horizontal divider (I) are best cut with the dado head. Note that the front edge of part E is cut at a 45-degree bevel.

After part F is made, all parts can be given a thorough sanding, working up to

220-grit. Assemble as shown using glue and wood screws, countersunk and plugged with screw buttons, to secure parts A, B, C, and E. Check for squareness.

Apply glue to the back half of the tenon on each end of part D, then apply glue to the front half of its mating dado in part A. When part D is slid in from the back, this gluing technique serves to spread the glue out evenly. Parts H and I can be added in the same manner. Following this, the plywood back (G) is secured in place with finishing nails.

The door panel (part M) will require edge-glued stock. The bevel is best cut on the table saw with the blade tilted at an angle of about 9 degrees. It's a good idea to clamp a tall (about 6 in.) auxiliary fence to your rip fence in order to support the panel as it's passed over the blade.

The panel groove in parts J and K can be cut on the table saw with the dado head. However, the panel groove in parts L is stopped, so a router will have to be used here.

After sanding all parts, the door is assembled as shown. Don't glue the panel in place; it must be free to float. Note that you'll need to add a doorstop (N) and a bullet catch to hold the door closed.

The project can now be stained to suit. We used two coats of Minwax Golden Oak Wood Finish followed by several coats of their antique oil finish.

If not available locally, the door hinge (called a combination hinge support) is available from Paxton Hardware, 7818 Bradshaw Road, Upper Falls, MD 21156; order part no. 5009.

Bill of Materials (all dimensions actual)			
Part	Description	Size	No. Req'd.
A	Side Panel	$3/4$ x $9^1/4$ x $41^3/4$	2
B	Top	$3/4$ x 6 x $29^1/4$	1
C	Upper Shelf	$3/4$ x $9^1/4$ x $29^1/4$	1
D	Middle Shelf	$1/2$ x 8 x $29^1/4$	1
E	Bottom	$3/4$ x $8^1/2$ x $29^1/4$	1
F	Front Panel	$3/4$ x 9 x $28^1/2$	1
G	Back	$1/4$ x $17^1/4$ x $29^1/4$	1
H	Vertical Divider	$1/2$ x $5^1/2$ x $8^1/2$	2
I	Horizontal Divider	$1/2$ x $5^1/2$ x 13	1
J	Top Rail	$3/4$ x 3 x 25	1
K	Bottom Rail	$3/4$ x 3 x 25	1
L	Door Stile	$3/4$ x 3 x $17^1/4$	2
M	Door Panel	$3/4$ x $11^7/8$ x $23^1/8$	1
N	Doorstop	$3/4$ x 1 x 2	1

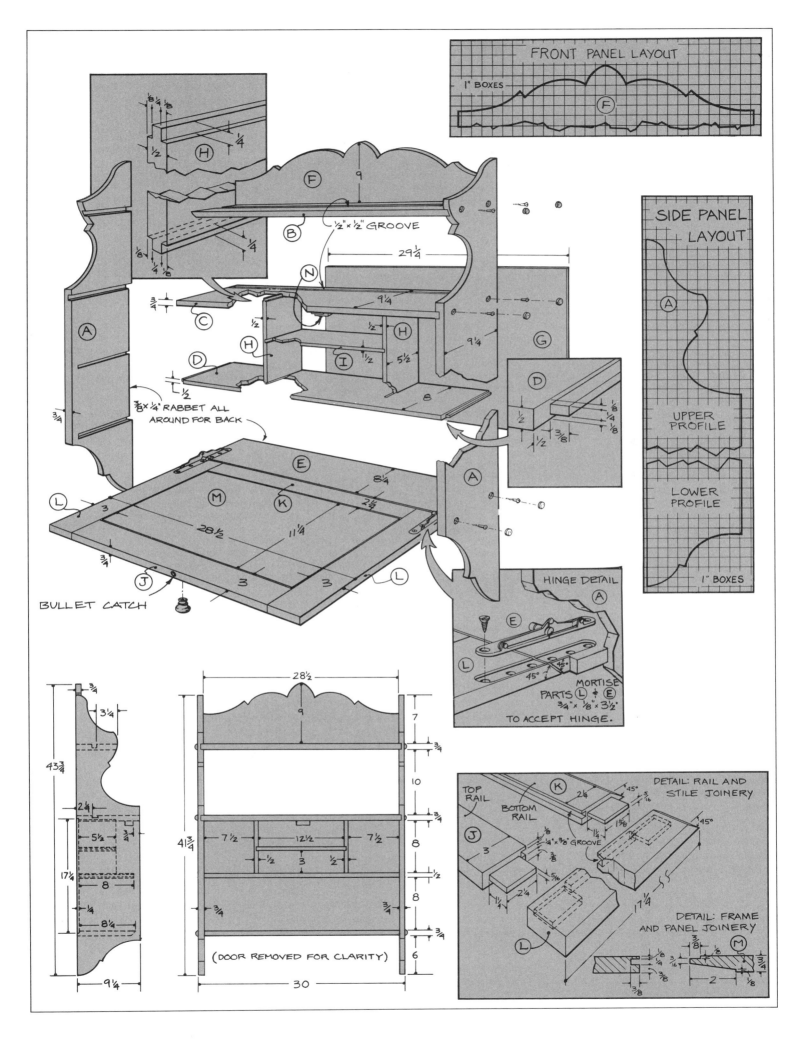

FRONT PANEL LAYOUT

1" BOXES

F

SIDE PANEL LAYOUT

A

UPPER PROFILE

LOWER PROFILE

1" BOXES

H

1/4

1/2

1/8

1/4

1/2

9

F

B

1/2" x 1/2" GROOVE

29 1/4

N

9 1/4

3/4

C

1/2

H

1/2

H

A

D

1/2

3/8 x 1/4" RABBET ALL AROUND FOR BACK

3/4

I

1/2

5 1/2

G

9 1/4

D

1/2

3/8

1/2

1/8

1/4

1/8

A

E

M

K

8 1/4

2 1/2

L

3

28 1/2

11 1/4

J

3

3

L

BULLET CATCH

3/4

HINGE DETAIL

A

E

L

45°

45°

MORTISE PARTS L & E 3/4" x 1/8" x 3 1/2" TO ACCEPT HINGE.

3/4

3 1/4

43 3/4

2 1/4

5 1/2

3/4

17 1/4

8

1/4

8 1/4

9 1/4

28 1/2

9

7

3/4

10

3/4

7 1/2   12 1/2   7 1/2

1/2   3   1/2

8

1/2

41 3/4

8

3/4

3/4

6

30

(DOOR REMOVED FOR CLARITY)

DETAIL: RAIL AND STILE JOINERY

K

2 1/4

45°

5/16

45°

TOP RAIL

BOTTOM RAIL

J

3

1/4" x 3/8" GROOVE

3/8

5/16

1 5/8

1/4

1 1/4

2 1/4

17 1/4

L

DETAIL: FRAME AND PANEL JOINERY

3/8

1/8

M

3/4

1/4

3/16

3/8

2

1/8

3/8

Shaker Chest of Drawers

The clean lines that typify Shaker style are very much evident in this handsome piece. Solid cherry, a wood commonly chosen by Shaker craftsmen, was used for all parts, except the drawer sides, backs, and bottoms.

The two sides (parts A) and the top (part B) can be made first. Since these parts are rather wide, it will be necessary to edge-glue two or more narrow boards in order to get enough width. It's best to cut the boards so that the glued up stock will be slightly wider and longer than necessary.

Perhaps most important to the success of an edge joint is a clean, smooth surface on both mating parts. This permits close contact between both surfaces and results in maximum glue strength. When a board is ripped on a table saw or radial-arm saw, it usually results in a fairly rough edge, so it's best to clean it up using the jointer.

When edge-joining boards of this length, it's a good idea to use three or four dowel pins. Although the pins don't add strength to this joint, they make it easier to keep the edges aligned when the boards are clamped.

Apply a thin coat of glue to both mating surfaces, then clamp the stock together with bar or pipe clamps. There's no need to add glue to the dowel pins. Avoid over-tightening the clamps which can cause too much glue to squeeze out, resulting in a weakened joint.

Once dry, remove the clamps and cut part B to overall length and width. Cut parts A to length, but don't trim them to final width yet. It's best to do that after the drawer frame dovetail grooves are cut.

The top, part B, can now be temporarily put aside while the two sides, parts A, are worked.

The dovetail grooves for the six drawer frames are made next. Carefully lay out the center line location of each groove, extending the line across the entire width of part A. Next, at a point 3/8 in. on each side of the center lines, scribe another line across the width. This pair of lines establishes the 3/4 in. thickness of the dovetail groove.

Equip the router with a 1/2 in. dovetail bit (we used a Sears bit, part no. 9-25531) and adjust it for a 3/8 in. deep cut. Cut a guidestrip of suitable length from straight stock and clamp it to the side. The distance between the guidestrip and the bit (dimension "A" in figure 1A) should be such that the cut establishes one leg of the dovetail. The guidestrip must be parallel to the guidelines. Make the cut with the router held firmly against the guidestrip.

Now, transfer the guidestrip to the other side of the slot and again clamp it in place. The distance between the guidestrip and the bit (Dimension A in figure 1B) should be such that it establishes the 3/4 in. dovetail width. With the guidestrip parallel to the guidelines, make another cut, again holding the router firmly against this guidestrip. Repeat this process for each of the drawer frames.

The two sides can now be trimmed to final width. Then, using the dado head cutter, add a 1/2 in. by 3/4 in. rabbet along the back edge as shown. This rabbet can also be cut by making repeated passes with a regular saw blade.

The dovetails that join parts A to part B can now be cut. Lay out the dovetails very carefully using a hard, sharp pencil. Once the tails have been laid out on the top (B), mark the waste material between the tails with an "X" to avoid confusion. In addition to scribing the tail layout on the face of the board, carry the lines across the end grain. Now clamp the top in a vise and use a fine-tooth dovetail saw to make the angled cuts that will establish the tails. Cut just on the waste side of the line, grazing but not removing it. Bring the cuts almost — but not quite — to the scribed bottom line. A coping saw is now used to cut across the grain and remove the waste. Take the top from the vise, clamp it flat on the workbench over a scrap board, and use a sharp chisel to dress the sides and bottoms of the cutouts.

The pins on the sides (A) should be laid out and marked using the finished dovetails as a template. To do this, clamp the side vertically in a vise, lay the dovetailed top in position on the side, and trace the dovetails with a sharp pencil or X-acto knife. Use a small square to carry the scribed lines onto the face of the board.

Mark the waste portion between the pins with an "X," then cut out using the same technique as for the dovetails. A well-fitted dovetail should fit together with only light tapping from a mallet and scrap block. If needed, trim further with a sharp chisel.

Next, cut part D, establish the dovetail on the ends, and notch the sides to fit the dovetail.

The six drawer frames are made next. The top frame consists of parts K, L, and M, the bottom frame consists of parts K, L, M, and N, and the remaining four frames consist of parts K and L. Note that a 1/4 in. wide by 1 1/4 in. deep groove is cut along the inside edge of each part K. This groove serves as a mortise for the tenon on each end of parts L.

Parts L for the top frame and the bottom frame require a 1/4 in. wide by 1 1/4 in. deep groove along the inside edge to accept the tenon for parts M. Parts L for the remaining four frames do not require any grooves.

Parts L and M have ¼ in. thick by 1¼ in. long tenons on each end. These are cut to fit in the mortises in parts K and L. Parts M also have a ¼ in. by ⅜ in. groove along each edge.

The dust panels, parts N, are made from ½ in. thick solid stock. Each edge is tapered to ³/16 in. (see cross-sectional view of drawer bottom for typical taper) to fit into grooves in parts L and M.

Once parts K, L, M, and N have been cut they can be assembled as shown. Use glue and clamp each frame securely. It's most important that the frames be square so check carefully and make adjustments as necessary. The dust panels (N) should not be glued in place. They should be free to "float" in the frame.

Part G and the five parts F can now be cut to size and glued in place. Use care here to make sure the top and bottom edges of parts F are flush with the top and bottom edges of the drawer frames. Only the top edge of part G should be flush.

The dovetails on each end of the drawer frames can best be cut using a router table. Using the same bit that cut the dovetail grooves, run the drawer frames on edge through the cutter. In order to better support the frames, it's best to clamp a temporary tall fence to the router table fence. Be sure to measure carefully when setting up, and make several practice cuts to check for accuracy. Properly cut, the dovetails should be snug yet slide into the grooves with a minimum of effort. Remember, when the glue is applied later on, the wood swells slightly, so try to allow for this when cutting. Since the dovetails only show at the front edge, it's most important that the fit be accurate at that point.

We used a molding-head cutter (Sear's part no. 93212) to cut the molding (part P). To increase safety, it's best to cut the molding on the edge of a wide piece of stock, then rip it to its 1 in. width. Use pushsticks to keep hands away from the cutter.

The dovetails on each end of part E are best cut with a dovetail saw. Once cut, transfer the profile to parts D and F, then use a sharp chisel to chop out the waste material.

After the remaining parts are cut to size, all can be given a thorough sanding. Begin assembly by joining the two sides (A), to the top (B). While gluing, use a pair of temporary stretchers to

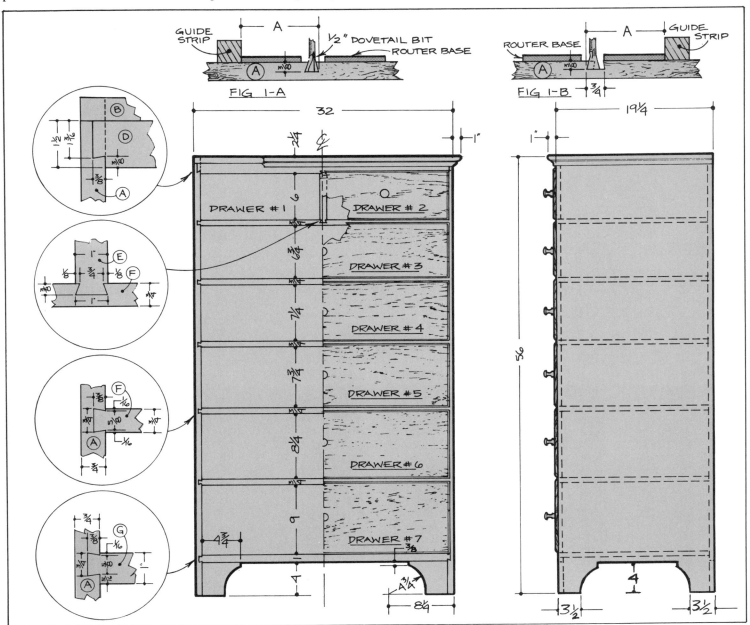

provide proper spacing across the bottom.

Once dry, the bottom drawer frame can be installed. Apply a coat of glue to the front half of the drawer support end (part K) and the back half of the dovetail groove in part A. When the drawer frames are slid in from the front, this gluing technique serves to spread the glue evenly. Once the frame has been slid in place, check for squareness and allow to dry. Once dry, follow the same procedure for all remaining drawer frames.

Although in theory we know that the cross-grain orientation of the drawer frames to the sides should create a serious wood movement problem, in practice, with a piece such as this, which is made of hardwood and has the sides essentially locked in by the series of dovetail frames, the problem never manifests itself. In case you wondered about the function of part J, it serves to prevent the two top drawers from tipping as they are opened.

The seven drawer knobs can be lathe-turned to the dimensions shown or a similar style can be purchased from Shaker Workshops, P.O. Box 1028, Concord, MA 01742.

All remaining parts can now be assembled. Each back piece (part C) is joined to the back of the drawer frames by a single screw through the center of each board. A single screw allows each board to expand and contract with changes in humidity.

The drawers are assembled as shown. Note that the dovetail spacing varies from drawer to drawer.

Give the chest a thorough final sanding, using 220-grit for the final effort. Check all drawers for a good sliding fit. Two coats of a good penetrating oil complete the project.

Bill of Materials
(all dimensions actual)

Part	Description	Size	No. Req'd.
A	Side	3/4 x 19 1/4 x 56	2
B	Top	3/4 x 19 1/4 x 32	1
C	Back	3/4 x 10 5/8 x 55 3/4	3
D	Stretcher	3/4 x 1 1/2 x 31 1/4	1
E	Divider	3/4 x 1 x 6 3/4	1
F	Edging	3/4 x 3/4 x 31 1/4	5
G	Edging	3/4 x 1 x 31 1/4	1
H	Foot	3/4 x 4 3/4 x 4	2
I	Glueblock	1 1/4 x 1 1/4 x 3 3/4	4
J	Guide	1 x 1 1/2 x 17 3/4	2
K	Frame End	3/4 x 3 1/2 x 17 3/4	12
L	Frame Front & Back	3/4 x 3 1/2 x 26 3/4	12
M	Frame Divider	3/4 x 3 1/2 x 13 1/4	2
N	Dust Panel	1/2 x 10 3/4 x 11 1/8	2
O	Runner	3/4 x 1 x 17 3/4	1
P	Molding	See Details	As Req'd
Q	Drawer	See Details	7

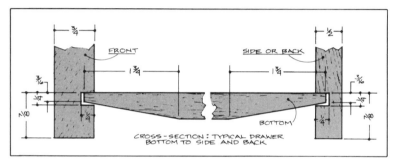

CROSS-SECTION: TYPICAL DRAWER
BOTTOM TO SIDE AND BACK

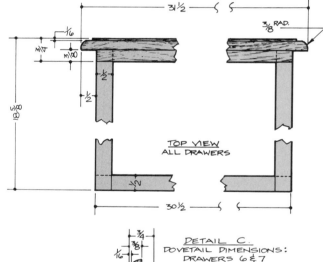

TOP VIEW
ALL DRAWERS

TABLE OF DOVETAIL DIMENSIONS

DRAWER	A	B	C	D	E	F	G	H	I	J	K	L	M	N	O
1 & 2	SEE DETAIL A.														
3	6 3/4	7/16	7/8	3/8	1/2	3/4	1/2	7/8	1	7/8	1 1/8	15/16	7/8	1	1 3/16
4	7 1/4	3/8	1	3/8	7/16	7/8	1/2	1	1	1	1 1/4	1 1/16	7/8	1 1/8	1 5/16
5	7 3/4	5/16	1 1/8	3/8	3/8	1	1/2	1 1/8	1	1 1/8	1 3/8	1 3/16	7/8	1 1/4	1 7/16

DRAWER	AA	BB	CC	DD	EE	FF	GG	HH	II	JJ	KK	LL	MM	NN	OO
6	8 1/4	3/8	15/16	3/8	7/16	13/16	1/2	5/8	1	7/8	1	1 1/16	7/8	1	1 1/16
7	9	3/8	1 1/16	3/8	7/16	15/16	1/2	5/8	1	1 1/8	1	1 1/16	7/8	1 1/4	1 1/16

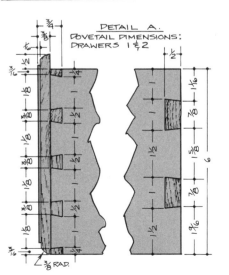

DETAIL A.
DOVETAIL DIMENSIONS:
DRAWERS 1 & 2

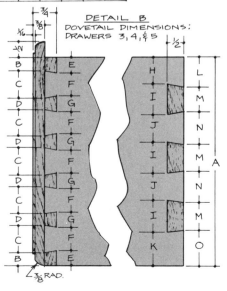

DETAIL B
DOVETAIL DIMENSIONS:
DRAWERS 3, 4, & 5

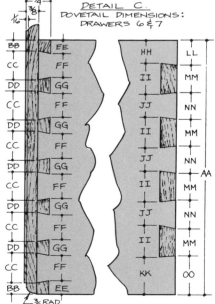

DETAIL C.
DOVETAIL DIMENSIONS:
DRAWERS 6 & 7

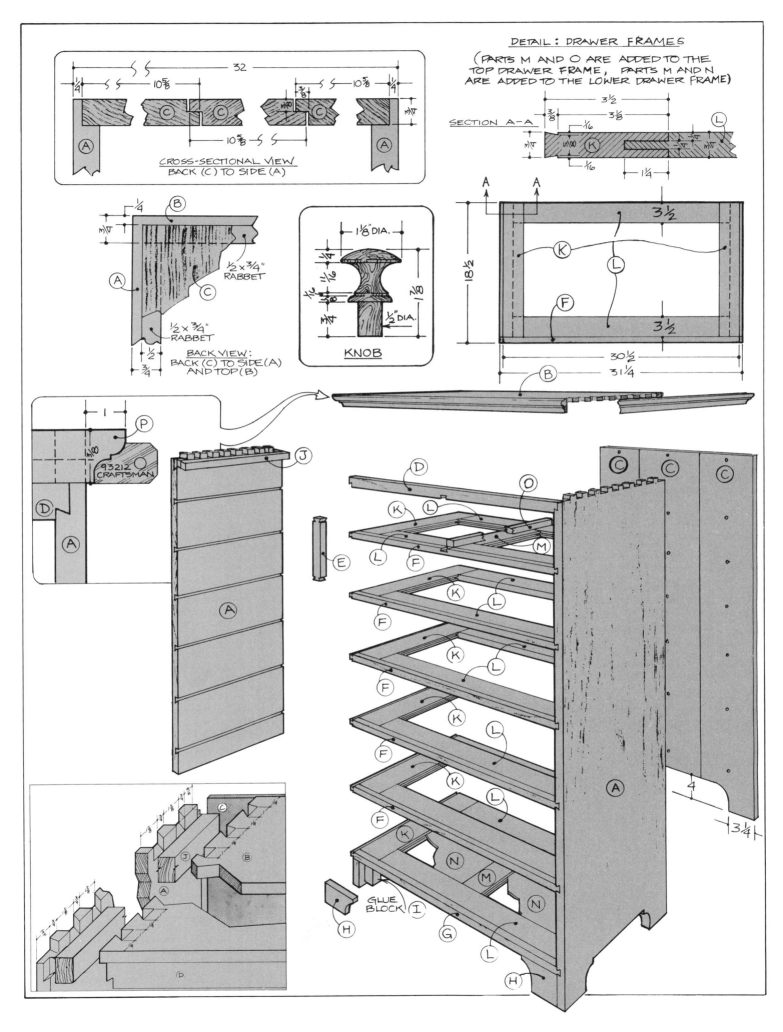

DETAIL: DRAWER FRAMES

(PARTS M AND O ARE ADDED TO THE
TOP DRAWER FRAME, PARTS M AND N
ARE ADDED TO THE LOWER DRAWER FRAME)

SECTION A-A

CROSS-SECTIONAL VIEW
BACK (C) TO SIDE (A)

½ x ¾" RABBET

½ x ¾" RABBET

BACK VIEW:
BACK (C) TO SIDE (A)
AND TOP (B)

KNOB

1⅛" DIA.

½" DIA.

93212 CRAFTSMAN

GLUE BLOCK

Toy Train

Generations of children have enjoyed wooden toy trains, and the appeal seems as strong today as ever. Rather remarkable, some might say, when you consider a wooden train doesn't contain a single micro-chip.

This one is a replica of a typical American type steam locomotive built around the turn of the century by the Baldwin and American Locomotive Works. It was the first locomotive in the world to set speed records and put the American steam locomotive in the forefront of steam motive power.

Use poplar for just about all parts. It's hard enough to stand up to rugged handling yet the cost is reasonable. For maximum durability, though, use maple or birch.

The locomotive main chassis (part A) is made from 1/2 in. thick stock and cut to the length and width shown in the Bill of Materials. To make the boiler (part B), face-glue 10 pieces of 13/16 in. thick by 3 in. square stock, then turn to 2 1/2 in. diameter. Once turned, use a drill press to bore holes for the various parts that will be attached later on. The boiler can now be trimmed to a 7 1/2 in. length on the table saw or radial-arm saw. Next, use a sanding block or sharp hand plane to apply a 1 in. wide flat along the bottom. This will provide a good surface for the boiler to be attached to the main chassis.

If you don't have a lathe, there's another way to make the boiler: use a 2 1/2 in. hole saw to cut 10 disks, then face-glue them together. Keep the edges flush when clamping. Allow to dry, then sand the surface smooth.

The four driver wheels (parts Q) are best turned on the lathe, although a hole saw, if you have one, will also do the job. An adjustable circle cutter will work too, but it may leave a ridge that must be sanded off. The pilot wheels (parts Y) can be made in much the same fashion.

To make the cowcatcher (part V), you'll need a piece of 3/4 in. thick stock measuring 2 3/4 in. by about 12 in. long. Set the table saw miter gauge at 45 degrees and tilt the sawblade to 45 degrees, then cut to the center point of the stock. Repeat this for the other side, then move both the miter gauge and sawblade to zero. Mark the location of the 1 in. rabbet, then cut out this material by making repeated passes on the table saw. Once the rabbet's been cut, the cowcatcher can be cut to its 3 1/4 in. length.

Parts W, CC, II, NN, OO, and PP can be lathe-turned or similar parts can be mail-ordered from K & K Woodcrafters, R.D. 4, Box 27A, Scotia, NY 12302.

Parts HH, KK, LL, and MM are all made from dowel stock. The banding (part QQ) is simply 3/16 in. wide strips of mahogany veneer that's bent around the boiler (B) and glued in place. The

cylinder (part EE) is a 1 1/2 in. length of 3/4 in. diameter dowel stock with a 3/8 in. hole bored 1 3/8 in. deep. Note that there is a 1/2 in. wide flat on one side.

The completed train should be given a complete sanding, taking special care to round all edges and sharp corners. The safest non-toxic finish is none at all.

Bill of Materials
(all dimensions actual)

Part	Description	Size	No. Req'd.
	Locomotive		
A	Main Chassis	1/2 x 2 3/4 x 10 1/2	1
B	Boiler	2 1/2 dia. x 7 1/2	1
C	Roof Support	1/4 x 1/2 x 3 3/8	2
D	Front Roof Support	1/4 x 1/2 x 1 3/4	2
E	Cab Floor	1/2 x 1 3/4 x 2 7/8	1
F	Cab Front	1/2 x 3/4 x 2 3/4	1
G	Cab Front	1/2 x 1/2 x 1 3/4	2
H	Cab Side	1/2 x 3/4 x 2 3/4	4
I	Cab Side	1/2 x 3/4 x 1 3/4	4
J	Cab Side	3/8 x 1/2 x 2 3/4	2
K	Cab Roof	1/4 x 3 x 4 1/2	1
L	Tender Linkage Bar	3/8 x 1 x 2 1/2	1
M	Tender Dowel	3/8 dia. x 1 1/4 long	1
N	Dowel Pin	1/8 dia. x 3/4 long	1
O	Driver Axle Support	1/2 x 1 1/2 x 2 3/4	2
P	Driver Axle	3/8 dia. x 3 7/8 long	2
Q	Driver	3 1/2 dia. x 1/2 thick	4
R	Pilot Truck Support	1/4 x 1 1/2 x 4	1
S	Cylinder Intake Block	1/2 x 5/8 x 1 1/2	2
T	Cross Member	3/4 x 3/4 x 2 3/4	1
U	Pilot Truck	5/8 x 3/4 x 3	2
V	Cowcatcher	3/4 x 2 3/4 x 3 1/2	1
W	Marker Light	(See Drawing)	4
X	Pilot Wheel Axle	1/4 dia. x 3 7/8 long	2
Y	Pilot Wheel	1 3/8 dia. x 1/2 thick	4
Z	Pilot Truck Dowel	1/4 dia. x 3/4 long	2
AA	Tie Rod	1/4 x 1/2 x 5	1
BB	Rod Connector Block	1/4 x 1/2 x 1 1/4	1
CC	Tie Rod Dowel Pin	(See Drawing)	5
DD	Push Rod	3/16 dia. x 3 1/2 long	2
EE	Cylinder	3/4 dia. x 1 1/2 long	2
FF	Lantern	3/4 x 7/8 x 1 1/4	1
GG	Lantern Support Pin	3/16 dia. x 1 long	1
HH	Number Plate	(See Drawing)	1
II	Stack	(See Drawing)	1
JJ	Whistle	(See Drawing)	1
KK	Dowel	3/16 dia. x 3/4 long	1
LL	Sand Dome	1 dia. x 1 1/4 long	1
MM	Throttle Dome	1 dia. x 1 1/2 long	1
NN	Dome Cap	(See Drawing)	2
OO	Dowel Pin	(See Drawing)	1
PP	Dome Dowel Pin	(See Drawing)	1
QQ	Banding	1/32 thick x 3/16 wide	4

Bill of Materials
(all dimensions actual)

Part	Description	Size	No. Req'd.
	Gondola		
A	Floor	1/4 x 4 x 10	1
B	Side	1/2 x 1 3/4 x 10	2
C	Front & Back	3/4 x 1 3/4 x 3	2
D	Type "A" Coupler	(See Detail)	1
E	Type "B" Coupler	(See Detail)	1
	Caboose		
A	Floor	1/2 x 4 1/4 x 7	1
B	Side w/ Windows	1/2 x 1 1/2 x 5 1/2	2
C	Front & Back	3/4 x 1 3/4 x 3	2
D	Side Roof Support	1/4 x 1/2 x 5 1/2	2
E	Roof	1/2 x 4 1/4 x 7	1
F	Cat Walk	1/8 x 1/2 x 2 1/4	2
G	Cupola	3/4 x 2 3/4 x 2 1/2	1
H	Cupola Roof	1/4 x 2 3/4 x 2 1/2	1
I	Locator	1/4 x 3 x 4	1
J	Rear Caboose Coupler	(See Detail)	1
K	Type "A" Coupler	(See Detail)	1
	Tender		
A	Floor	1/4 x 4 x 7 1/2	1
B	Side	1/2 x 2 1/2 x 7 1/2	2
C	Front & Back	3/4 x 2 1/2 x 3	2
D	Front Tender Coupler	(See Detail)	1
E	Type "B" Coupler	(See Detail)	1
	Box Car		
A	Floor	1/4 x 4 x 10	1
B	Side	1/2 x 2 1/2 x 10	2
C	Front & Back	3/4 x 3 x 3	2
D	Side Rail	1/2 x 1/2 x 10	2
E	Roof	1/4 x 4 x 10	1
F	Cat Walk	1/8 x 1/2 x 10	1
G	Locator	3/16 x 1 x 3	2
H	Type "A" Coupler	(See Detail)	1
I	Type "B" Coupler	(See Detail)	1

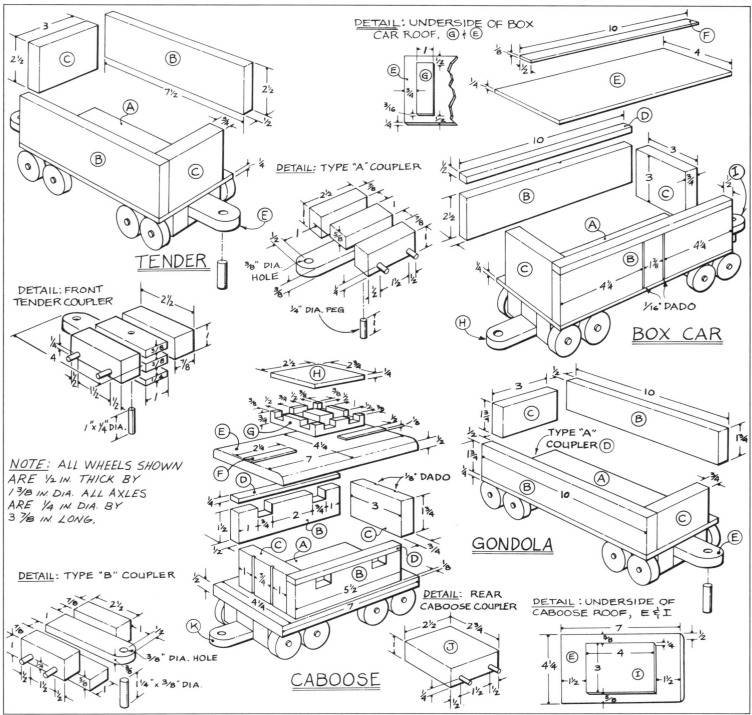

DETAIL: UNDERSIDE OF BOX CAR ROOF, G & E

DETAIL: TYPE "A" COUPLER

TENDER

DETAIL: FRONT TENDER COUPLER

NOTE: ALL WHEELS SHOWN ARE ½ IN. THICK BY 1 3/8 IN. DIA. ALL AXLES ARE ¼ IN. DIA. BY 3 7/8 IN. LONG.

DETAIL: TYPE "B" COUPLER

BOX CAR

CABOOSE

GONDOLA

DETAIL: REAR CABOOSE COUPLER

DETAIL: UNDERSIDE OF CABOOSE ROOF, E & I

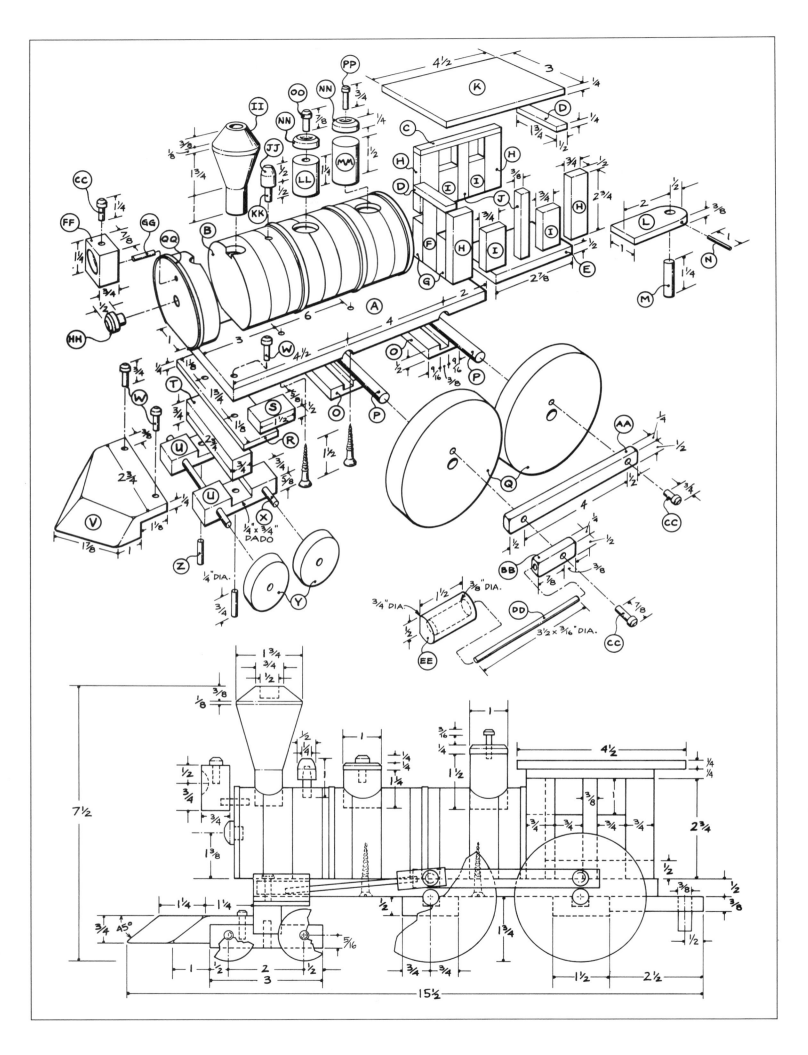

Waterbed

We think many readers will be surprised to learn how easy it is to build this handsome queen size waterbed. The joinery is relatively basic and shouldn't present any special problems to woodworkers of intermediate skill.

The frame dovetail joints and the pedestal joints are not glued, but rather they are connected by corner brackets — a feature that permits the bed to be easily disassembled and moved if necessary. The frame dovetails and half-pins are designed to protrude 1/8 in., a nice detail that effectively lends itself to disassembly. Red oak was used for all parts except the inserts and deck.

From 1 in. thick stock, cut the pedestal sides (parts A), pedestal ends (parts B), frame ends (parts G), and frame sides (parts H) to overall length and width. Referring to the frame dovetail detail, lay out the location of the tails on each end of parts G, keeping in mind that the tails are 1/8 in. longer than the frame thickness. Scribe the lines carefully and use a sharp, hard pencil for added accuracy.

Once scribed, use a dovetail saw or back saw to cut out the waste stock. Make the cut slightly on the waste side of the line, then use a sharp chisel to pare the stock exactly to the line.

Now, using the tails as templates, scribe the dovetail half-pin on each end of parts H. As you scribe them, label each mating end to avoid confusion later on. Use a dovetail saw or back saw to establish the 1 1/8 in. depth of cut, then chop out the remaining material with a sharp chisel. Work from one side and cut only one-half way through, then flip the piece over and cut through the other side. Some paring may be necessary to achieve a good fit.

A 1/8 in. chamfer is now added to all edges of the pedestal (parts A and B) and frame (parts G and H). A router equipped with a piloted chamfer bit will come in handy here, although the chamfer can also be done by hand with a file and sandpaper. Even if you use a router, you'll still find some hand chamfering will have to be done near the dovetails and pins.

The center insert (part C) and the two cross inserts (parts D) can now be cut to length and width from 3/4 in. thick particleboard. Part C measures 9 in. wide by 6 ft. long, while parts D measure 9 in. wide by 4 ft. long. Note that part C has a pair of slots, each located 23 1/2 in. from the ends, and measuring 3/4 in. wide by 4 1/2 in. long. Parts D also have a 3/4 in. wide by 4 1/2 in. long slot cut in the center.

Carefully scribe the location of the slots, then cut out with a back saw and sharp chisel. Once cut, check the parts for a good fit.

The deck (parts E and F) is made from 3/4 in. thick particleboard. A standard 4 ft. by 8 ft. sheet, ripped down the middle, will yield parts E. On the headboard end, nip the two outside corners at 45 degrees. The cut need only be big enough to allow heater wires to pass through later on. Part F can then be ripped to width.

Next, attach the side and end battens (parts I and J) to the frame parts. Locate the battens 3/4 in. from the bottom of the frame members (see detail), and about 3 in. from each end. Use glue and wood screws to join them in place.

The two headboards (parts L and M) are made next. Cut each piece to final width, but allow a little extra on the length (about 1 in.) Set the table saw miter gauge to 30 degrees, then cut the two pieces to 62 in. overall length.

Next, the three spacers (part N) are made from 1 in. thick stock.

Cut each one to 1 in. wide by 3 in. long. Like the pedestal and frame parts, a ⅛ in. chamfer is applied to all edges of the headboards and spacers. Following this, the headboard cleats (parts K) are cut to 3 in. wide by 20 in. long. *Editor's Note: In the photo below, note that the headboard cleats (K) are narrower than 3 in. After building the bed, we decided to beef them up, so the width was changed to 3 in. on the drawing.*

Give the headboards (parts L and M) and the headboard cleats (parts K) a thorough sanding, finishing with 220 grit. Now, glue and clamp the spacers (N) in place between the headboards as shown.

Now, sand all the frame and pedestal parts, again finishing with 220 grit. Once all parts have been sanded, the final finish can be applied. We used Waterlox (available from Woodworker's Supply of New Mexico, 5604 Alameda Place N.E., Albuquerque, NM 87113), a quality penetrating oil that provides good water resistance. Allow to dry, then rub down thoroughly.

The bed can now be assembled. Join each of the four corners of the pedestal members (parts A and B) with a pair of 2 in. by 2 in. corner brackets. Space the brackets 1 in. from the top and bottom edges. Assemble the two cross inserts (parts D) to the center insert (part C) then set the decking members (parts E and F) in place.

Assemble the frame (parts G and H) next. Begin by attaching the headboard (parts K, L, M, and N) to the frame end (part G) with 1¾ in. long by no. 10 flathead wood screws.

Next, place the frame end (with the headboard) on top of the particleboard in its proper position, then add the frame sides and the remaining frame end. Just dry assemble the frame member dovetails, don't glue them in place. To join the frame members, use 2 in. by 2 in. corner brackets located 1 in. from the top and bottom.

When the mattress is installed and water is added, the mattress tends to push out on the frame members (parts G and H), causing them to bow. To prevent this, use a 2 in. by 2 in. corner bracket to join the center of each frame member to the decking.

Before adding the mattress and its associated parts, be sure to square the frame members to the pedestal unit. This is a simple matter of checking for a 5 in. overhang all around.

A complete water-bed mattress system consists of four basic parts: a stand-up liner, which serves to contain the water in the frame in the unlikely event of a leak, a heater pad to keep the water warm (otherwise hypothermia could result), a control box with a heat sensor (to provide adjustable heat) and the mattress. Just about any waterbed store will carry these parts; in fact, they are usually sold together as a package deal.

Attach the thermostat control box to the outside of the frame at the head of the bed. Connected to the box is a heat sensor which will run through the mitered corners of the deck into the frame and lay about 12 in. from the frame side. The heater pad is then placed in the center of the bed at least 12 in. from the heat sensor. The cord for the heater pad runs out the same mitered corner and plugs into the control box. Next put the stand-up liner inside the frame.

Now place the mattress in the frame and center it. Add a bottle of algicide (available at most waterbed stores), then connect a water hose and begin to fill. Fill the bed about one-quarter full and check for squareness. Add water until you are unable to touch bottom at the center of the bed when you are in a sitting position.

Add mattress pads, then plug in the heater. The bed will be ready to use in about 24 hours.

Caution: Never place the heater pad or sensor inside the liner. Should the mattress ever spring a leak, then a short could occur.

Part	Description	Size	No. Req'd.
Bill of Materials (all dimensions actual)			
A	Pedestal Side	1 x 9 x 74	2
B	Pedestal End	1 x 9 x 48	2
C	Center Insert	¾ x 9 x 72	1
D	Cross Insert	¾ x 9 x 48	2
E	Outer Deck	¾ x 23¾ x 84	2
F	Inner Deck	¾ x 12½ x 84	1
G	Frame End	1 x 9 x 62¼	2
H	Frame Side	1 x 9 x 86¼	2
I	Long Batten	¾ x ¾ x 37	4
J	Short Batten	¾ x ¾ x 20	4
K	Headboard Cleat	1 x 3 x 20	2
L	Lower Headboard	1 x 4 x 62	1
M	Upper Headboard	1 x 6 x 62	1
N	Spacer	1 x 1 x 3	3

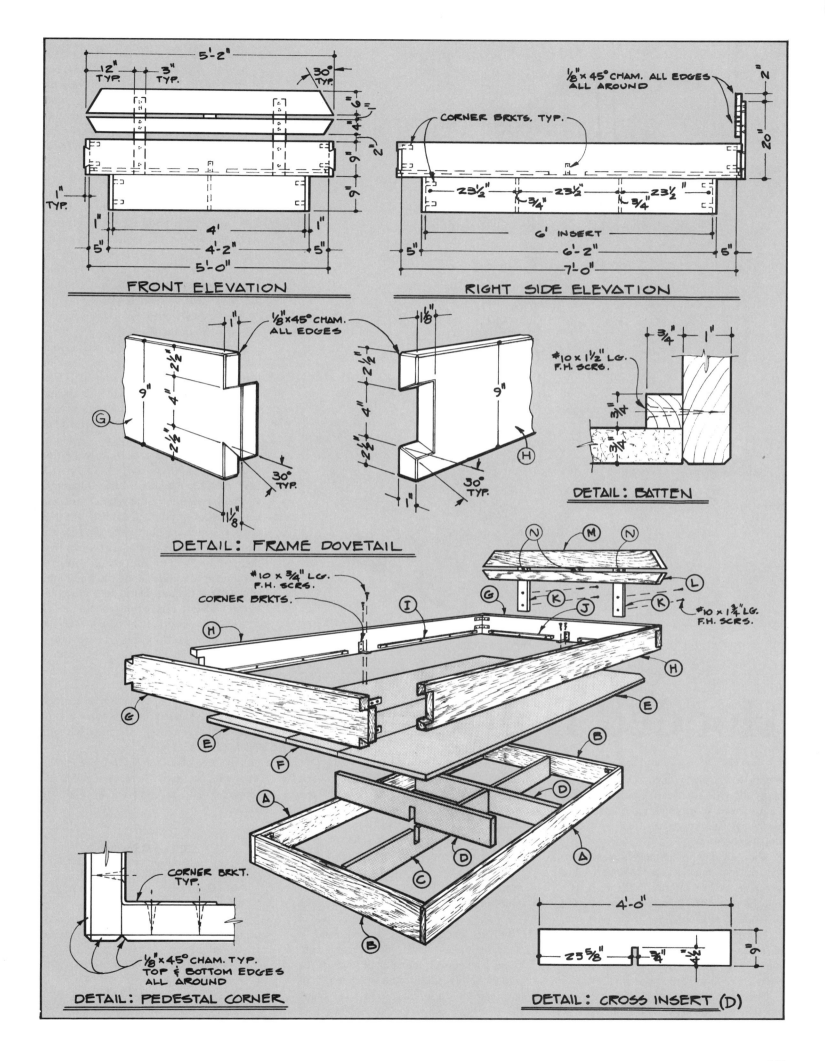

FRONT ELEVATION

RIGHT SIDE ELEVATION

DETAIL: FRAME DOVETAIL

DETAIL: BATTEN

DETAIL: PEDESTAL CORNER

DETAIL: CROSS INSERT (D)

111

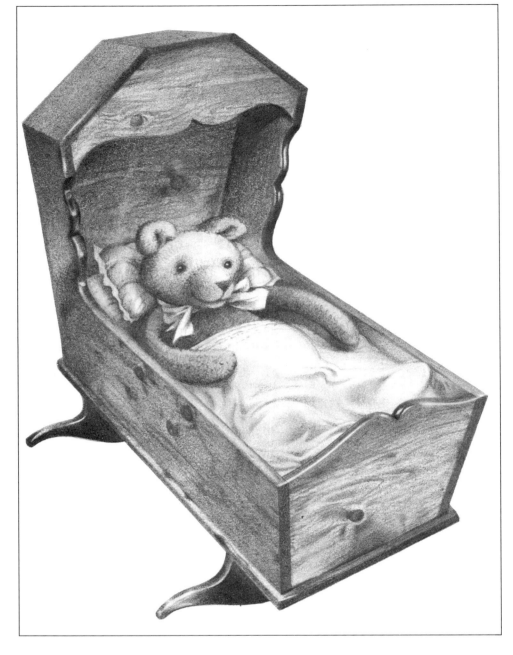

Hooded Doll Cradle

This scaled down version of an Early American cradle is made from 1/2 in. thick pine, although a hardwood such as cherry, oak or walnut can also be used.

With its compound angles this piece may at first glance seem challenging, but once the sides (A), front (B), back (C) and bottom (G) have been made and assembled, the remaining hood parts (D, E, F) are simply cut to fit. Since the hood parts are cut to fit after assembly, the dimensions in the Bill of Materials for parts D, E, and F are approximate.

Once you've prepared stock for the sides, front, and back, use the table saw to cut these parts to final size. Since the sides, front, and back of the cradle tilt out at 10 degrees, the butt joint where these parts meet will be a compound angle. The compound angle tables tell us that for a four-sided butt miter (with sides tilted at 10 degrees), the table saw miter gauge should be angled 9³/4 degrees, while the blade is tilted 1¹/2 degrees. However, if you are unable to achieve such accuracy on your table saw, we discovered that a 10-degree miter gauge setting and a 2-degree blade tilt will yield a good tight joint. The cuts on the ends of parts A, B, and C should establish the finish length of these pieces. Next, tilt the table saw blade 10 degrees, and use the rip fence to establish the bevel on the bottom edge of parts A, B, and C.

Now set the miter gauge at 90 degrees, tilt the saw blade 22 degrees, and with the back edge of part A against the miter gauge, establish the bevel along the top. Next, lay out the curved profiles on the sides and front, using the grid patterns as a guide, and cut these profiles out with a scroll saw, jigsaw, or band saw. Also, on the table saw, establish the 32-degree angle on the top edge of the back, which will support the hood. These angles are accomplished on the table saw with the miter gauge tilted 22 degrees, and the ends of part C backed up to the miter gauge. Just make sure that the angle on the back will fall on a plane with the 22-degree bevel cut you made earlier on the top edge of the sides.

After cutting the bottom to size, assemble the sides, front, back and bottom, using both glue and finishing nails. All the remaining parts, except the rockers (H), will be cut to fit the cradle case. Start with part D, which has the same compound angle cut on its ends as you cut on the ends of parts A and B. Although we show a finish length of l0³/16 in., part D may have to be cut a little longer or shorter in order to fit the actual dimension across your cradle. Establish the 32-degree angles on the top of part D, and trim the ends until you have a perfect fit to the cradle. Then transfer the profile, and cut the curved shape along the lower edge of part D. After part D has been glued and finish nailed in place, you can cut parts E and F to fit. Note that one end of each part E and both ends of part F are cut at l6-degree angles. Let the other end of parts E run long so it overhangs the sides, then hold it in position, scribe a line along the underside where it overhangs, and trim flush. This cut to trim parts E flush with the sides must be made with the blade tilted 22 degrees.

Cut the rockers to size, lay out and cut their profile, and assemble them to the cradle. Final sand, stain if desired, and finish.

Bill of Materials
(all dimensions actual)

Part	Description	Size	No. Req'd.
A	Side	See Detail	2
B	Cradle Front	1/2 x 5¹/4 x 8³/4	1
C	Back	1/2 x 10¹/4 x 9⁷/8	1
D	Hood Front	1/2 x 2¹/2 x 10³/16	1
E	Hood Top	1/2 x 4³/4 x 4¹/4	2
F	Hood Center	1/2 x 4³/4 x 4¹/4	1
G	Bottom	1/2 x 8¹/2 x 16	1
H	Rocker	1/2 x 2 x 13	2

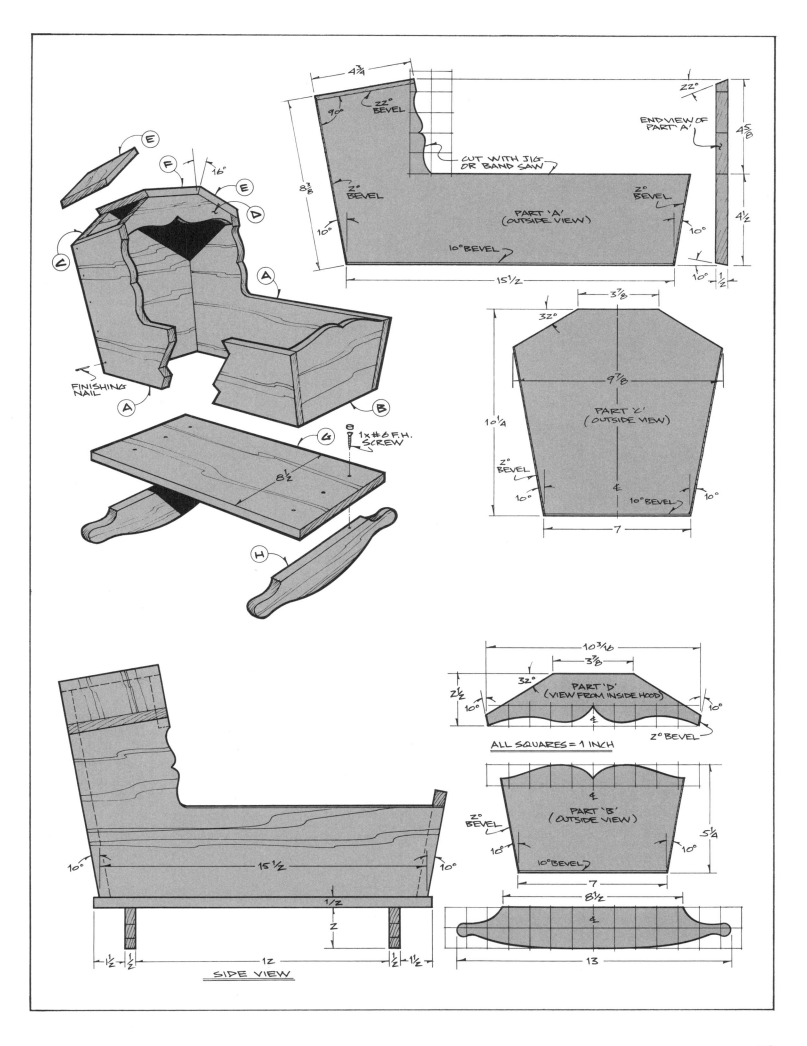

4¾

90° 22° BEVEL

8⅜

2° BEVEL

10°

10° BEVEL

15½

22°

END VIEW OF PART 'A'

4⅝

4½

PART 'A'
(OUTSIDE VIEW)

CUT WITH JIG
OR BAND SAW

2° BEVEL

10°

10° ½

E

F 16°

E

D

C

A

A

FINISHING
NAIL

B

3⅞

32°

9⅞

10¼

2° BEVEL

10°

PART 'C'
(OUTSIDE VIEW)

₵

10° BEVEL 10°

7

G 1x#6 F.H.
SCREW

8½

H

10³/₁₆

3⅜

32°

2½

10°

PART 'D'
(VIEW FROM INSIDE HOOD)

10°

₵

2° BEVEL

ALL SQUARES = 1 INCH

2° BEVEL

10°

PART 'B'
(OUTSIDE VIEW)

₵

5¼

10° BEVEL 10°

7

8½

₵

10°

15½

10°

½

2

½ ½

12

½ ½

SIDE VIEW

13

113

Canning Jar Storage Shelves

I f you're one who enjoys putting garden products up in jars, as we do, we think you'll find this project to your liking. It's a solidly constructed storage rack with room for plenty of canning jars. The one shown is made from solid oak stock, with oak plywood for the shelves (parts F). However, for a project like this, just about any wood can be used, even pine.

The two front legs (parts A) and the two back legs (parts B) can be made first. Cut each leg to overall width and length, then lay out and mark the location of the mortises for the rails (parts C).

To cut each mortise, use a $^1/_4$ in. diameter drill bit to bore a series of holes. This removes most of the waste material. What remains can be cleaned out with a sharp chisel. Be sure to cut the mortise about $^1/_{16}$ in. deeper than the tenon length in order to allow room for excess glue. If you neglect to add this extra depth, and there is excess glue, the joint won't close.

A well made mortise should be square to both the edge and face surfaces of the leg. A drill press, if you have one, will make this step fairly easy. However, if done with care, a hand brace or portable electric drill will do as good a job.

The stretchers (parts D) and back (part E) are joined to the legs with single half-lap through dovetails. This joint is not as difficult to make as you might think, and it adds considerably to both the strength and visual interest of the piece. Cut parts D and E to overall length and width, then lay out the location of the $^3/_8$ in. deep by $^3/_4$ in. wide dado that's cut to accept the shelves (parts F). This cut is best made with a dado head cutter, although you can get the same result by making repeated passes with a regular saw blade.

Next, using the same procedure, cut a $^3/_8$ in. deep by $^3/_4$ in. wide rabbet on the end of each part D and E. This step forms the half-lap portion of the joint.

Now, referring to Details A and B, lay out the dovetails as shown. For maximum accuracy, it's best to use a sharp knife or pencil to scribe the lines. Use a dovetail saw or a fine tooth backsaw to remove the waste.

The dovetail pins on the front and back legs (parts A and B) can best be laid out and scribed by using the finished dovetails as a template. Use a square to carry the scribed lines to the face of the board. The next step is to make the two saw cuts establishing the angled sides. Again, use a dovetail saw or fine tooth backsaw to make these cuts. For an accurate cut, lay the saw blade on the waste side of the scribed line, just grazing it.

The waste between the cuts is removed with a chisel and mallet. With a sharp knife, score the original line at the base of the waste. Next, with the bevel of the blade down, use a chisel to make a V-cut into the line. This prevents the grain from splintering behind the line. Now, lay the flat of the chisel against the back of the V-cut and proceed to chop away the waste material. When halfway through, flip the stock over and start from the other side.

A well fitted joint should go together with only light tapping from a mallet. If necessary, trim further with the chisel.

The shelves (parts F) can now be cut to overall length and width. The edging (parts G) is glued to both ends as shown. Use pipe clamps to secure until dry. It's best to cut the edging a bit wider than necessary. After clamping it can be planed flush.

The rails (parts C) can now be cut to overall length and width. The tenon can best be cut using the dado head cutter.

Sand all parts thoroughly, then assemble parts A, B, and C as shown. Use glue and pipe clamps. When dry, assemble part E and the three back stretchers (parts D), again with glue and clamps. Finally, complete assembly by adding the shelves (parts F) and the four front stretchers.

Final sand, then finish with two coats of polyurethane varnish.

Bill of Materials
(all dimensions actual)

Part	Description	Size	No. Req'd.
A	Front Leg	$^3/_4$ x 2 x $38^1/_2$	2
B	Back Leg	$^3/_4$ x 2 x $40^1/_2$	2
C	Rail	$^3/_4$ x 2 x $6^3/_4$	4
D	Stretchers	$^3/_4$ x 2 x 30	7
E	Back	$^3/_4$ x 5 x 30	1
F	Shelving	$^3/_4$ x $8^1/_4$ x 28	4
G	Edging	$^1/_4$ x $^3/_4$ x $8^1/_4$	8

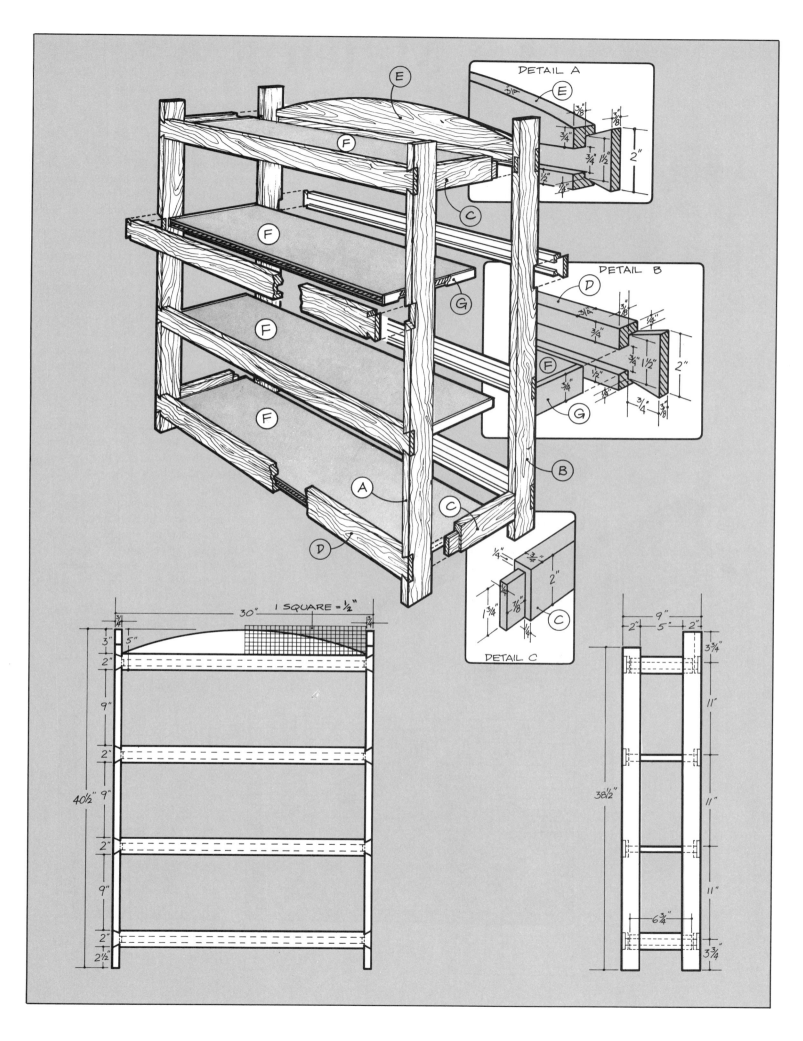

DETAIL A

DETAIL B

DETAIL C

E

F

C

G

F

F

D

A

C

B

G

F

D

G

1 SQUARE = ½"

30"

3"
5"
2"
9"
2"
9"
2"
9"
2"
2½"

40½"

9"
5"
2"

38½"

11"
11"
11"

3¾"

6¾"

3¾"

115

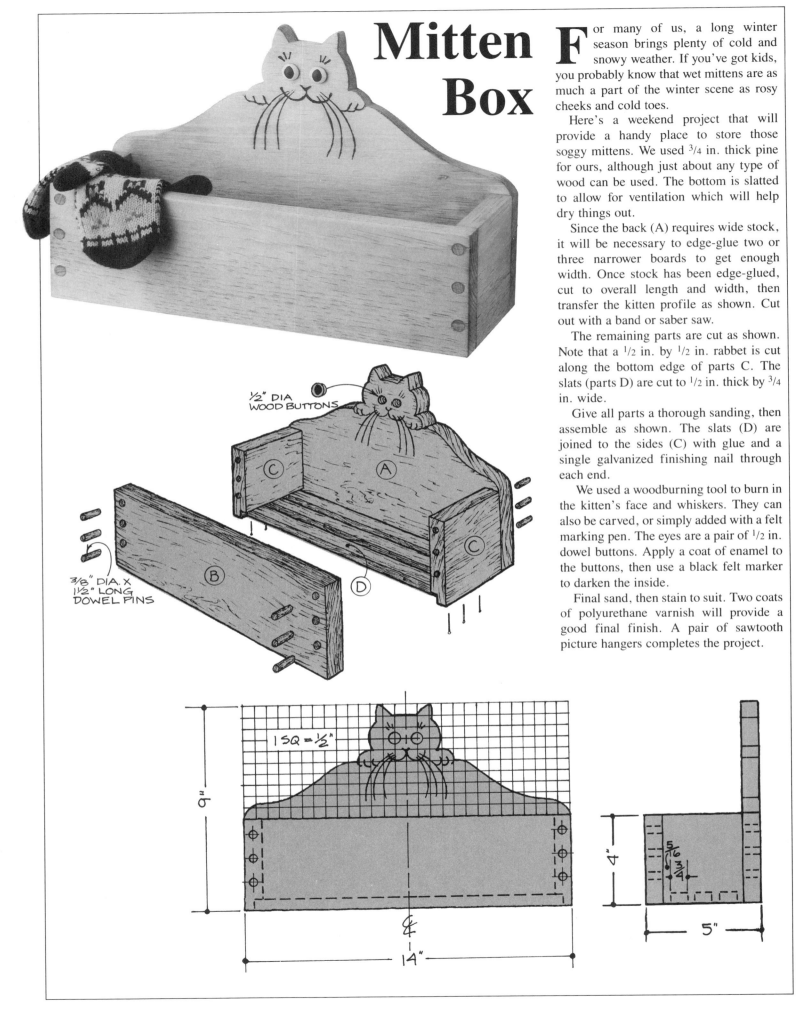

Mitten Box

For many of us, a long winter season brings plenty of cold and snowy weather. If you've got kids, you probably know that wet mittens are as much a part of the winter scene as rosy cheeks and cold toes.

Here's a weekend project that will provide a handy place to store those soggy mittens. We used ³/4 in. thick pine for ours, although just about any type of wood can be used. The bottom is slatted to allow for ventilation which will help dry things out.

Since the back (A) requires wide stock, it will be necessary to edge-glue two or three narrower boards to get enough width. Once stock has been edge-glued, cut to overall length and width, then transfer the kitten profile as shown. Cut out with a band or saber saw.

The remaining parts are cut as shown. Note that a ¹/2 in. by ¹/2 in. rabbet is cut along the bottom edge of parts C. The slats (parts D) are cut to ¹/2 in. thick by ³/4 in. wide.

Give all parts a thorough sanding, then assemble as shown. The slats (D) are joined to the sides (C) with glue and a single galvanized finishing nail through each end.

We used a woodburning tool to burn in the kitten's face and whiskers. They can also be carved, or simply added with a felt marking pen. The eyes are a pair of ¹/2 in. dowel buttons. Apply a coat of enamel to the buttons, then use a black felt marker to darken the inside.

Final sand, then stain to suit. Two coats of polyurethane varnish will provide a good final finish. A pair of sawtooth picture hangers completes the project.

½" DIA WOOD BUTTONS

3/8" DIA. X 1½" LONG DOWEL PINS

1 SQ = ½"

9"

14"

4"

5/16

3/4

5"

Not too many years ago, the coal scuttle was an important piece of equipment in many homes. We used pine to make this charming adaptation of one, and found that it can be put to a number of uses around the home. We use it to hold magazines, but it also serves well as a planter or wastebasket. Kindling wood stacks nicely in it too.

The sides (parts A) can be made first. Since each side is 14½ in. wide, you'll need to edge-glue two pieces of 1 by 8 stock (which actually measures ¾ in. thick by 7¼ in. wide). Apply glue to both mating surfaces, then use bar or pipe clamps to clamp the stock together. Once dry, remove the clamps, then transfer the curved profile from the drawing. Cut to shape with a band saw or saber saw.

Note that the front (part B), the back (part C), and the bottom (part D), all require wide stock, so it will be necessary to edge-join material for all these parts.

Assemble with glue and finishing nails. To prevent splitting, be sure to first drill pilot holes.

Give all parts a thorough sanding, taking care to round over all edges. To give ours an antique look we did some judicious distressing with a hammer.

For a final finish we applied two coats of Minwax's Golden Oak stain followed by an application of their Antique Oil finish.

Bill of Materials (all dimensions actual)			
Part	Description	Size	No. Req'd.
A	Side	¾ x 14½ x 16¾	2
B	Front	¾ x 8¾ x 9¾	1
C	Back	¾ x 14¼ x 9¾	1
D	Bottom	¾ x 13¼ x 12½	1
E	Arm	¾ x 2½ x 12	2
F	Handle	1 dia. x 12¼ long	1
G	Pivot Pin	⅜ dia. x ⅞ long	2
H	Handle Pin	¼ dia. x 1 long	2

Coal Scuttle

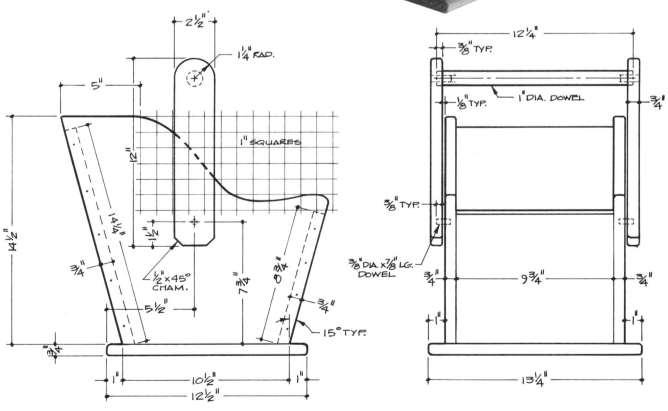

ere's a delightful toy that we think kids are sure to enjoy. And, like the real elephants that roam the plains of Africa, this one moves its head up and down as it rolls along.

Our thanks to the people at Cherry Tree Toys for providing us with the plans. If you'd like a catalog of all their toy designs, send $1.00 to them at P.O. Box 369, Belmont, OH 43718. Their catalog also includes hardwood toy wheels and parts.

Maple or birch will provide maximum durability, but just about any wood, even pine, can be used. Begin by cutting a piece of $1\frac{3}{4}$ in. thick stock to a width of 6 in. and a length of $8\frac{1}{4}$ in. Lay out the profile as shown on the grid pattern, then cut out with a band saw or saber saw.

The $\frac{11}{16}$ in. wide slot is cut by hand with a back saw or dovetail saw. Make two parallel cuts to establish the width, then remove the waste with a sharp chisel.

Cut all remaining parts, then assemble. Parts A, B, and C can be made as shown or purchased from Cherry Tree Toys.

Give the final assembly a thorough sanding. Round over all sharp edges and corners. Since some finishes can be toxic, we feel the safest finish is none at all.

Bill of Materials
(all dimensions actual)

Part	Description	Size	No. Req'd.
A	Eye	See Detail	2
B	Cam	See Detail	1
C	Wheel	See Detail	4
D	Pivot Pin	$\frac{1}{4}$ dia. x $1\frac{1}{4}$ long	2
E	Axle	$\frac{3}{8}$ dia. x $3\frac{3}{8}$ long	2
F	Push Rod	$\frac{3}{8}$ dia. x $2\frac{3}{4}$ long	1
G	Body/Head	$1\frac{3}{4}$ x 6 x $8\frac{1}{4}$	1
H	Ear	$\frac{1}{2}$ x $2\frac{1}{2}$ x $3\frac{1}{4}$	2

Elephant Push Toy

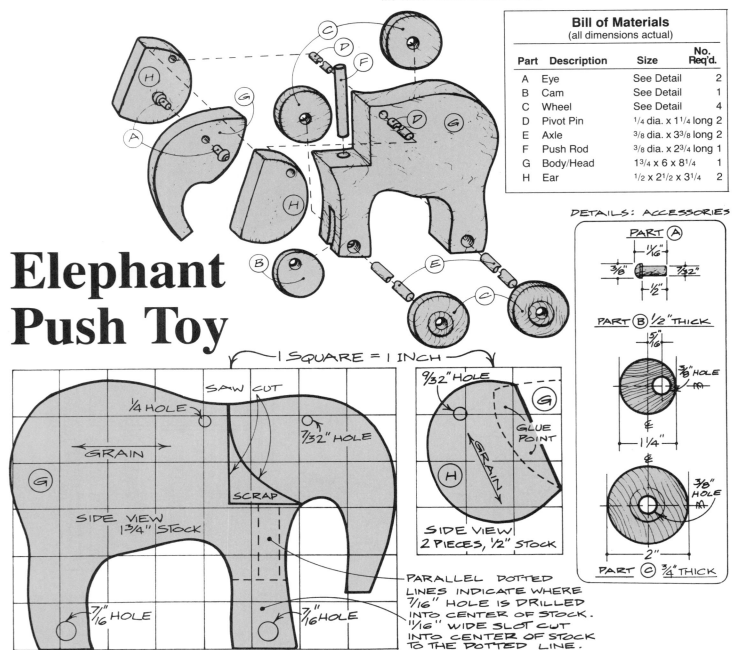

DETAILS: ACCESSORIES

PART A
$1\frac{1}{16}$"
$\frac{3}{8}$"
$\frac{7}{32}$"
$\frac{1}{2}$"

PART B $\frac{1}{2}$" THICK
$\frac{5}{16}$"
$\frac{3}{8}$" HOLE
$1\frac{1}{4}$"

PART C $\frac{3}{4}$" THICK
$\frac{3}{8}$" HOLE
2"

1 SQUARE = 1 INCH

G
SAW CUT
$\frac{1}{4}$ HOLE
$\frac{7}{32}$" HOLE
GRAIN
SCRAP
SIDE VIEW $1\frac{3}{4}$" STOCK
$\frac{7}{16}$" HOLE
$\frac{7}{16}$" HOLE

$\frac{9}{32}$" HOLE
G
GLUE POINT
H
GRAIN
SIDE VIEW
2 PIECES, $\frac{1}{2}$" STOCK

PARALLEL DOTTED LINES INDICATE WHERE $\frac{7}{16}$" HOLE IS DRILLED INTO CENTER OF STOCK. $\frac{11}{16}$" WIDE SLOT CUT INTO CENTER OF STOCK TO THE DOTTED LINE.

Sources of Supply

The following pages list companies that specialize in mail order sales of woodworking supplies

United States
General Woodworking Suppliers

Constantine's
2050 Eastchester Rd.
Bronx, NY 10461

Craftsman Wood Service
1735 West Cortland Ct.
Addison, IL 60101

Frog Tool Co.
700 W. Jackson Blvd.
Chicago, IL 60606

Garrett Wade
161 Avenue of the Americas
New York, NY 10013

Highland Hardware
1045 N. Highland Ave., N.E.
Atlanta, GA 30306

Shopsmith, Inc.
3931 Image Dr.
Dayton, OH 45414-2591

Trend-Lines
375 Beacham St.
Chelsea, MA 02150-0999

Woodcraft Supply Corp.
210 Wood County Industrial Park
P.O. Box 1686
Parkersburg, WV 26102

Woodworker's Supply of New Mexico
5604 Alameda, N.E.
Albuquerque, NM 87113

Hardware Suppliers

Anglo-American Brass Co.
Box 9487
4146 Mitzi Dr.
San Jose, CA 95157

Horton Brasses
Nooks Hill Rd.
P.O. Box 120
Cromwell, CT 06416

Imported European Hardware
4320 W. Bell Dr.
Las Vegas, NV 89118

Meisel Hardware Specialties
P.O. Box 70
Mound, MN 55364-0070

Paxton Hardware, Ltd.
7818 Bradshaw Rd.
Upper Falls, MD 21156

Period Furniture Hardware Co.
123 Charles St.
Box 314, Charles Street Station
Boston, MA 02114

The Wise Co.
6503 St. Claude
Arabi, LA 70032

Hardwood Suppliers

American Woodcrafters
905 S. Roosevelt Ave.
Piqua, OH 45356

Austin Hardwoods
2119 Goodrich
Austin, TX 78704

Berea Hardwoods Co.
125 Jacqueline Dr.
Berea, OH 44017

Craftwoods
10921-L York Rd.
Hunt Valley, MD 21030

Croy-Marietta Hardwoods, Inc.
121 Pike St., Box 643
Marietta, OH 45750

Educational Lumber Co.
P.O. Box 5373
Asheville, NC 28813

Kountry Kraft Hardwoods
R.R. No. 1
Lake City, IA 51449

K & S Specialty Lumber
P.O. Box 125
Hills Lane Rd.
Carthage, TX 75633

(continued on next page)

McFeely's Hardwoods & Lumber
P.O. Box 3
712 12th St.
Lynchburg, VA 24505

Wood World
1719 Chestnut
Glenview, IL 60025

Wood Finishing Suppliers

Industrial Finishing Products
465 Logan St.
Brooklyn, NY 11208

The Wise Co.
6503 St. Claude
Arabie, LA 70032

Wood Finishing Supply Co.
100 Throop St.
Palmyra, NY 14522

WoodFinishing Enterprises
1729 N. 68th St.
Wauwatosa, WI 53212

Clock Parts Suppliers

The American Clockmaker
P.O. Box 326
Clintonville, WI 54929

Klockit, Inc.
P.O. Box 542
Lake Geneva, WI 53147

S. LaRose
234 Commerce Place
Greensboro, NC 27420

Mason & Sullivan Co.
586 Higgins Crowell Rd.
West Yarmouth, MA 02673

Miscellaneous

DML. Inc. (router bits)
1350 S. 15th St.
Louisville, KY 40210

Formica Corp. (plastic laminate)
1 Stanford Rd.
Piscataway, NJ 08854

MLCS (router bits) P.O. Box 4053
Rydal, PA 19046

Homecraft Veneer (veneer)
901 West Way
Latrobe, PA 15650

Canada
General Woodworking Suppliers

House of Tools Ltd.
131 12th Ave. S.E.
Calgary, Alberta T2G 0Z9

Lee Valley Tools
1080 Morrison Dr.
Ottawa, Ontario K2H 8K7

Stockade Woodworker's Supply
291 Woodlawn Rd. West, Unit 3C
Guelph, Ontario N1H 7L6

Tool Trend Ltd.
420 Millway Ave.
Concord, Ontario L4K 3V8

Treen Heritage Ltd.
P.O. Box 280
Merrickville, Ontario K0G 1A0

Hardware Suppliers

Home Workshop Supplies
RR 2
Arthur, Ontario N0G 1A0

Pacific Brass Hardware
1414 Monterey Ave.
Victoria, British Columbia V8S 4W1

Hardwood Suppliers

A & C Hutt Enterprises Ltd.
15861 32nd Ave.
Surrey, British Columbia V4B 4Z5

Longstock Lumber & Veneer
440 Phillip St., Unit 21
Waterloo, Ontario N2L 5R9

Unicorn Universal Woods Ltd.
4190 Steeles Ave. West, Unit 4
Woodbridge, Ontario L4L 3S8

Clock Parts Suppliers

Hurst Associates
405 Britannia Rd. E., Unit 10
Mississauga, Ontario L4Z 3E6

Kidder Klock
39 Glen Cameron Rd., Unit 3
Thornhill, Ontario L3T 1P1

Murray Clock Craft Ltd.
510 McNicoll Ave.
Willowdale, Ontario M2H 2E1

INDEX

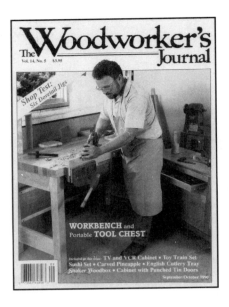
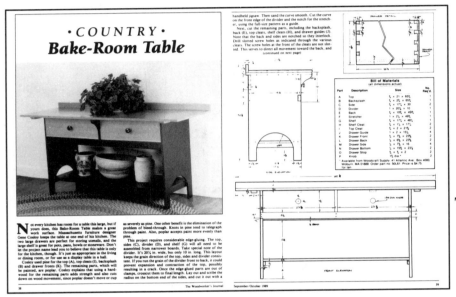